Hull City AFC: 20 Legends

David Bond

VERTICAL EDITIONS

www.verticaleditions.com

First published in the United Kingdom in 2011 by Vertical
Editions, Unit 4a, Snaygill Industrial Estate, Skipton,
North Yorkshire BD23 2QR

www.verticaleditions.com

ISBN 978-1-904091-55-4

A CIP catalogue record for this book is available from the
British Library

Cover design by HBA, York

Printed and bound by MPG Books, Bodmin

Dedicated to the memory of Alan Plater: a great Hull City supporter, a great playwright and an even greater person.

CONTENTS

David Bond was born in Hull in East Yorkshire in 1949 and started specialising in sports writing as a journalist and author in 1975. David has written or co-written eight books, covering four different sports—football, cricket, rugby league and squash. He regularly gives talks on a variety of sports and has scouted extensively.

ACKNOWLEDGEMENT

We are grateful to Geoff Lawes for his permission to reproduce the lyrics of his 2008 song 'Hull City Heroes' and acknowledge his authorship and copyright of it. He can be contacted on Geoff@lawes223.karoo.co.uk.

INTRODUCTION

Writing a book about 20 Hull City legends seemed to be a good idea at the time. It was to be part of a series featuring other football and rugby league clubs, but the style of its content was open to individual interpretation. Outwardly it might not be simpler, but in reality it was not long before a big doubt set in.

The problem was how to select the 20 legends because it will never be simple when the club concerned are long-established. Basically the choice can never be definitive because Hull City have now been playing League football for 106 years and it means that someone has to be veritably ancient to have seen all the possible candidates personally since the club's formation. A certain amount of judgment, therefore, has to be based on statistics, records and maybe a bit of hearsay in the interest of obtaining a proper balance from the Tigers' history.

Then there is the tricky question of how to define a legend. Is there an argument for saying that the 20 in City's case should be chosen only from those who played for them when they finally reached the top flight of English League soccer for the only time so far for two seasons between 2008 and 2010? And should the list preclude all those who played for the club only in the lower divisions? So where would that leave Ian Ashbee, who played for the club in all four divisions of the Football League? Presumably he would be half a legend! Then there might also be a consideration that City's early players represented them in the Second Division when the Football League still had only two divisions. Accordingly they appeared in the second tier and the bottom flight at the same time!

There is clearly much more to ponder and playing success certainly has to be a part of the selection process—whether a legend achieved it individually or as part of a team. But it is also obvious that some of City's greats experienced the bad times with the good and their status was underlined by the way in which they showed the character to fight back from adversity.

Then there are the fans' heroes and those represented by their fellow professionals: the twain have not always met, of course. Then there is the factor as to whether the choices should be drawn from what players did for their Tigers only or from what they achieved in abundance here, there and everywhere throughout their careers as well. In other words, Stuart Pearce played one game for City's reserves on trial on a wet night in Grimsby, but does his stunning subsequent career qualify him as a legend overall? Then there is the question as to who should be left out. There are surely more than 20 players who would meet the general legendary criteria even at a club such as City with their constant ups and downs.

The final choice then is not borne out of an exact science. But mine at least includes prominent goalkeepers, prolific goalscorers, some who combined managing the club as well as playing for them and, above all, those who gave plentiful service to the Tigers—a facet that should arguably be of paramount importance in these often greedy, grasping times when loyalty in football is generally at a premium. At the same time there are also some who made short, sharp impacts that will never be forgotten.

I am confident then that my final choice has lots of balance in terms of both City's achievements and their history. I am equally happy that my 20 are worthy candidates because they have all had a special quality—even if it is definable in different ways. And I am absolutely sure that I have still managed to upset a lot of people— from those who have been excluded from my list to the fans who disagree fundamentally with it. They are, of course, always entitled to their views—even if they might be convinced that I am already surrounded by men in white coats!

Maybe, then I should publicly apologise to some of those who have just missed out. There are loyal, long servants such as local lads Roger de Vries, Peter Skipper and Malcolm Lord. There is goalscoring winger Ian Butler, a member of a great forward-line who are otherwise well-represented in my final choice. And there are regular goalscorers such as Sammy Stevens, who was even before my time, Keith Edwards and Bill Bradbury.

I am sure, too, that there are a few other omissions who might cause multiple raising of eyebrows. It is obvious that a survey of fans would certainly throw up many choices of 20 City legends that would be different from each other and different from mine.

All I can say is that I firmly believe that my final 20 all qualify as legends in various ways. And we do know that football is a funny old game and it is always full of funny old opinions, so I hope that everyone will look on me as sympathetically as possible when they discover my final choice. Above all, though, I do hope that the stories produced in the book of my 20 legends will still at least provide plenty of insights for those interested in Hull City's fortunes.

David Bond, 2011

1

JOHN 'JACKIE' SMITH

On April 30, 1910, the fledgling Hull City were optimistic about clinching promotion to the top flight of English football for the first time. All they needed to do was to earn a point at Oldham in their final game of the season, but they lost 3–0. As a result, Oldham Athletic went up to the First Division with champions Manchester City on goal average and the Hull area's football public were left with a ghost that it was to take 98 years to exorcise.

One reason why City's fans had had high hopes at Oldham was that they had a goalscoring talisman at their disposal—John 'Jackie' Smith. His name might outwardly have been plain, but his record as a marksman was extraordinary and he was at the peak of his form as the climax of the 1909–10 season approached. After all, Smith, who might arguably have been described as the Tigers' early North-East version of 'Wor Jackie,' had just notched 10 goals in seven games. In addition, he had scored in every home game that he had played against the Latics, but could he help the Tigers to promotion with one last gargantuan effort at Boundary Park? But it was not to be for Smith or the Tigers on a sloping quagmire of a pitch in a hostile atmosphere. Manchester City were the champions by one point as Oldham, City and Derby County all finished on 53 points from their 38 games: it was that close. And Oldham and City both finished with the same League records of winning 23, drawing seven and losing eight.

On a personal note Smith, who was born at Wardley, near Newcastle, in November 1886, at least ended the season with the distinction of being the leading marksman in Europe in 1909–10 with 32 in the League, who then comprised a total of 40 clubs. And the honour took him a stage further than he had gone in the 1907–08 season when he had first been the top goalscorer in the country with 31 in the League as, what turned out to be, his truncated career gained impetus. Smith had joined the Tigers in 1905 as they prepared for their first League programme, having had one season since their formation when they played friendlies apart from entering the FA Cup. Smith's road to becoming City's first goalscoring hero had started relatively quietly, but he arguably had two assets—the right name and the right origin.

For a start, he was not the only Smith who was trying to establish City as a force. In those formative days the club's chairman was Alwyn Smith, whose family had been bankers in Nottingham dating back to medieval times and had had East Yorkshire business links with the descendants of slavery abolitionist William Wilberforce. And forward Augustus Smith had scored 17 goals in 34 friendlies in 1904–05 although he did not stay on to play any League football for the club. John Smith, meanwhile, was soon followed to City by another forward, Joe 'Stanley' Smith, in September 1905. Later on two more forwards called Smith—Wallace and Ned—joined the Tigers in March 1909 and May 1910 respectively although the four of them never quite managed to play in the same League side for the club.

City, in fact, were fastidious with surnames in those early seasons. After all, they had Dan, David and Ted Gordon, Anthony, George and Tommy Browell, Gordon and William Wright, William and Frank Martin, Tom and George Hedley and Ellis and Harry Hall all on their books at the same time as some of the Smiths.

In addition, Smith's background in the North-East might also have counted in his favour because it was a major recruiting ground for City's player-manager Ambrose Langley. In the club's first season in the League Langley included Martin Spendiff, Harry Simmon, John Smith, Joe Smith, George Browell, Peter Howe, David Wilson, Tom Hedley and Patrick Lavery, all of whom had links with the North-

East's hotbed of soccer. Others followed bit by bit: in fact, Langley was so determined to sign the third Browell, Tommy, in April 1910 that he and director Fred Stringer rowed across the River Tyne to get to the family's home territory of Wallbottle on the outskirts of Newcastle!

John Smith's arrival was ordinary in comparison. As City braced themselves for life in the League, chairman Alwyn Smith presided at an extraordinary meeting of club members at Hull's Grosvenor Hotel in late June 1905 to consider increasing the capital of the company from £2,000 to £8,000 by the creation of 12,000 new shares at 10 shillings each and to amend the memorandum and articles of association. At the same time the signings of John Smith and R.R. Young, both of whom hailed from Hebburn Argyle, 'a Northern Alliance club on the banks of the Tyne,' were announced. Little more was heard about Young, who was described as a bustling 5ft 10in half-back, but Smith's potential was patent because it was reported:

> He is considered to be one of the finest forwards in junior football and his services were sought by at least two Second Division sides. He can play either right or left inside-forward and much is expected of him.

In mid-August 1905 City played a practice match at Hull's Newland Cottage Homes when the Whites beat the Stripes 3–0. John Smith scored twice and Augustus Smith was also on the mark. But Augustus Smith joined Goole Town soon afterwards because he had been upstaged by his namesake John Smith, of whom it was then written: 'He is a sharp, shrewd chap and, being one of the youngest members of the team, he should be heard of again because he meant business all the way through.'

A week later and a week before their entry into League football, City held what was described as a full dress rehearsal at Anlaby Road cricket ground, coming amid a claim in the Press about the players' fitness: 'There are several who need to undergo the reducing progress before the stern fighting of a 90-minute League game is undertaken.' The practice game began at 6pm after a cricket match between Hull An XI and Welton—which had included an all-run six— and Smith, who had started in the Possibles, had to face a fitness problem of another kind. He and Simmon were switched to the Probables at halftime of a game that ended 2–2, but Smith was hurt in a collision with Laurence Traynor and omitted from the side announced three days later for the big kick-off at home to Barnsley.

City beat Barnsley 4–1, but then they scored only once in each of their next three outings, so Langley took decisive action, making three changes, two of them in the forward-line. The same line-up had been retained for the club's first four League games, but it was reported:

> The weakness of the City forwards against Burnley has resulted in wholesale changes against Leeds City at Elland Road. Last Saturday City Reserves defeated the Leeds second string 7–3 at Holbeck and the brilliant form exhibited by two of the forwards, Jack Smith and Harry Simmon, has resulted in these young players substituting for George Spence and George Rushton. Both promoted players are strangers to League football. Their record for the current season is six goals each in two matches, so they are adept as marksmen and a couple of young and active men such as Smith and Simmon should liven up the front line immensely.

But the Tigers lost 3–1 at Leeds, Langley immediately signed Joe Smith and George Browell from Newcastle side West Stanley and Jack Smith and Simmon were dropped because it was said: 'The reconstructed 11 did worse than ever . . .'

Smith's response was to end September 1905 by scoring seven goals in City Reserves' 14–0 win at Driffield White Star in the East Riding County League after travelling to the game by train, but he still found first-team chances hard to come by. His next nudge to the management came in bizarre circumstances at the end of October when City were amazingly double-booked. They were told that they would have to play both a League game against Manchester United at the Boulevard—it attracted their first five-figure League attendance of 12,000—and an FA Cup tie in the second qualifying round at Midland League leaders Denaby United on the same day. The first team played the League game and lost 2–0, but Smith was in the 'reserves' for the cup tie and scored both their goals in a 2–0 win. Billy Thornton, later to join Denaby, made the first and the second was said to be 'one of the finest single-handed efforts ever witnessed.' The 2,000 crowd had an early glimpse of Smith's goal-grabbing ability because it was written:

> Receiving the ball in his own half, he tricked man after man in a marvellous manner and finished up with a shot that gave the goalkeeper no earthly chance. Smith's effort was generously applauded and it thoroughly deserved it.

The situation brought about a ruling that clubs were 'precluded from playing reserve teams in cup ties,' while it earned Smith a first-team recall a fortnight later because Howe had a damaged shoulder and he scored his first League goal for the Tigers in a 3–0 home win over Stockport County. But then he was left out again as George Rushton was recalled. Smith made one more isolated League appearance and added another FA Cup goal, but he had to wait until January 1906 to establish himself, playing in 17 out of the last 18 games of the season. His first away League goal came in a 2–1 victory at Blackpool in mid-March and two more followed in wins at Bradford City and Chesterfield before Smith wrapped up his first League season with his fifth goal at home to Lincoln City. Smith's return from 20 League starts was relatively modest, especially in contrast with his 23 goals for the reserves. He had had a struggle to impose himself on League football and there had been few hints of what was to come.

But then Smith started the 1906–07 season in stunning style, scoring in the first five games and taking his tally to seven goals from the first seven. There was then a lull until he started 1907 equally as emphatically, scoring in the first six League games of the year, including two in a 5–0 home win over Glossop. There was another spell of four goals near the end of the season when City won three games on the trot. Smith had finally made a big impact, finishing as the Tigers' leading goalscorer with 19 goals in all and underlining his reputation as being a lucky omen. After all, City won only four of their last 18 League games of the season from the start of 1907—and Smith was on target in them all.

Smith received much better support in the goalscoring stakes in 1907–08 after City had signed two other forwards from the North-East—schoolteacher Joe Shaw and Arthur Temple. Shaw had shown some promise at Sunderland and the younger Temple arrived from

Wallsend Park Villa, but they scored 14 and 18 League goals respectively in their first season with City. Yet Smith outscored them radically as they formed a formidable inside-forward trio—all three of whom were on target in a 4–1 FA Cup giantkilling triumph at Woolwich Arsenal in a replay in January 1908—because he sensationally hit 31 goals in 37 League games to become the top marksman in the country that season. Smith, who missed just one League fixture throughout the season, began with an opening burst of 11 goals in the first nine games. Another productive run of nine goals in eight League games began on Christmas Day, 1907, before Smith added a further eight in the final nine matches of the season during March and April 1908.

The lethal inside-forward trio scored all but 10 of the Tigers' League goals in 1907–08 and Smith also chipped in with a club record. It happened in October 1907 when he became the first City player to score four goals in a League game as they beat Clapton Orient 5–0 at home. Defender William Robinson, the brother-in-law of City teammate Walter Dagnall, got the other as Smith hit a first-half hat-trick into the teeth of a gale. He was close to two more before adding his fourth late on. Orient had Frank Thacker sent off, while ex-Tiger William Martin was injured and ended up as a passenger, but it still took City to the top of the Second Division table with six wins out of eight. And it was reported:

> The feature of the winners' display was the wonderful shooting by Jack Smith, whose four goals brought his record up to more than one per match. In this respect he is without an equal in either the First or Second Division of the League.

Smith's goalscoring exploits also earned him a representative call-up for the Football League against the Scottish League at the end of February 1908 and it was written of him: 'Although only a small man, he is endowed with any amount of trickery, but prefers to bustle his opponents and seems to take glory in charging a 6ft back.'

In 1908–09 Smith had a more modest return and discovered that he had become a marked man. He and City had not started the season too well and things reached a head in a 2–0 home win over Blackpool in mid-October 1908. Smith scored one and made one for

Temple, but he was switched out to the right-wing 'on account of a bad kick he received early on.' As a result, Smith, who was also described as having been 'crippled early in the game,' missed the next nine matches and was out until Christmas Day when he scored on his return against Bradford Park Avenue.

Smith's value was again underlined when he and Temple led a revival as City won seven and drew one of their first eight League games of 1909, but this time Temple ended up as the club's leading goalscorer with 17 in the League.

Strangely, though, he finished at right-back for the final four games when City took seven points out of eight and Smith added a final flourish with three goals in the sequence of an injury-hit season. He still scored 10 goals in 23 League appearances and it meant that the Tigers had their best season to date, finishing a distant fourth despite some inconsistent results.

It raised hopes of a genuine promotion push in 1909–10 and that was just how it turned out with Smith well and truly to the fore. Again he began in style with eight goals in the first seven games and the longest that he went without scoring during the whole season was a four-match sequence during October. Smith added 11 more League goals in a mid-season run of 10 games as City got up a head of steam from December, which began with a 7–0 home thrashing of Birmingham City. It was the Tigers' biggest League win to date and Smith scored twice although Temple outshone him on this occasion with a hat-trick. City's form had been modest in October and November, but the trouncing of Birmingham started them on a run in the League in which they won 16 and drew three of their next 21 games. Smith took his tally for the season to 32 with four hat-tricks—in a 3–1 home win over Leeds City, a 4–0 home win over Oldham Athletic, a 5–1 victory at Stockport and a 5–1 home win over West Bromwich Albion, the penultimate game.

The victory over Albion was the only occasion on which three players with the same surname scored for the club—John Smith, Joe Smith and Wallace Smith—and it had been preceded by an odd indication that the fans were getting behind the team because it was reported:

Quite a titter of amusement went round when a procession, headed by a fantastic device borne aloft, wended its way along Spion Kop a quarter-of-an-hour or so before the start. The device consisted of a wooden shield, painted a dingy yellow, surmounted by a prehistoric representation of a tiger.

At the same time the tension was mounting as the season reached its climax and it was also written: 'The Spion Koppers have all been fidgets lately and no wonder.

City, meanwhile, believed that they had had found a pre-match formula that worked in their favour: they visited the seaside before their final three games. They had trained at Cleethorpes before winning 1–0 at Gainsborough Trinity, they had trained at Withernsea before thumping West Bromwich and this time they trained at Blackpool before the visit to Oldham. Could they hold their nerve and could Smith, their goalscoring talisman, deliver the goods on one last crucial occasion? The omens looked good. He had scored a hat-trick against them earlier in the season and in the final match of 1908–09 he had scored the winner when City signed off with a 1–0 win over them.

All it needed was an action replay from Smith and the Tigers were in the First Division. But it was not to be. City, who were without defender Jack McQuillan, another of their recruits from the North-East, began the game two points clear of Oldham, whose promotion push had been based on a sound home record. The Boundary Park pitch was described as being 'in an absolutely abominable state,' the crowd were known to be particularly partisan and Oldham were reckoned to be a physical side. The Tigers accordingly slumped to a 3–0 defeat in the cauldron as Oldham secured the runners-up spot behind Manchester City with goals by Tommy Broad, Alf Toward and David Walders. Smith had, for once, fired blanks and what made matters worse was that Toward, whose goal had a suspicion of offside about it, had left the Tigers midway through the season after having struggled to dislodge him and gain a regular place in the side. Toward was another of City's recruits from the North-East, he and Smith had twice scored in the same League game for the club during 1908–09 and he had also featured in the final game of the season when City had beaten Oldham a year earlier.

There was briefly hope that an extra promotion place might have been available for City to claim because First Division strugglers Woolwich Arsenal were amazingly going through a financial crisis, but again it was not to be. And it was going to be a very long time before the Tigers would ever have it so good. But for Smith it was tragically never going to be as good ever again. From being Europe's top goalscorer in 1909–10, he found that his career would enter a downward spiral in the aftermath of the dual anti-climax.

In 1910–11 Smith scored only once—in a 2–1 defeat at Bolton—in his first seven games for City and it soon became ruthlessly clear that no-one was indispensable to the club. He last played for them in a 2–0 win at Leicester Fosse in November 1910 when it was reported that Smith, who had cost the Tigers just £10, missed 'a certain score.' It was—in two senses—his last chance: two days later he was transferred to Sheffield United in a £150 deal to fulfil his ambition of playing the First Division football that had eluded him so narrowly with the Tigers the previous season. It was indicated: 'In view of the fact that he had a guaranteed benefit of £175 this season, the sum paid by the Blades for his services will readily understood to be a substantial one.' He had scored 98 times for City in just 158 League games and his goals in the FA Cup and friendlies, which also included some in Holland and Sweden while on tour, took him comfortably past the century mark overall. Furthermore, he still remains fourth in the club's all-time goalscoring list.

City's fans, meanwhile, soon had a new goalscoring hero to support Temple—Tommy 'Boy' Browell, the third of the brothers from the North-East. Smith and Browell had played in only three League games together early in the 1910–11 season, but the new order was emerging. Browell was soon switched from outside-right to centre-forward, he immediately scored hat-tricks against Stockport County and Barnsley in successive home games and Smith was to appear only once more in the No. 9 shirt that he had latterly made his own.

Smith scored seven times in 12 League appearances for the Blades, but his stay at Bramall Lane was brief because Nottingham Forest became his third club of the season when he cost them £350 in March 1911. But Smith, who scored once for them in three League outings, was unable to help them to avoid relegation from the First Division as they finished bottom. And he became disillusioned with League football on his return to the Second Division, leaving it for good the following September when he signed for Nelson. A year later he moved to York City, he returned to Hebburn in January 1913 and he finished his career with Heckmondwike—playing as a full-back in the Yorkshire League. His fall from grace was spectacular and it still begs the question as to how different it might have been for him if he had secured promotion for City in April 1910.

There was a perverse justice that Oldham would have gone on to snatch the League title for the only time in their history—if they had won their last game of the 1914–15 season. But tragedy awaited Smith because he enlisted for the 1914–18 War with the York and Lancashire Regiment and was killed in action early in September 1916, aged just 29. There was further pathos on two other counts. Patrick Lavery, briefly one of Smith's teammates in City's first League season, had already died in action with the Highland Light Infantry. And David Wilson had collapsed and died during a game for Leeds City only three months after having played alongside Smith on his League debut for the Tigers in September 1905. And the following year Smith had scored in a benefit match between the two sides to help the dependants of Wilson, whose nickname had been 'Soldier . . .'

Smith himself left a large family—including two sons, Jack and Jim, who played rugby league for Hull Kingston Rovers—and a lasting legacy as City's first great goalscorer. His brief life and relatively-short football career had been a roller-coaster ride and that was what it would become for the Tigers, too . . .

2

TOMMY BLEAKLEY

Many of Hull City's early players came from the hotbed of football in the North-East of England, but there was another fruitful early breeding-ground for the club—Lancashire. And that was where half-back Tommy Bleakley originated because he was born at Little Hulton, just south of Bolton, in May 1893. His playing career began with five seasons at Clegg's Lane in the nearby Farnworth League and a spell with Walkden Central before it was blighted by the outbreak of the 1914–18 War. Bleakley represented Bolton Wanderers in wartime football, but then crossed the Pennines to join the Tigers. His debut came in a 3–0 home win over Huddersfield Town in early October 1918 when it was reported that City's team had a strong military flavour: it included Private Tommy Bleakley! It was the first of his 10 games for them in the Midland Section Principal Competition that season, but he also played in three of the club's six games in the Midland Section Subsidiary Competition before League football resumed from the 1919–20 season.

On every occasion Bleakley played at left-half and he went on to make the No. 6 shirt virtually his own for more than a decade with the Tigers. During the 1920s there were other players, such as Bob Coverdale, Bert Mills, Bill Johnson, Cornelius Sullivan and Sammy Weaver, who also played a fair few games at left-half, but they could not dislodge Bleakley from the side. Quite simply, he wore the No. 5

shirt instead even though he was scarcely the biggest to be a centre-half because he was only 5ft 6in tall. But Bleakley was renowned as a good header of the ball even though he was small—a point that was underlined in a 4–0 home win over Millwall in April 1929 when future England international Ronnie Starling scored the first goal of his hat-trick after a remarkable build-up involving headers between Bleakley, Ken McDonald and Sam Smith. It was also curious that, when Bleakley started to struggle to keep his place in the side on a regular basis in 1929–30, the No. 6 shirt usually went to future Northern Ireland international Bill Gowdy, who was only 5ft 7½in tall himself! And the idea of a small centre-half did not always hinder City because Paul Feasey, who was regarded as 5ft 8in during his one-club senior career, played in 45 out of 46 League games in the No. 5 shirt when he captained them to promotion in 1958–59. Maybe both just followed Bleakley's lead . . .

The concept of consistency was always a more important factor anyway and Bleakley, it seemed, had that quality in abundance. He made his League debut in August 1919 in a 4–1 defeat at Birmingham City—the Tigers' first game in the Second Division after hostilities had ended—and he immediately became a regular. City finished 11th and for the most part Bleakley featured in a half-back line that also comprised Joe Edelston, whose Hull-born son, Maurice, later became a noted BBC football commentator, and Charles Deacey.

And Bleakley was rarely out of the side once he had made his mark. His constant appearances in City's defence during the 1920s stressed his dependability. For nine seasons he just totted up the League games—35 in 1919–20, 37 in 1920–21, 38 in 1921–22, 38 in 1922–23, 26 in 1923–24, 42 in 1924–25, 37 in 1925–26, 36 in 1926–27 and 33 in 1927–28. He was an ever-present for the only time during the 1924–25 season—42 League games and five FA Cup ties—as part of a formidable half-back line with Irishman Mick O'Brien and Scotsman John Collier. Fellow defender Jimmy Lodge once said: 'I had to try to keep a move ahead of the play because that was the way it was with Tommy Bleakley and Jack Collier. Tommy was one of the best in his day.'

The only setback was in the 1923–24 season, which got off to a bad start for Bleakley. On the opening day City drew 1–1 at home to Leicester City, but eight minutes in he was carried off after a collision. Perhaps significantly, Leicester scored while Bleakley was off the field for repairs, but he had a twisted ankle and early in the second half he was forced to come off for good. He missed the next 15 League games and did not return until early December for a 3–2 home win over Coventry City. Incidentally during the game against Coventry, new signings George Richardson—at £1,000 the second most expensive player in the club's history after Scottish international centre-half Michael 'Rubberneck' Gilhooley—and Harry Havelock, whose father had been a forward with Hull FC, made their debuts.

But Bleakley did prove a point in the FA Cup. City lost 4–0 in a replay against holders Bolton in the third round in January 1924, but Bleakley shone against his home-town club in the first meeting at Anlaby Road. It ended 2–2 after the squad had prepared at a special training base at Ben Rhydding in West Yorkshire and it was only a late equaliser by another Bolton-born player, England international David Jack, that prevented the Tigers from causing a major upset. Bleakley was said to have had 'a storming game' and it was reported:

> Bleakley distinguished himself by relieving much congestion near City's goal. He was also the brains of the Tigers' attacks and repeatedly surprised his followers by the brilliance of his moves and the tricky nature of his footwork.

It sounded impressive for a centre-half, but Bleakley had, in fact, made his mark alongside Gilhooley. City, though, lost 4–0 in the replay as he suffered an unhappy return to his home town.

Bleakley also enjoyed his flirtations with the FA Cup on other occasions early in his City career. Most memorably, he was in the side who shocked English football in the third round of the competition in February 1921. Burnley were on their way to the First Division title on the strength of a record run of 30 League games without defeat. They had been unbeaten for 26 games—24 in the League and two cup ties—when they visited Anlaby Road, but the Tigers trounced them 3–0 and it was reported: 'One could hardly count the number of times that Tommy Bleakley intercepted the passes from Billy Nesbitt to Robert Kelly in the first half.'

There was another sensational giantkilling episode the following season when Bleakley scored his first goal for the Tigers as they thrashed Middlesbrough, who were on their way to finishing eighth in the First Division, 5–0 at home in the first round in January 1922. Bleakley was said 'to have scored the goal that he deserved.'

But the magic of the FA Cup started to wear off in January 1923 when City were drawn at home to West Ham United in the third round, so they went away to Filey for a few days to prepare for the tie. At one stage Bleakley and his teammates Dan Bew, Tom Eccles, Jimmy Lodge and Bert Mills were spotted fishing off Filey Brig, but then everything suddenly started to go wrong when manager Percy Lewis resigned two days before the game and then the Tigers were beaten 3–2!

The following season Bleakley again scored in the FA Cup when the Tigers beat Crystal Palace 3–2 at home in the second round in January 1925, but, more significantly, he unwittingly found himself involved in controversy during the 1929–30 season when City reached the FA Cup semi-finals for the first time.

Bleakley had played in 12 of the first 13 League games that season, but he was not always a first-team regular by the time that the competition got under way in early 1930. He did not play in City's first five ties although he was back in first-team favour again by March after a long absence. But he was again omitted for the Tigers' first semi-final meeting with the mighty Arsenal, which ended 2–2 at Leeds. But City made one change for the replay at Villa Park in Birmingham, bringing in Bleakley for the injured Jimmy Walsh. They lost 1–0 to a controversial goal and had centre-half Arthur Childs sent off, but a further argument ensued because there was a strong feeling that the balance would have been tipped City's way if Bleakley had played in the first meeting at Elland Road. City commentator Keith Martin observed:

> Tommy Bleakley's skills were tailored for the crises of the first match and might have swung the tie. Even though past his best, he was needed in that traumatic semi-final in his last season. They needed him desperately, but in retrospect played him in the wrong game—in the replay.

But City's manager Bill McCracken, a former Northern Ireland international, harshly saw it differently as it became clear that Bleakley's career was nearing its end. McCracken had assembled a group of youngsters from minor footballing circles—Douglas 'Dally' Duncan from Aberdeen Richmond, Ronnie Starling from Washington Colliery, George Goldsmith from Loftus Albion, Sam Weaver from Sutton Town and Stan Alexander from Percy Main Amateurs—and they became known as his 'diamonds in the rough.' And he insisted:

> The team that year were very much on the young side. I wanted simplicity—the ability to defend as a unit and a fast and direct service between halves and forwards. Our success in cup ties resulted from this. We began the season with Tommy Bleakley and Sam Weaver at half-back, but Jimmy Walsh and Bill Gowdy had come in by the time of the cup ties. Tommy's best days were behind him and we had problems when Sammy left for my old club Newcastle United. Walsh and Gowdy were picked because they were ball-winners who were able to give us impact and a maximum of possession. Without making excuses, the injuries to Walsh and 'Paddy' Mills in the first semi-final were crucial. We had them going by halftime, but lacked balance and full fitness in the last half-hour. It slipped away from us then.

McCracken, in fact, had previously shown his ruthlessness in dealing with Bleakley, who had been as regular as usual in City's side at left-half and then centre-half during the 1926–27 season. During the summer McCracken had gone back to Newcastle to sign wing-half Edward Mooney and Bleakley found himself out of favour for the opening game of the 1927–28 season at Barnsley. He was instead chosen to play in the game at Anlaby Road between the two clubs' reserve sides. Mooney, who had helped the Magpies to beat Aston Villa 2–0 in the 1923–24 FA Cup final, played in 11 out of City's opening 12 League games, but by then Bleakley had been reinstated in the first-team line-up after missing the first seven fixtures. And Mooney never reappeared for the Tigers after his opening burst as Bleakley became a regular again for the rest of the season, so the natural order was duly restored.

It came as no surprise, therefore, that Bleakley's days with the Tigers were finally numbered at the start of the 1930s. And there was a sad ending because he played the final League game of his one-club career in a 2–1 defeat at Bury in late April 1930 as they slipped towards relegation for the first time in their history. During the game Bleakley was given a warning 'for vigorous play,' but he was also close to scoring an equaliser. And, as it turned out, it would have been enough to save City from the drop at Bristol City's expense if the game had ended in a draw.

As it was, Bleakley missed the last three games of the season and, two days after finishing their disappointing programme with a 2–0 home win over Wolverhampton Wanderers, City announced their retained list. Former Scotland international Jimmy Howieson, Tom Flannigan and Walsh were transfer-listed and 10 players, including Bleakley, were released. It was reported:

> It will be seen that the services of Tommy Bleakley, the popular left-half who has been at Hull for 11 seasons, are not to be retained. He will be given a free transfer, but there is still plenty of football left in the Lancastrian and he will have the best wishes of everyone in any future engagement in the game.

Bleakley played in a total of 365 League games, all of them in the Second Division, for City and at the time it briefly put him at the top of the club's all-time appearances list—just ahead of his defensive colleague Matt Bell, who soon overtook him. But Bleakley remains joint ninth in the list with Doug Clarke, who ironically was also from Bolton, and he did occasionally score in the League. It happened five times and there was a sort of symmetry about his goalscoring. Three of his League goals came in one season—1922–23—and three of them were scored against Port Vale. He also scored in both the League and the FA Cup against Crystal Palace. And he also scored against Leeds United in both a League match—a 3–1 home win in March 1923—and a cup competition.

And in turn the feat also provided a sort of symmetry about Bleakley's two goals in friendlies because both were scored inside the penalty area in different ways. In April 1922 he scored with a penalty when 'Paddy' Mills, City's other goalscorer, was fouled in the 43rd minute of a 2–1 win over Leeds in Hull Hospital Cup. In May 1923 Bleakley and Mills were also on target in the same competition when the Tigers beat Bradford City 4–1. This time City were awarded an indirect free-kick inside the penalty area when Bradford's former Scotland goalkeeper John 'Jock' Ewart was penalised for 'overcarrying' and Bleakley was on the mark when his fellow half-back John Collier tapped the ball to him.

Bleakley's last appearance of any kind for the Tigers also came against Leeds in the Hull Hospital Cup in late April 1930. Maybe it was typical of the way in which the luck had been turning against him when City lost on the toss of a coin after a 2–2 draw. But Bleakley was not yet finished with football even though he was only a few days off his 37th birthday when City released him. He promptly moved into non-League football with Goole Town, Bridlington Town and then Wombwell.

Bleakley skippered Goole during the 1930–31 season and was a useful acquisition because they had just lost their captain and centre-half Jack Gilling to Doncaster Rovers. One contender to replace him was local teenager Stan Denby, but A.N. Other was named as Town's centre-half for their second game of the season and it later became clear that the mystery man was Bleakley. Denby found himself in the cold, but at least he had the chance to learn from a master and, ironically, the Tigers snapped him up two years later.

And there were initial signs that Bleakley had not lost any of his defensive ability. Town came back from two goals down to draw 2–2 at Yorkshire Amateur on his debut and it was reported:

> Goole have had a lot of trouble filling the centre-half position, but there seems little doubt that Bleakley is going to be the right man for the job. During the opening half he was somewhat strange, but he settled down and played a great game after the interval. To him was entrusted the captaincy and he held the side together wonderfully well. What he lacks in inches he makes up in nippiness and he was a commanding figure in Goole's defence.

A week later Goole won their first game—2–1 at Selby OCO—and Bleakley's impact was again underlined because it was said:

> At an estimate he kicked the ball twice as often as any other player on the field and metaphorically stood head and shoulders above the rest. Always in the thick of the fray, he was the complete captain and opened out the game splendidly.

Much later Bleakley again proved that there was still some football left in him. At the end of the 1939–45 War, City relinquished their link with the Anlaby Road ground, but Bleakley regained his when he took charge of Hull Amateurs, who were accepted into the Yorkshire League with five other clubs—Bradford City, Bradford United, Firbeck Main Colliery, Ossett Town and Wombwell Athletic—at the end of hostilities. But the first moves to form the new club as a section of Hull Town Cricket Club, who were also based at Anlaby Road, had been started while the War was in full flow—as early as the summer of 1941. When the Tigers ended their tenancy at Anlaby Road and 'a dog-track concern' had obtained an option on the land, an approach was made for facilities for a new football club. The project progressed further at a meeting in November 1943, the East Riding County FA gave their approval in April 1944 and the following autumn a committee, including City's former winger Arthur Bullock, the one-time England schoolboy international, was formed.

It was then stated in the club's inaugural annual report:

> During the summer of 1945 the club obtained entry into the Yorkshire League and started playing on September 1 after several weeks' training. Among the preparations were the acceptance of the offer of Tommy Bleakley to act as honorary trainer. And Jimmy Lodge was demobilised when we were at our wits' end, so he was immediately signed on as groundsman and assistant trainer. No other amateur club in Hull had the facilities for training and massage.

It was a gesture that was typical of Bleakley's innate enthusiasm, as was the fact that on one occasion he even turned out for Amateurs himself even though he was in his early 50s. But he found it tough going and Amateurs, who also included his son Arthur, finished bottom of a tough, 15-strong Yorkshire League including sides representing Huddersfield Town, Bradford City, Scunthorpe United, Halifax Town and York City, conceding 100 goals in 28 games. Bleakley at least snapped up one impressive signing—winger Jack Major, who had moved north after a spell on Watford's books. Major went on to play for the Tigers, become an England amateur international and win an FA Amateur Cup winner's medal with Bishop Auckland before settling in Hornsea. And Bleakley even got the chance to lead Amateurs against City when they met each other twice in a week near the end of the season. One game was a friendly, in which Arthur Bleakley, who wore the No. 4 shirt, scored, and the other was in Hull Hospital Cup. But things were again difficult in 1946–47—on one occasion a game at Selby Town had to be abandoned at halftime when four Amateurs players collapsed and were unable to continue—and the club resigned from the Yorkshire League at the end of the season.

But Bleakley did have another link with football, returning to his roots to scout for Bolton. Hull-born defender Bob Dennison, who had 1½ seasons with Wanderers before playing in the League for the Tigers in the 1950s, recalled:

> Tommy took me there after he'd seen me playing for the East Riding. He came across afterwards and said he wanted to send me to Bolton. Bill Ridding, who was a nice man, was the manager then, but Tommy didn't send anyone else from the area to them. I was working for Rose, Downs and Thompson's, but they let me go and play in A-team games for Bolton. On a Saturday I would get the milk train from Hull via Sheffield to Salford and then either be given a lift or get a taxi the rest of the way. While I was at Bolton, I would still train with City's juniors on Tuesdays and Thursdays. Tommy, who was a caring man, would come down to the sessions and ask how things were going for me in games for Bolton, whether everything was to my liking and if I had any complaints.

And Bleakley maintained a parallel sporting interest right through his football career—in cricket. He had played in the Lancashire League in his early days and in the 1920s he had spells with Hull Town, turning out alongside his City teammates Billy Mercer and Charlie Flood, and South Holderness at Hedon, east of Hull. Bleakley scored a century and took a hat-trick during his time with South Holderness and it was said of him:

> During Archie Knight's time as honorary secretary he was instrumental in persuading Tommy Bleakley to act as player-coach. Bleakley was a very good all-rounder at cricket—an excellent bat and medium-fast bowler who had been very successful in Lancashire League cricket. He coached the youngsters and the standard of cricket had quite an uplift during the three or four years that he was with the club. His presence in the First XI assisted with bringing many a success, both collectively and individually.

And when Bleakley left the Tigers in 1930, it was reported: 'He is likely to remain in local cricket during the summer.' Within days he took up an appointment as cricket coach at Hull's Hymers College and a report from the school, whose head of sport at the time was former England rugby-union international Bill Cobby, observed:

> Taking the achievements of all the teams into consideration, it can safely be said that this cricket season has been far more successful than any experienced by the school in recent years. This year a coach has been engaged and players in all the teams have derived much benefit from his useful advice.

And Bleakley, who also coached the East Riding and Hull University, completed a sporting double after the 1939–45 War when he played both football and cricket in his 50s. His 53rd birthday came early in the 1946 cricket season when he made four first-team appearances for Hull Town in the Yorkshire Council, taking 12 wickets at an average of 12.30 apiece. His notable contemporaries still included Flood as well as George Cawthray, who played for Yorkshire and became the head groundsman at Headingley, Douglas Greasley, who later had five years with Northamptonshire, and Joe Wheater, who was to go to three successive Olympic Games in the clay-pigeon shooting.

In addition, Bleakley, whose son Arthur played for Coal Exporters, had a remarkable trait for a cricketer because Dennison added:

> He was said to be a good, regular player who was quite slight in terms of build and he had a thumb and only three fingers on one hand. Nobody knew how it happened, but there was a joke that went round about him in football that, when he tried to signal that there were only five minutes left, he told you that there were only four!

Bleakley ran a sports outfitter's ship with Mercer, another colleague in football and cricket, when he retired and also had a spell as a publican. He lived in Hull's Swanland Grove before moving to the city's Westlands Road, which is where he died at the start of October 1951. But he maintained his immense passion for sport to the end because he saw City lose 2–1 at home to Luton Town on the Saturday, he spoke at length to East Riding County FA president Wilf English on the Sunday and he passed away suddenly on the Monday.

And City commentator Keith Martin summed up his football career when he later wrote:

Tommy Bleakley was a wing-half of quiet, but massive efficiency and his great virtue was consistency. Match in and match out, it set him apart from other, more fundamentally-talented players to whom it was a gift as elusive as quicksilver. His football never illuminated a match, as did the individually-styled play of Michael Gilhooley, and yet they were an effective and integral half-back combination. Gilhooley's cry of 'Tammy!' as he prepared to give a deft nod to his little left-half became a well-known and much-loved sound to the crowd and was part of the folklore at Anlaby Road. Bleakley never again struck the kind of rapport that he enjoyed with Gilhooley with the succession of centre-halves the club had in the 1920s, but, as a 'method' half-back of his age, his special, if unadorned functional qualities could not be minimised. For 11 seasons his lack of display and ostentation served as a sop to some of the extrovert characters around him. Bleakley was the rudder. He was guidance and sanity when all else failed and, when things were going wrong, he was a tower of refuge to his colleagues in distress. He was big in heart as well as in utility and lacked the height and weight which might have powered him to representative honours, but such conjecture was simply to belie his temperament and style.

3

MATT 'GINGER' BELL

Hull City have been blessed with some special goalkeepers during the course of their history, but a statistical quirk of fate means that arguably one of the most successful of them made his name as a full-back—Matt 'Ginger' Bell. By the time that Bell left the Tigers in 1931, he had played in more League games for the club than anyone else—393—and he had played at left-back in all except 31 of them, mainly in his first season in 1919–20. He had worn the No. 2 shirt on those other occasions, but there had also been an amazing instance when he had actually donned the goalkeeping jersey at the start of an FA Cup tie.

The spectacular saga started in January 1925, by when Bell had long established himself as a first-team regular as a full-back. First-choice goalkeeper George Maddison damaged his wrist in a third-round cup tie at home to City's Second Division rivals Wolverhampton Wanderers and Bell took over from him in goal when he went off. The game ended 1–1, but Maddison, who had only recently established himself in the side, was ruled out of the replay five days later and remarkably it was then predicted:

> With no available understudy, the breach is likely to be filled by Matt Bell, who is very keen on operating between the sticks and in his own mind is confident that he could make as good a success in that position as in any other he has occupied.

City stayed at the Regent Hotel in Leamington Spa as they prepared for the replay and Thomas Dyke, the reserve goalkeeper, travelled with them, but there was a doubt about his eligibility for the tie. But it was optimistically reported: 'Bell has given satisfactory examples of custodianship at Leamington and, not being without experience, it is felt that he will capably discharge his new duties.' In the end Bell kept a clean sheet in a tie that tested his powers of concentration because it went into extra time and City won 1–0 with a goal by Bert Mills, who converted a cross by George Richardson after 104 minutes. And it was said of Bell:

> The City 'keeper evoked an encouraging cheer from the few Hull supporters present. Bell made a brave show in the circumstances, but his strangeness to the position was obvious. He acquitted himself with wonderful security and throughout the whole match only once perhaps gave the least suspicion that the job was comparatively strange to him. His display was most encouraging in the circumstances he found himself in. His colleagues never hesitated to kick the ball back to him when the occasion warranted it and he disposed of high shots and low shots with coolness and promptitude.

Maddison was, in fact, ruled out for a month, but Bell's conversion to goalkeeping soon became a stopgap measure. After all, it was reported after the replay: 'The search for an effective understudy to Maddison is being made in earnest.' City signed 31-year-old Herbert Bown, who had retired the previous summer, and two days later he made his debut in a 5–0 home win over Crystal Palace. But he added further irony to the tale because he had been a goalscorer during his spell with Halifax Town. In fact, Maddison later described all his goalkeeping rivals during his time with City as 'good 'uns,' adding:

> My first challenger was a chap called Herbert Bown, who had been at Leicester City. In a match at Hull I had my wrist broken, so Matt Bell, our famous back, went into goal and played very well. Then the club signed Bown and he was in the side until my wrist was mended.

The experience arguably put Bell on a par with a later City goalkeeper, Ron Capewell, who appeared in one League game for the club and kept a clean sheet when they beat Bury 1–0 at home in April 1955! And there were, in fact, some noteworthy sequels to Bell's emergency role:

much later he himself was again to deputise in goal for the Tigers and in November 1986 regular goalkeeper Tony Norman injured himself on the team coach en route to a full Members' Cup tie at Southampton, so defender Peter Skipper had to start in his place.

Bell had another flirtation with goalkeeping in September 1929 when City drew 2–2 at Southampton and again he kept a clean sheet in a topsy-turvy game in what was going to be a topsy-turvy season. Maddison pulled a thigh muscle early on and Bell temporarily replaced him. City went 2–0 up with Bell still in goal, but Maddison had returned when the Saints reduced the arrears just before halftime. But he went off again after Bobby Weale had equalised for Southampton eight minutes after halftime when it was reported: 'Maddison was limping and found that he could not move across his goal to stop the ball and was compelled to retire from the game, Bell again going in goal.' It left the Tigers to fight a rearguard action because George Goldsmith, Tommy Bleakley and Ronnie Starling were also carrying knocks, but it was written: 'Bell made some excellent saves. City showed not a single slackness in defence and Bell was never at fault. There was some fierce play in front of Bell, but he was safe in goal.'

Bell then acquired further goalkeeping experience in a Third Division North game at Lincoln City at the end of January 1931. City, in fact, fielded three different goalkeepers in what was described as a 'chapter of casualties.' They started out with Fred Gibson in goal because Maddison was already out of action with another wrist injury. But Gibson, who had been in the side for the previous two months, was carried off on a stretcher with a badly-bruised back after half-an-hour, so Bell once more stepped into the breach. But this time he himself had to be led off injured early in the second half, reducing City to nine men in those pre-substitute days. Arthur Childs then became City's third goalkeeper of the day, but they went down 3–0 as it was noted: 'Vigour came before science in Lincoln's game.' At least something had briefly worked in skipper Bell's favour because he had won the toss and taken first advantage of a strong cross-wind.

And Bell, who was born at West Hartlepool in July 1897, had one good reason for taking his chances in goal. After all, it is highly unlikely that he would not have been with City in the first place if it had not been for a goalkeeper—his brother Albert. In September

1915, Albert Bell, who was in business in Hull, played in goal in a wartime game for City when they beat Derby County 4–2 in the Midland Section Principal Competition. Matt Bell, meanwhile, played in Army football during the 1914–18 War and was then with West Hartlepool before joining City in August 1919 when he was demobilised. Manager David Menzies fixed him up with a trial after he had come to Hull from Hartlepool to join his brother and he cost the Tigers only a signing-on fee when he was taken on.

But Bell was another City hero whose participation in League football began the hard way. He made his League debut in a 3–1 defeat at Stoke in September 1919—and was then dropped for the next game at Leeds City. But his replacement, Arthur Betts, then pulled out with a foot injury, Bell was promoted from the reserves and City won 2–1. He began to be a first-team regular and it was said of him: 'Bell makes up in enthusiasm and vigour for what he lacks in experience, but he has the makings of a big, powerful defender when he becomes accustomed to Second Division tricks.'

But First Division Sunderland brought about his next omission because he gave away a penalty when they won 6–2 at Anlaby Road in the FA Cup third round in January 1920 and the legendary Charles Buchan recorded a hat-trick. Bell, though, was soon back in favour until he lost his place through suspension the following month and his first-team contribution was over for the season. He did not reappear for the first team until November 1920 after 'showing improved form with the reserves' and Jimmy Lodge was rested, but he was to remain a regular fixture after that.

And early in his career Bell played against Burnley in the FA Cup third round in February 1921 when the Tigers pulled off a major giantkilling coup. Burnley's 26-match unbeaten run was ended and it was written:

A word of praise is due to Matt Bell and Sam Cheetham for their clever defence when Burnley's wingmen got away. The times that Bell dispossessed Eddie Mosscrop were beautiful to witness. Bell played a more scientific game than any other back on the field and kept the ball continually going to his own forwards. Not only was he the best defender, but he was also a fine asset to the attack.

Eleven months later Bell played in the City side who demolished First Division Middlesbrough 5–0 at home in the FA Cup. He had become a first-team regular, he was to captain the club for nearly eight years and he soon became a fans' favourite, but he also played a vital, strategic role in a defensive system for the Tigers that changed the course of football history.

Bill McCracken, who succeeded Harry Lewis as City's manager in February 1923, had been dubbed 'the offside king' during his illustrious playing days with Northern Ireland and Newcastle United even though he had not originated the tactic. He tried to confuse opposing forwards by manoeuvring them into static positions and it had made him unpopular as a player, but that did not deter him from employing it rigorously as a manager and Bell was at the forefront of implementing it on the pitch. He and fellow full-back John 'Jock' Gibson, an American who was brought up in Scotland from the age of 13 and joined City in May 1922, combined with goalkeepers Billy Mercer and Maddison to organise McCracken's offside trap and Bell said: 'We knew instinctively what each would do in almost every possible circumstance.'

The direct outcome was that City forced the offside law to be changed in 1925 when it was decided that an attacker would then need to have only two opponents between himself and the goal instead of three. McCracken recalled: 'I know we were criticised in some quarters for persisting with the offside game, but it was justified with the playing strength we had. The trouble was it was a less reliable tactic under the amended laws than in my playing days.' And the alteration to the ruling in 1925 brought a surfeit of goals the following season as defenders initially struggled to cope with it: in 1925–26 6,373 goals were scored in the Football League—compared with 4,700 the previous season. At the same time McCracken and Bell in particular continued to utilise the offside trap when they could while they remained together at City.

And it was written of the Tigers' defence at the peak of Bell's era:

In 1926–27 the Hull City defence became the talk of the football world and the envy of clubs bearing famous names. In the first 12 games in the Second Division that season City conceded only four goals. At this stage every other club except Stoke City had at least 10 goals against them and some had more than 30 in the goals-against column. These were the days of the George Maddison, John 'Jock' Gibson and Matt Bell defensive combination and one First Division club were so impressed that they offered the Tigers an open cheque for all three!

And it was joked that Bell and Gibson 'used to build a brick wall in front of the goal.' In addition, his teammate Jimmy Lodge, who knew a full-back when he saw one, said of Bell: 'He was another Mick Gilhooley in his value as a clubman, but he never quite touched international class.'

Ironically, Bell played in more than half of City's League games in all his 12 seasons, but he was never an ever-present. The closest that he came was in 1923–24 when he missed only one game through injury after 15 minutes of a 1–0 defeat at Bury. He strained groin muscles as 'he was reaching forward for the ball when an opponent charged him from behind' and missed a 1–1 draw at Manchester United.

But Bell earned himself some consolation soon afterwards because he scored his only goal for City in a 2–0 home win over fellow strugglers Bradford City on Easter Saturday, 1924. The Tigers were on the fringe of the relegation zone after winning just two League games in 16—a double over South Shields—since Boxing Day 1923. In addition, they had not scored more than once in a game during that run, so Bell's goal, which followed one by Harry Lewis, marked a turning-point. Bell himself had proved a point, though, because a week earlier he had been blamed for a miskick that led to Bradford's first goal in a 2–1 win over City. The Tigers' relief after Bell's goal, set up by Scottish winger Alec Thom, was evident because it was reported:

> Quite apart from the brilliant and remarkable character of the goal registered by Matt Bell, City's popular left-back, in the closing stages of the game, the fact that it counted as a second goal for the first time in a League match by the Tigers in 1924 caused the spectators almost to lift the roofs of the stand with their shouts of enthusiasm at the success. The Scotsman promptly responded to Bell's signal to middle the ball, which the full-back drove with great force into the net.

But Bell's defensive capabilities usually earned him the plaudits and he was awarded two benefit matches. The first was in a 1–0 home defeat against Wolves, who gained revenge for his goalkeeping exploits a month earlier, in February 1925. The second was a joint benefit game with Maddison and Bleakley in March 1930 when City lost 3–0 at home to Blackpool at a crucial phase in the club's history and at a point when Bell had been in and out of the side. But it was later said of him:

> When the talk is of great clubmen, Hull City fans between the two World Wars go back instinctively to the almost palmy days of Matt Bell, a great warrior of a full-back. No honours came the way of this great-hearted player even though he shared in some of the club's greatest triumphs and would have led them on to the Wembley turf for a cup final with a little luck.

As the 1929–30 season unravelled, there was a stark contrast between City's inconsistent League form and their FA Cup heroics. They actually began the Second Division programme well, winning four and drawing one of their first five League games, but then Bell missed a game at Bristol City and they lost 4–0. It was reported: 'The absence of Bell was an undoubted handicap.' It was the start of a run in which the Tigers won only one of 10 League games, they started to leak goals and Bell never managed to play more than nine League games in succession in what developed into a topsy-turvy season for him personally, too. He still managed 29 League appearances, but City found themselves in relegation danger after a run of only one win in 12 League games in the second half of the season. And the outcome was that they went down a few weeks after reaching the FA Cup semi-finals for the first time.

Bell had 'had a notion that City would do well in cup ties' in 1929–30 and the run began with wins at Plymouth, who became the Third Division South champions, and at home to Blackpool, who became the Second Division champions. City faced a much tougher task at Manchester City in the fifth round and Bell was ruled out by a foot injury. He had been hurt a fortnight earlier in a 4–1 League defeat at Notts County and failed a fitness test shortly before the tie. But he was positive because he said: 'It is rather a big thing to say, but the spirit is there and that means a lot.' City went behind early on, but equalised by halftime when the watching Bell observed: 'When the teams were level at halftime, I felt sure that we should not lose.' In fact, the Tigers won 2–1. Bell himself also missed the next League game at Millwall, but he was back for the quarter-finals against Newcastle United when City won 1–0 in a replay after a 1–1 draw at St James' Park. And the Tigers' winner was scored by Scottish international inside-forward Jimmy Howieson, who had actually been played out of position at left-back in Bell's absence in the success at Manchester City.

That meant a semi-final against Arsenal at Leeds and City were 2–0 up after half-an-hour, but they suffered a series of injury setbacks and Bell was one of the victims although he returned to the action after halftime. The knocks unsettled the Tigers, particularly because it was felt that Bell and fellow full-back George Goldsmith had worked the offside trap well to frustrate the Gunners, who changed their tactics, got back into the game and eventually earned a replay eight minutes from time. City returned to dine at Hull's Royal Station Hotel and a large crowd assembled outside in Paragon Square, so Bell was called to address them, saying: 'Only injuries to some of our players prevented us from winning, but I have every confidence that we shall be able to beat the Arsenal in the replay.' The feeling in City's camp was that they still had the upper hand and Bell later added: 'We showed that we could master Arsenal in the first half at Leeds and we shall be out to do the same again. Only the Tigers will on no account relax their grip this time.'

But City's FA Cup history has been dogged by controversy at crucial moments during their most compelling runs—and the replay at Villa Park, Birmingham, was one of them. Arsenal won 1–0 with a suspicious, 11th-minute winner by England international David Jack and the Tigers had defender Arthur Childs sent off. Both Bell and fellow defender Billy Gowdy thought that the ball was on its way out of play in the build-up to Jack's goal, so they left Joey Williams unchallenged as he set it up. City's goalkeeper Fred Gibson felt that the winner had been legitimate, but Bell always insisted that the ball had crossed the line and gone out of play before it was put into the middle.

City's season collapsed and it was becoming clear that Bell's career with the club was approaching its end. He made 25 League appearances at Third Division North level for the first time, but in mid-March 1931 he was injured in a 3–2 defeat at York City. It was reported: 'The Tigers had established a two-goal lead, but Bell's injury necessitated his removal to the left-wing, where he was more or less a limping passenger. Bell played soundly before his injury.' In fact, he had sustained rib injuries, which kept him out of the final 11 games of the season.

As it turned out, manager Bill McCracken left shortly before the end of the 1930–31 season after failing to get City back into the Second Division at the first attempt and it fell to Bell as captain to present him with an English crystal electric table-lamp as a token of the players' appreciation of him. It was reported: 'Bell made happy reference to the relationship between the players and the manager and regret was expressed about his retirement.' McCracken responded that he had had his criticisms of his players, but he had never intended them to be personal or destructive. And he certainly did not retire. He remained involved as a scout into his 90s and on this occasion he was back in the game as Gateshead's manager in September 1932. What was more significant was the fact that McCracken as manager and Bell as captain had been very close. And fate seemed to dictate that once one had left City, then the other might soon follow, which is exactly how it turned out.

City appointed Haydn Green as McCracken's successor soon after their last game of the season—a 4–0 home win over Nelson, which Bell missed because of injury—and soon disclosed that four players were to be transfer-listed—defender Arthur Childs, wing-half Robert Turner, winger Billy Taylor and inside-forward Martin Davin. Green, meanwhile, took up his duties five days after his appointment and his arrival at once coincided with an announcement that Bell and fellow defender Jimmy Walsh had been transfer-listed because they had 'not accepted the amended terms for next season.' Ironically, Walsh had started the 1930–31 season as City's captain, but then the role had been restored to Bell.

Goalkeepers Maddison and Gibson had re-signed for the club, but there was a suggestion that Bell was not going to be one of Green's men because City had signed a potential new captain soon after the end of the season—centre-half Charles Wrack, who had led Grimsby Town and twice helped them to promotion. As it turned out, Wrack was to make just three League appearances for the Tigers and Bell was on his way out of Anlaby Road.

Making Bell available had led to shock waves because it was reported:

> He is one of the best-known and respected players in League football and has always been an outstanding personality in the City defence. He played in only minor football before he developed on sounder lines while in the Army in France. When he was demobilised, he joined Hull City and quickly reached the League team, with whom he practically kept his place throughout his connection with the club.

But there was to be no turning back even though Bell did not find a new club straightaway—and there was a curious irony in the circumstances when he did. Green, whose wife came from Hull, had joined Nottingham Forest as an amateur 16-year-old, playing for them against the Tigers at Anlaby Road in 1906, and then gone on to play for Manchester United, Aston Villa and Reading. He had also been born in Nottingham, so maybe it was no surprise that in mid-August 1931 Bell duly signed for Forest . . .

It gave Bell, who had had a £350 price tag placed on his head when City transfer-listed him, the chance to return to Second Division football after one season away from it. The move was tied up a fortnight before the new League season began and it was reported:

> The arrangement between the two clubs on the subject of the transfer fee has been completed and it was left with the Forest authorities to settle with the player himself. The ex-captain of the Tigers welcomed a return to Second Division football and also expressed regret that such a long association with Hull City had been broken. Bell has earned the respect of everyone during what is a record for the length of playing service with the club and opposing teams have frequently gone out of their way to pay a tribute to the good sportsmanship of the City left-back.

Bell was by then top of the Tigers' appearances list and he remains sixth overall. But he was disappointed about his departure because he said: 'I always cherished the wish to end my career where I started it—with Hull City.' It was said at the time that he intended to retain his business interests in the Hull area and at one stage he had a newsagency and confectionery shop on the city's Anlaby Road close to the ground that he had graced. Bell scored once for Forest in 85 League games for them and stayed in football when his playing days were over as part of their backroom staff. And in the late 1930s he moved to Holland to coach, managing Heracles at one point. But he was forced to flee as the Germans overran the country—and was always reluctant to talk about it. On returning to England he continued to take an interest in football because he regularly watched Doncaster Rovers for a while.

But eventually Bell returned to Hull, moving to the city's Albert Avenue after having lived in the Doncaster area. And in January 1962 he died at the age of 64, leaving a widow Nora; children Fred, Bernard, Denis and Barbara and grandchildren Tony, Michael, Lisa, Paul, Jeremy and Philippa. Fittingly for someone who was always rated as one of City's best-ever defenders, he passed away on the day that they kept a clean sheet in a goalless draw at home to Southend United.

Bell had been someone whose playing ability had always been respected by his contemporaries. In 1922 his fellow defender Mick Gilhooley won his only cap for Scotland just before leaving City for Sunderland in a British record deal worth £5,250, but his career failed to flourish: he had injury problems, but later he also admitted that Bell was one of the teammates that he had missed most. And future England inside-forward and FA Cup-winning captain Ronnie Starling once said:

> I had some very happy years with Hull City. Bill McCracken signed me and he was a very good manager. He was a very honest man and he knew the game inside out. And we had a good side in those days with Fred Gibson, Matt Bell, Jimmy Howieson and Stan Alexander.

Bell's leadership qualities had also been significant, as was shown in a game at Stoke in December 1927 when City led at halftime, but then lost 3–1. At one stage he even adopted a cricket principle because it was reported: 'Bell appealed to the referee against the bad light. The wonder was that he had refrained from doing so before.' All in all, it was no wonder that he was once described as 'a prince of full-backs . . .'

4

JIMMY LODGE

Hull City stalwart Jimmy Lodge could legitimately have posed the age-old question: 'What's in a name?' For a start, the long-serving Lodge did not just make a name for himself with City—he made two! The explanation is that he joined the club as William Barrass and then became Jimmy Lodge. Furthermore, his job titles during his yeoman service with the Tigers in two spells had even more names— for example, player, trainer, coach, scout, masseur and physiotherapist—with a few variations thrown in for good measure.

But Lodge, who was born into mining stock at Felling-on-Tyne in County Durham in January 1895, had always used the surname of Barrass because he was unaware that he had been orphaned when he was only a few months old and he was raised as part of his maternal grandparents' family. As a result, it was said that his true identity came to light only when he got married. He was supposed to be changing his bride Mary's surname: instead he ended up changing his own, too!

The practical outcome was that he technically played as Barrass in his first two seasons at Anlaby Road and then as Lodge in the following three. It meant, therefore, that he made the first 35 of his 81 League appearances for City as Barrass in 1920 and the first part of 1921 and the remaining 46 as Lodge between the summer of 1921 and 1923. The bland description of him as 'the new back' when he unexpectedly made his League debut for the Tigers in January 1920 might have kept everything a lot simpler . . .

And when Lodge, who was one of six brothers, talked about his origins, he again confused matters by using different names. Although he was born at Felling near the southern bank of the Tyne, he was brought up at Gosforth on its Northumberland side. As a result, Lodge considered Gosforth to be his home town. But much later he muddied the waters even more when he wickedly described his home town as 'Gosforth and Hull!'

But it was much more certain that football was always in Lodge's blood even though he had to wait until his mid-20s to gain League recognition, partly, of course, because of the demands of the 1914–18 War. In fact, he had been so keen on it that in his youthful exuberance he played in goal for his school team in the mornings and as a full-back in a junior side in the afternoons. Lodge eventually became a miner when he left school and it was then that his football career began in earnest as an amateur when he played for Newcastle side Coxlodge. In 1911 he joined the Territorials as a 16-year-old and two years later he was snapped up by Northern Alliance club Scotswood.

Dedicated service was to become an integral part of Lodge's life and the 1914–18 War soon made sure of it in a dramatic manner as his football career was largely put on hold. He did play some Army football, but his service during the so-called Great War was viewed as exemplary. There are conflicting reports as to whom Lodge actually served when he joined up in August 1914. One indicates that he was in the Northumberland Fusiliers for three years, taking part in some bloody fighting on the Western Front. Another insists that he served as a lance-corporal—or a 'one-striper'—with the 50th Division (Signals) of the Royal Engineers.

It is undisputed, though, that Lodge received the Military Medal for bravery in action in 1915 and the following year a Bar was added to it in recognition of his efforts at the Battle of the Somme, where he was wounded. He recovered and returned to active service, fighting twice at Ypres and also at Arras, Passchendaele, Langemarc, where he got shrapnel in his elbow, and High Wood, where he was shot in the shoulder. Lodge then received two further awards for action 'beyond the call of duty' when he was awarded the

Distinguished Conduct Medal at Le Cateau, followed by the addition of a Bar for further gallantry in the Mormal Forest.

When the conflict ended, Lodge, who had been awarded a gold medal while playing football for the 50th Division in 1916, became a semi-professional with Northern Alliance club Newburn in the North-East, from whom City signed him in December 1919. He initially played in a trial match for the club and then signed in the buffet at Newcastle's railway station two days before the end of the year. The war years had taken their toll to a degree, but Lodge said: 'When I came out of the Army, I was never one for covering the ground quickly, but I relied on positional sense and judgment to be in the right place at the right time.'

Curiously, City had just beaten Wolverhampton Wanderers 10–3, but Lodge soon found that he had arrived relatively quietly at a time of potential crisis when 1920 dawned. The Tigers began the year by losing 7–1 at League newcomers South Shields and then going down 6–2 in a rearranged FA Cup tie at Sunderland. There were plans to reshuffle their side for the return game against South Shields—it was the first season when clubs usually played each other home and away in succession—but Lodge was not included in the original squad of 13. He suddenly appeared, though, as 'the new back' and then William Barrass as City made three defensive changes, bringing in Billy Mercer in goal and naming a new full-back partnership of Billy Stephenson and Lodge, whose middle name was William, instead of Matt Bell and the injured Charlie Betts. Early on it was reported that 'Barrass was applauded for a fine tackle' as City turned the tables on South Shields with a 3–0 win. Lodge kept his place for a 3–2 defeat at Leicester when it was then claimed that he was 'not speedy enough' and the directors, who picked the side in those days, dropped him for one game before he played out the 15 remaining ones of the season—all at left-back.

One reason why Lodge was able to settle in quietly was that much more was made of fellow full-back Jimmy Middlehurst's return to City after the second game against South Shields. Middlehurst had played in two League games in 1914–15 before returning on his demobilisation after fighting in Mesopotamia. This time he was given a reserve game against Notts County when it was claimed that he needed 'only a little training to bring him up to his old condition of fitness.' A second reserve game followed against Chesterfield and it was then reported: 'On the form shown Middlehurst would not strike the directors as the man they need for strengthening the first-team defence.' As it was, he stayed to partner Lodge at full-back in seven games, but was then released. The unheralded Lodge, meanwhile, was still serving the Tigers until his death in 1971 . . .

Another of Lodge's full-back partners was Ernie Blenkinsop, who joined City from Cudworth United Methodists in South Yorkshire for £100 in October 1921. Again they played only a handful of games together, but Lodge had a pivotal role in Blenkinsop's development because he said:

> He came as an inside-forward, but he couldn't find his true position until I suggested that he should partner me at full-back in the reserve team at Rotherham because he had such a good left foot. I had to go in goal when Arthur Briggs was hurt, but Ernie carried on fine with the aid of a few instructions from the goalmouth.

And Lodge's advice instigated a good career move for Blenkinsop because he went on to play for England 26 times at full-back during a long stay with Sheffield Wednesday!

Lodge's own playing career, though, was unexceptional. He made just 81 League appearances for the Tigers although he had no doubt as to what provided the highlight of his spell with the club. It was an FA Cup first-round tie in January 1922 when City thrashed First Division Middlesbrough, whose forward-line contained internationals Jackie Carr, Andy Wilson and George Elliott, 5–0 at Anlaby Road. And Lodge recalled: 'It was one of those games when everyone rose to the occasion. We had the will to win and good team spirit and it was certainly the best game I played in.'

Lodge eventually moved on to Halifax Town, for whom he made 42 League appearances, during the summer of 1924, but he lasted only seven months even though he was an ever-present in their side. During the 1925–26 season he played non-League football for Nuneaton Borough and York City before the Tigers' manager Bill McCracken brought him back to Anlaby Road at the request of club chairman Dr Clifford Durham-Pullan. It was August 1926 and Lodge was called assistant trainer, he helped out McCracken's No. 2 Joe

Beck and he coached the reserves. Titles, though, were never important to him: service was and this time no-one would dislodge Lodge from his work for the Tigers.

Lodge later qualified as a masseur and physiotherapist, treating rugby-league players from Hull Kingston Rovers and Hull FC, Yorkshire county cricketers and dancers from the Scottish ballet in his time. He became City's faithful, old retainer and was once dubbed 'the man with the magic hands.' He outlasted Beck, who, however, continued to watch the Tigers from the Well in post-war years: Lodge himself would usually stand close to it near the players' tunnel—a moustachioed figure in his trademark white coat.

Lodge was universally liked, but he was never short of an opinion—even in his early days with City. For example, he spoke highly of his teammates, including Scottish international centre-half Mick Gilhooley:

> We used to call him 'Rubberneck.' He was a great header of the ball and a wonderful clubman. Mike had no equal as captain, centre-half and team man. He was a great worker and a great leader. He would run himself into the ground for Hull City and there was not a nicer fellow walking.

And he said of another fellow defender Billy Mercer: 'He was a fine goalkeeper. I played in front of him and he never tried to pass on the blame if he made a mistake.' Lodge also played briefly in the same team as prolific centre-forward Sammy Stevens, insisting: 'He was the best centre-forward City ever had. He was a footballer and a bustler and had a fine shot.' And he also had high praise for forward David Mercer: 'He was the best in England even when he was with City. He was equally as good at inside-forward as he was on the wing.'

Lodge also had a scouting role with the Tigers and was instrumental in the acquisition of players such as future England wing-half Sam Weaver and long-serving defender Cliff Woodhead. He had seen long-throw expert Weaver play for Sutton Town while with the reserves and said: 'He took to professional football like a duck to water and practically walked into the first team.'

And if Lodge had a high regard for many of the people he encountered during his long service with City, then the feeling was mutual. Former England wing-half Cliff Britton, who was just retiring from football with the Tigers when Lodge died, said:

> I got to know him as a loyal and devoted servant to everything in the interests of the club. He was a knowledgeable man in so many features of the game and he was always ready to use his knowledge for the help of any young player. He was a quiet, unassuming and likeable man who represented everything that is best in football in so many ways.

The long-serving Andy Davidson added:

> Jimmy was a terrific character who was idolised by the players. I don't think there was ever a player at the club who didn't like him. He was like a father to me and a great friend. He was a wonderful character, a fine man and one to whom you could always turn for advice and help. If anything went wrong, you went to Jimmy and he talked you through it. He would watch matches from the tunnel and tell you if you were rubbish, but he was never wrong. He was a kind person and he was a gem.

Other post-war players were quick to praise him because Benny Bridges said: 'When I was at City, Jimmy ran the reserves and Fred Smith looked after the A team. I think that Jimmy was the cornerstone of the club because he'd been there for so long.' Brian Bulless added: 'Jimmy Lodge was a great fellow who gave us all a lot of encouragement. He was a nice fellow, as was George Lax, who was also on the backroom staff.' Len Sharpe recalled: 'He was a lovely bloke and so laid-back about everything.' Bob Dennison said:

> Everybody liked him and he must have worked for the club for peanuts. He was a very nice chap, but quiet and had apparently been a very good player. He knew his football. He didn't do a lot of coaching, but nobody did because it was nothing like it is now. He would do the physiotherapy and the massages during the week and then take the reserves on Saturdays when he would do reports on all the players for the managers such as Bob Jackson and Bob Brocklebank.

And inside-forward Dave King, who scored twice on his League debut in a 3–1 win at Sunderland in December 1959, was said to have benefited from being 'mothered and fathered' by Lodge.

Pain played a major part in Lodge's life, especially when he suffered it during the 1914–18 War. But it was easier for him during the 1939–45 conflict when he worked in Civil Defence until 1941 before volunteering for the Royal Signals, the equivalent of his old formation. He became a sergeant instructor until he was demobilised in June 1945 and observed: 'It was cushier the second time. If they'd given me four blankets and sheets in 1914, I'd have thought the War was over!' And Lodge was not averse to inflicting pain—albeit playfully—during his time with the Tigers.

It seemed that Lodge's general goodwill and benevolent bonhomie evaporated in the treatment room on occasions because Davidson recalled:

> Jimmy looked after people and was dedicated to the club. He was a great character, but he used to make up a potion with a paste and some linen and tell you: 'This won't hurt, you son.' All of a sudden it would burn you and you'd jump up off the treatment table. He would let out a little giggle and they'd be just about sweeping you off the ceiling!

Dennison added:

> It was a mixture that he made up himself. It was red-hot and it looked like a black-molasses paste. He would put it on his hands and give you a rub-down with it. I think that it was his magic potion for anybody who had an injury. But even though he used it mainly for injuries, he would then rub it all over so that it would burn and the victims would then have to jump into the bath to cool down as quickly as they could!

And sometimes, it seems, Lodge would merely try to hoodwink his patients because Ken Houghton reflected: 'Jimmy was a lovely fellow, but, if you went to him with niggling knocks when he was physiotherapist, he would kid you into thinking that you had nothing wrong with you.' But Bulless insisted: 'Jimmy loved getting his thumbs stuck into you!' And Davidson added:

> He would start to feel your leg gently, but he was very subtle and suddenly there would be a click with his hands and he'd stick his thumbs in while talking to you. He would then drag you off the couch and say: 'Who are you kidding? Get out and train. There's nothing wrong with your leg.'

There was a fleeting period after the 1939–45 War when Lodge was no longer with the Tigers as they sought to regain their active existence at their new Boothferry Park base. On demobilisation, Lodge instead took what he called a job as 'groundsman, etc.' with the newly-formed Hull Amateurs before City's new manager Major Frank Buckley and director Henry Needler heard about his return from war service and offered him a job with the re-formed club as assistant trainer. Lodge himself welcomed the opportunity because he said: 'The directors did everything they could to give the game a good start in the city again because it was never on strong legs before.'

Lodge himself went from strength to strength in one role or another with City and was singled out for public praise when they held a celebration dinner at Hull's Royal Station Hotel after winning the Third Division North title in 1948–49. And as Lodge moved towards the 40th season since he first joined them as a player, he was presented with a television set by the club in February 1959. Vice-chairman Ron Buttery said that the presentation represented the high esteem in which Lodge was held and a tribute to his devotion to the club. There had been contributions towards the gift, according to Buttery, from different sources such as manager Bob Brocklebank, directors, players, ground staff, office staff, the supporters' club and the auxiliary group, all of which prompted Lodge to say that it left him 'truly speechless.' But he did manage to say: 'The fact that so many people have joined in to help to make it possible shows just how much team spirit and friendship there is between us.' In fact, Lodge had been attending to duties at Boothferry Park with trainer Johnny Mahon on the previous Sunday morning while a television aerial had been put up at his home in his absence to maintain the surprise element!

And in April 1970 Lodge was awarded a testimonial match to mark 50 years since he first joined the club. It took place against Brian Clough's Derby County in April 1970 and finished 2–2 in front of an 8,937 crowd. It was attended by his close friend Alan Hardaker, the Hull-born secretary of the Football League who had played briefly for City's reserves, and the tributes poured in. Manager Cliff Britton said: 'Everyone who has been closely associated with Jimmy

Lodge knows him to be an honest and likeable man. His outstanding service to the game and devotion to Hull City is unsurpassed.' And skipper Chris Chilton added: 'We are very grateful for the care and attention we have received from him for our injuries and also for the help and advice which is always available from one who has had such long and varied experience in the game.' Lodge's long-standing colleague Wally Chapman, who also had a variety of backroom roles in a part-time capacity with the club, was chairman of the match committee and Derby's side included Les Green, Kevin Hector and John McGovern, all of whom were to have links with City to varying degrees. In addition, two of Lodge's former City teammates, Charlie Flood and Bert Mills, were present, as were two other club stalwarts, Cliff Woodhead and Billy Bly. On this occasion Lodge's match-day tasks were duly left to coaches Andy Davidson and John McSeveney, who observed: 'It's not until you have all Jim's jobs to do that you realise just how much he gets through.' Lodge himself mused afterwards: 'It has been a night I shall never forget. So many people have been so good to me. I shall never be able to thank them all.'

Not surprisingly, he never officially retired. Lodge lived in Hull's Woodlands Road, he had two daughters Elsie, who emigrated in 1948 after marrying an American serviceman, and Muriel. He was the grandfather of twin girls, but he was a widower when he died after a short illness in Hull's Kingston General Hospital in October 1971, aged 76. His funeral, which was directed by the family firm of former City chairman Arthur Shepherd, was attended by FIFA's president Sir Stanley Rous and Alan Hardaker.

The official club tribute read:

> Everyone at Boothferry Park was saddened by the death of Jimmy Lodge, who had given more than 50 years' loyal service to Hull City. His record as player, trainer and masseur has scarcely any rival in either length or devotion and it is surpassed only by the respect and admiration in which he was held by everyone who knew him. His name grew to be synonymous with that of Hull City and it will be more than a little heart-rending not to see him busying himself with all those jobs which help to make a football club tick. Every one of the countless players who have come and gone while Jimmy steadfastly served the Tigers has had good cause to be grateful to him. And each of the managers he served will not deny that they reaped the benefit

of his experience and his readiness to help in any way he could. Jimmy was the kind of man who could never find a wrong word to say about anyone. But what is an even greater tribute to a man who served Hull City so well and for so long is that no-one could find a wrong word to say about him. It was typical of a man who was decorated for gallantry four times during the 1914–18 War that, even in failing health, he should still be serving the club he loved until a week before his death. Jimmy once said: 'I'll pack in when Hull City tell me they don't want me anymore.' That day would never have come.

Lodge had served 12 different managers in different guises—David Menzies, Percy Lewis, Bill McCracken, Haydn Green, Jack Hill, Ernest Blackburn, Major Frank Buckley, Raich Carter, Bob Jackson, Bob Brocklebank, Cliff Britton and Terry Neill—and two months before his death he had been made a life member of the Ex-Tigers' Association for the club's former players at their inaugural meeting in City's social club at Boothferry Park.

The loyal Lodge once said: 'If I had my time to go over again, I would still play soccer and I would stick to it after my playing days, too. I'd also say that Hull City are fairer to players and everyone else than any club I have known.' But City's first post-war chairman and benefactor Harold Needler summed it all up best in the build-up to that testimonial match when he said: 'Few clubs have had the good fortune to have a Jimmy Lodge.'

5

BERT 'PADDY' MILLS

Bert Mills was born in India and brought up to speak Hindustani, but nothing was ever simple in his case. His birthplace was Multan, which was then in India and later in Pakistan, and it became even more of a circus because his real name was Bertram, but in the end everybody knew him as Paddy. The nickname is said to have arisen from a boyhood altercation when he 'fought like a Paddy', but none of it prevented him from becoming one of Hull City's earliest goalscoring heroes in two spells with the club. And despite his beginnings Mills was eventually brought up locally—on the south bank of the Humber at Barton-upon-Humber, which is where he returned to live at the end of his career.

Mills' Army father, John, was from Liverpool, his mother, Annie, was from Skegness and he himself was the youngest of seven children. He first came to England as a five-year-old, settling with the family in Barton-upon-Humber two years later. And Mills, who was born in February 1900, admitted: 'I didn't know any English when I came over. When I first went to school, I often used to break into Hindustani!'

Mills first joined the Tigers in September 1920 from Barton Town after having a trial. His wage was £2 a week and it was a while before he was given his chance in League football. In fact, it almost came out of desperation because City had been struggling for goals all season, a situation which worsened when they failed to score in six successive League games during the late autumn of 1920. Mills was given his debut in the No. 9 shirt in the penultimate of them—at Nottingham Forest in December 1920.

It was tough for Mills as he was in and out of the side at first and City went 10 League games without a win in early 1921. But he scored his first goals for the club—at home to Sheffield Wednesday and in a 4–1 defeat at Notts County, whom he was later to join—during the run. Two more goals followed as he ended up playing in 15 games during 1920–21, latterly showing signs of developing a useful partnership in attack with the popular Charlie Flood.

Mills became more of a first-team regular in 1921–22, playing in 24 League games, but his goalscoring was spasmodic. He played in six of the first 11 League games, but failed to find the mark. Then in November 1921 City won four League games in succession and Mills scored a total of nine goals in them. But his brief purple patch began with four in a 7–1 home win over Stoke—they did not become Stoke City until four years later—who amazingly went on to win promotion to the First Division as the runners-up to Nottingham Forest that season.

Mills' goals came in a 27-minute spree—after 23, 33, 42 and 50 minutes—underlining his value when he was on song: And it was written of his feat:

> Undoubtedly, the hero of the game was 'Paddy' Mills, who has been the subject of much discussion in local-football circles during the season. When he was playing hard and doing everything but score, there was a feeling that he was hardly mature enough for the position of leader of the Tigers' line. But on this occasion he would undoubtedly have got two more goals but for being tripped when in a favourable position to shoot. His success was due as much to his own abilities as to the work of his comrades. Three of his goals were obtained by solo efforts which took him from the halfway-line to the goal area. During the past week he has been indulging in ball practice and dribbling to shoot on the run and how well he followed this up! He has only to add finishing power to his work to become one of the greatest centre-forwards in the Second Division.

In addition, Mills had to be carried off on trainer Joe Beck's back with badly-bruised ribs in the closing stages.

Oddly enough, Mills scored in only one other League game that season—with two in a 2–0 win at Crystal Palace in January 1922—so it was felt that he still had plenty to prove. At any rate there was some belated recognition of his embryonic value towards the end of the season when City, who still had one League game left, visited Barton Town at the start of May to play in what became known as 'the Bert Mills transfer match.' The Tigers won 2–1 in front of a 2,000 crowd after being behind at halftime, but Mills aptly equalised from Northern Ireland international Danny McKinney's cross before Tom Eccles scored the winner. Even more fittingly, Mills scored both City's goals when they returned to Barton for another friendly and again won 2–1 exactly a year later.

There were also early comparisons of Mills with three of the Tigers' immediate post-war goalscoring heroes—Sammy Stevens, Tom Brandon and Flood—and teammate Jimmy Lodge once said of him: 'He was not quite a Sammy Stevens, but he was one of the fittest men who ever played. There was no limit to his stamina.' Mills had, in effect, been signed as a potential replacement for Stevens, who had moved to Notts County during the summer of 1920. At that stage Stevens had been second only to John 'Jackie' Smith in the blossoming City's League goalscoring ranks, but Mills would eventually overtake them both—only, though, after he himself had had a spell with County.

Mills, meanwhile, still struggled to have any consistency in his goalscoring. He was out of the side for much of the first half of the 1922–23 season, during which time he was on the mark only once. But he scored seven times in the League in the second half of the campaign, including three in four games, when he featured more regularly. The pattern continued during 1923–24 when he was again slow out of the goalscoring blocks although he played most of his games at left-half until Christmas. When Mills was restored to the centre-forward berth, though, the switch soon paid dividends. He broke his duck for the season when he hit a hat-trick in a 5–0 win over Bristol City at Anlaby Road and in the next home game on Boxing Day he added a further treble when City beat Fulham 4–2. He also scored in the FA Cup against Bolton Wanderers even though he was carried off at one point. And a promising partnership with

George Martin continued to develop as Mills missed only one League game out of 42 that season.

In the four seasons since Mills' arrival and Stevens' departure, though, the Tigers had not been particularly prolific goalscorers in the League as a team—43 in 1920–21, 64 in 1921–22, 52 in 1922–23 and 46 in 1923–24. Mills had scored 34 of them, but the burden on him was increasing. Fortunately for him and City, the best was yet to come.

In 1924–25 City moved up seven places to finish 10th in the Second Division table, but it would have been a vastly-different tale if Mills had not had by far his best season to date. In fact, he quite simply carried the side in terms of goalscoring. City managed just 50 League goals and Mills scored half of them. The record included only 10 away goals and Mills scored six of them. And they scored just 12 goals in the first 10 games with Mills getting seven of them. He scored at some point against seven of the top-eight clubs with only runners-up Manchester United curbing him. Mills also scored eight times in four successive home games, he twice scored in four consecutive League games and he added a further four to his tally in five FA Cup ties.

He matured and became a marked man, a factor which was amplified in a 5–0 victory over Portsmouth, who finished fourth, on their first visit to Hull in January 1925. Mills scored twice early on, but had to be carried off just before halftime after a foul by Harry Foxall. He did return, but went off for good early in the second half. And it was written of him:

> 'Paddy' Mills became a firm favourite of the Anlaby Road crowds. Previously unconvinced, they took warmly to his sharp, penetrative style of play, his bags of bustle and his clever shooting ability. As a centre-forward of compact rather than huge build, he was alert, mobile and adroit, ever ready to trade all-out endeavour for space in the penalty area.

It was also reported:

> 'Paddy' was not a big 'un, but he was tough enough to shake the best and biggest of centre half-backs, so, although he could take up any position in the attack, it was at centre-forward that his natural talents and great pace found an outlet.

Mills continued in the same goalscoring vein during the 1925–26 season and had better support in attack from George Whitworth, but a turning-point was approaching. He scored five goals in four League outings when the Tigers began the season promisingly and he then scored three in three games despite missing three fixtures during the run. But City were losing ground and, even though he rallied them with six goals in six mid-season League games, the crunch eventually came.

In March 1926 Mills scored twice in a 3–3 draw at Middlesbrough and a week later he had his benefit game when City beat struggling Stockport County 4–0 at home. It earned him £350, but soon after the start he was switched from inside-left to outside-right, which was reckoned to be 'incomprehensible to many of the onlookers.' Two days later Mills was on his way as Notts County, whose long-serving secretary-manager Albert Fisher had been at the game, instigated a £3,000 deal although the fee was later amended to £3,750. They were desperate to land a marksman in their battle against relegation, but they still went down in bottom place as the lowest goalscorers in the First Division. County, for whom Mills' brother Percy made 409 League appearances and scored 21 goals, had beaten Burnley for his signature, while Huddersfield Town had also been interested. But it was indicative of Mills' value to the Tigers and the pressure that he had been under to keep knocking in the goals that he was still their leading marksman by the end of the season with 17 in 27 League appearances. And his move provoked a boardroom revolt because two directors resigned in a protest about the way in which their colleagues had tried to balance the books by allowing Mills to go.

Mills had another goalscoring brother, Arthur, who was on the mark 14 times in 36 League starts for Luton Town and 12 times in 33 starts for Gillingham, but Bert was the one who was once dubbed 'the lionheart of Lincolnshire.' When he left City, he had played in 173 League games, scoring 76 goals. At that point he was also third in the club's all-time goalscoring list. He had also scored four times in three FA Cup ties in 1924–25 and been on the mark abroad twice during City's summer tour of Sweden in 1924. Ironically, the Tigers finished higher than Notts County, for whom he scored 35 goals in 76

League appearances, during the next two seasons, but it was not until the summer of 1928 that Mills was adequately replaced when Ken McDonald, a Welshman who had started his prolific career in Scotland, moved to Anlaby Road from Bradford Park Avenue. County improved during 1928–29 and it meant that Mills earned a mid-season return to the top flight with Birmingham City, but it was not to last too long and he scored three times in his 13 League appearances for them.

And during Christmas week of 1929 Mills rejoined the Tigers. McDonald had scored 22 League goals by Christmas Day 1928, including all five at home to Bristol City, and he also began the 1929–30 season well with five in the first seven League games. City had taken nine points out of a possible 10 at the start of the season with McDonald developing a useful partnership with Stan Alexander, but they won only once in their next 10 League games and Mills was seen as one of the solutions to their problems. He and McDonald, who was transferred to Halifax Town in March 1930, never played together in League football as the Tigers had one of the most inconsistent and baffling seasons in their history. Mills' return heralded both relegation for the first time and their best-ever FA Cup run as they progressed to the semi-finals.

Mills was back in harness in time to play in the Tigers' first game of 1930 when they drew 2–2 at home to Cardiff City and it seemed that little had changed for him in one sense. It was reported: 'Mills' form did not appear to have undergone much change from the last time that he appeared at Anlaby Road although it seemed that the remainder of the team relied too much on him.' Mills was out of the side for seven successive League games as City lost their way in the Second Division, but he soon made his mark in the Cup.

The run began with a 4–3 win at Plymouth, who were on their way to the Third Division South title, in the third round and it continued a fortnight later when Mills was on the mark in a 3–1 home win over Blackpool, who, in turn, were on their way to the Second Division title. The fifth round brought the Tigers a trip to Manchester City, who had just knocked out Swindon Town 10–1 in a replay, and they were a goal down after just three minutes. Ernie Toseland gave Manchester City, who were to finish third in the First

Division that season, the lead, but then winger Billy Taylor made one and scored one for the Tigers to stun the Maine Road crowd of 61,574. Taylor had a drive diverted home by Mills with his head for the equaliser after half-an-hour and then grabbed the winner in the second half.

Mills missed the two quarter-final ties against Newcastle United, who were then struggling in the First Division, because of injury when City won 1–0 after a 1–1 draw at St James' Park, but he was back to face Arsenal in the last four. Arsenal, then mid-table in the First Division, in theory posed less of a threat than Manchester City, but luck deserted the Tigers in the end.

City led 2–0 at halftime in the first encounter at Elland Road, Leeds, but Arsenal adopted a more physical approach after the interval and George Goldsmith, Matt Bell, Jimmy Walsh and Mills all picked up knocks. Walsh had to move on to the wing with Mills taking up his wing-half role after switching from centre-forward, but he himself was struggling with a shoulder injury and failed to cut out the danger posed by future England international Cliff Bastin on his way to scoring Arsenal's equaliser eight minutes from time. Mills was also hurt in the replay at Villa Park, Birmingham, four days later because he was carried off five minutes from time when Arsenal won 1–0. But the damage had been done by then because it was claimed that the ball had gone out of play in the build-up to David Jack's 11th-minute winner and City had had centre-half Arthur Childs sent off five minutes after halftime. Jimmy Howieson and Mills had gone close to grabbing an equaliser, but Long Eaton referee Arthur 'Algie' Kingscott angered City even more at the end. Mills explained:

> As we were running off the field, the referee said: 'Never mind, Paddy, there are two good teams in the final!' I'd never heard anything like it, so I reported it to the manager Bill McCracken when we got back to the dressing-room. He asked if I were sure about what the referee had said and, if so, whether I would repeat it in front of the directors and the FA. I said I'd tell it to anybody.

City's chairman Dr Clifford Durham-Pullan resigned as a protest against the refereeing and it was curious that Kingscott's father, Arthur senior, who was then the FA's treasurer, had been involved in the same kind of goal-line controversy when he had refereed the FA Cup final.

City, meanwhile, were left to face a battle against relegation for the first time as they won one League game in 12. Mills had failed to find the mark in his first five League games back at Anlaby Road. And when he did so, it was in a 7–1 defeat at West Bromwich Albion. He scored again in a 2–0 home win over Tottenham Hotspur, but the Tigers still went down—with Mills' old club Notts County. And it was observed after relegation: 'Mills was buffeted about too much in the cup ties to be able to produce his old thrustfulness and power of finish in subsequent League matches on the hard grounds.'

It turned out that City's first involvement in football in the Third Division North brought them abundant goals although defences were generally more lax and disorganised in those days. Their League record was 99 goals in 42 games in 1930–31, 82 in 40 games in 1931–32 and 100 in 42 games in 1932–33 when they were promoted for the first time. Mills, who played at inside-right in a 3–1 defeat at the ailing Wigan Borough in September 1931 in a match that was subsequently expunged from the record-books when they resigned from the League soon afterwards, played his part in the first two seasons, but there was a distinct shape to his goalscoring exploits.

In 1930–31 Mills played 30 League games and was fourth top goalscorer on 12 behind Stan Alexander on 24, future Scottish international winger Douglas 'Dally' Duncan on 18 and Simon Raleigh on 15. Mills wore the No. 9 shirt 13 times, but played more often at wing-half. But it is open to debate as to what he might have achieved if Bill McCracken had played him more regularly at centre-forward because all his 12 goals came in two spells there. He scored five in the first five games and then seven in five towards the end of the season as City's No. 9 and it included a quickfire hat-trick when the goals came after six, 25 and 46 minutes in a 5–1 win on the club's first-ever visit to Carlisle in April 1931.

There was the same kind of pattern during the 1931–32 season when Mills wore five different shirts. Again he was fourth top League goalscorer behind Duncan on 19, Russell Wainscoat on 16 and Fred Speed on 12. This time Mills, who had played at centre-forward for the Whites against the Amber-and-Blacks in City's in-house, pre-season practice match and then been left out of the side for the opening game of the season, scored 11 goals in 37 League games, but new manager Haydn Green gave him the left-half berth for most of the first half of the season. But in mid-January 1932 Mills finally played his first game of the season at centre-forward and promptly hit a hat-trick in a 3–0 home win over Walsall. It was written: 'Mills made goalscoring look easy. He imparted wonderful enthusiasm into his play, his third goal especially being a bright example of the will-to-win spirit. He was so much of a live force on a ground just to his liking.' He then scored in the next two games, too. Coincidentally, he wore the No. 9 shirt on 10 occasions and it brought him eight of his 10 goals.

The last game of the season in May 1932 produced Mills his final goal for the Tigers in a 5–0 home win over Wrexham and it proved to be a watershed in his career with the club. He stayed on to help City to promotion in 1932–33, playing in 19 League games. But he was never given the centre-forward role again and played every game as a wing-half or inside-forward. Instead newcomer Bill McNaughton took over the No. 9 shirt and recorded a club-record 41 League goals in it as City scored 111 goals during the season—100 in the Third Division North and 11 in four FA Cup ties.

The last of Mills' 269 League games for the Tigers was in a 2–1 win at York City in late April 1933. Nine days later the scoreline was the same in the return game at Anlaby Road and City clinched the one promotion place open to the Third Division North champions. Mills had finished as the club's leading marksman overall with 101 League goals and remains third in their all-time charts behind Chris Chilton and Ken Wagstaff. He had overtaken Sammy Stevens, who had scored 84 in the League, and John Smith, who was on 98. And while Mills and Stevens had both left City to join Notts County, there was more in common between Mills and Smith. Both had played for City alongside forwards who were to die tragically while involved in games—Smith with David Wilson and Mills with Simon Raleigh. In addition, Mills had played alongside Sammy Hamilton, who also died young, during 1923–24. Smith and Mills had both scored regularly for City on summer tours to Sweden and both were prolific marksmen who ended their careers playing predominately in more defensive roles.

Mills, who was a month short of his 94th birthday when he died in

January 1994, may have played his part in ensuring that City regained their Second Division status in 1933, but he was not kept on to taste it again. He and full-back Arthur Rodgers were not re-signed and Mills moved back into non-League football. He initially joined Scunthorpe United, who were not a League club until 1950, and then Gainsborough Trinity, who had been a League club in City's early years before the 1914–18 War. Later in life Mills, who at one stage had the distinction of being the oldest-surviving player to have been with the oldest-surviving League club in England—Notts County— became a security officer at Scunthorpe's Redbourn Steelworks. And he never lost the all-action, never-say-die approach that had typified his football because he reflected much later: 'I drove a car until I was 85 and my biggest mistake was selling it!'

6

GEORGE 'GEORDIE' MADDISON

If goalkeepers are expected to be extroverts as a matter of course, then George 'Geordie' Maddison fitted the bill perfectly—both on and off the field. After all, Freddie Cowell, later Hull City's youth education officer, said: 'He was a character, he always wore a flat cap and he was a very good goalkeeper.' And it was once written of Maddison: 'The bigger the event the greater the confidence with which he plays.' Born at Birtley in County Durham, Maddison was acknowledged as an outgoing character who was the subject of a fund of anecdotes, some of which might well have been exaggerated in keeping with his personality. He was said to have lived life to the full before dying relatively young, but even that is shrouded in uncertainty. It is certain that he was a showman to the end because he died while singing on the stage of a Hull club in April 1959. But it was reported that he was 58 and yet confusion surrounds his age— simply because there is a doubt as to when he was actually born. The record-books tend to say that he was born on either August 14, 1901, or August 14, 1902. But his family firmly believe that he was born on August 13, 1902, which would, of course, have made him only 57 when he died.

Maddison's charisma also meant that there was always a

likelihood that tales about him as City's long-serving goalkeeper might also be inaccurate. For example, it was said that he would smoke a sly cigarette on the pitch or take a pint of beer out with him. And his grand-daughter Carole Bradford did confirm: 'He always smoked Woodbines . . .' But his great-grandson Paul Bradford insisted: 'Stories about him smoking and drinking on the pitch were made up. He did like a drink socially, but he was totally dedicated as a footballer and wouldn't have done anything that stood in the way of that.' In addition, Maddison and his teammate Cliff Woodhead would often walk down to Hull's Walton Club after home games at Anlaby Road in the 1930s, but Woodhead's son Don said: 'The two wives would make supper while they were there. But they never went on the pitch drunk.'

But some larger-than-life stories about Maddison do have a ring of authenticity about them. For example, Paul Bradford believes that it is true that he used to smuggle lads into games free under his overcoat. And he added: 'They used to say that, when he picked a pint glass up, you couldn't see it because his hands were so big.' Furthermore, Maddison's son-in-law Joe Last disclosed:

> He always wore a silk silver thread round his neck. He had once had a bout of quinsy and a gypsy had told him that he wouldn't get it back if he wore a silver string round his neck—and he never seemed to have a sore throat again!

And there are other accounts which suggest that Maddison was naturally superstitious—he would always put on his left boot first and then fasten its lace; he always insisted on being the last man to leave the dressing-room on his way out on to the pitch; and he even made a point of always stepping over certain sinks on his way to matches at Anlaby Road!

And some of Maddison's antics did occur during play. For example, he used to attract hordes of supporters behind his goal and maintain running commentaries to them during games! When nothing was doing at his end, he might toss sweets to youngsters behind his goal or throw them pennies that had gone astray from collection sheets! And on one amazing occasion when he had little to do on a cold day while playing for the reserves, a group of fans went to fetch a workman's brazier which, they knew, was close at hand and brought it for him to keep him warm! It is thought that Maddison then put it in his goalmouth until the referee stopped the game and told him that he could keep it behind the dead-ball line so that it was not interfering with play!

Maddison had his eccentric moments as a goalkeeper, too, because it was once written of him:

> Clever, but unorthodox, he had a razor-sharp eye and judgment, which kept him out of difficulties, and a consistent brilliance, which astonished many and drew the admiration of all. 'Geordie' Maddison was a cavalier among goalkeepers. He was a dominant figure—big and powerful—and a man who refused to be put down or kept in his place. His methods and techniques were calculated to upset the most composed of opposition and inspire his own side. He could catch the most powerful of shots in full flight while roaming loosely around his goalmouth. The whole basis of his goalkeeping was eye and timing and there was a fine sagacity about his play, which wasn't always appreciated. He took pains to be master of his own penalty area and it involved a keen understanding with a succession of backs. And there was the wry humour of his native Durham in everything he did.

He also disliked staying on his line, so he would occasionally leave his penalty area and beat an opponent before kicking upfield! And City teammate Stan Dixon once said: 'He would never allow a wall of players to stand in front of him for free-kicks and I cannot remember him ever conceding a goal from one. He wanted to see where the ball was and he would catch it.' And there might just have been more method than madness because Maddison himself insisted: 'In the olden days you had to do as you were told.' At any rate his technique served him well enough with the Tigers because he played for them from 1924 to 1938, he was an ever-present during four seasons, he once played in 115 consecutive League games and he remains third in their all-time League appearances list.

He had started his career with Birtley, which was also the birthplace of one of City's first goalkeepers, Ernest Storey, in the Northern Alliance before joining Tottenham Hotspur, where he made 40 League appearances and played alongside England internationals Fred 'Fanny' Walden, Arthur Grimsdell and Jimmy Dimmock, in

November 1922. But then the Tigers returned from their successful close-season tour of Sweden during the summer of 1924 to find that manager Bill McCracken had made two signings—Irish international centre-half Mick O'Brien from Leicester City for £750 and Maddison from Spurs for nothing. At Tottenham, though, Maddison had been under the wing of their manager Peter McWilliam, the former Scotland half-back who had been a teammate of McCracken at Newcastle United, and he was ready to make an impact with the Tigers.

But he had first to dislodge Billy Mercer, who had been a regular fixture in City's goal since early 1920, and his chance came at the start of November 1924. City, who had been improving after a poor start to the season, lost 1–0 at Chelsea to a goal from ex-Tiger and future England international Jackie Crawford, whose shot rolled over Mercer's arm and into the net. Mercer was said to be 'in need of a rest after his very strenuous work', so Maddison was given his opportunity a week later when City beat Stockport County 3–0 at home. Mercer sought a transfer and four days later he moved to First Division Huddersfield Town, whose legendary manager Herbert Chapman's brother Harry, had once been in charge of City. It was a good move for Mercer because Huddersfield were on their way to completing a hat-trick of First Division title wins, but Maddison never looked back with the Tigers after that first clean sheet.

He was a first-team regular for the rest of the season although he suffered an injury setback in the FA Cup first round against Wolverhampton Wanderers in January 1925 and amazingly his initial deputy was full-back Matt Bell. The tie at Anlaby Road ended in a 1–1 draw and Maddison was said to have suffered 'a maimed hand.' It was reported:

> Maddison went down to meet the ball and sustained the injury that may keep him out of the game for a few weeks. He is not having the best of luck since his promotion to the first team. Even if he betrays a somewhat excitable disposition, he is a great custodian and two of his clearances, including the one in which he injured himself, were worthy of his predecessors in Hull City's goal.

Maddison was back in harness on St Valentine's Day when City had the heart to beat Barnsley 2–1 for only their second away League success of the season and he did not miss another game until the start of December 1927. And it was during this period that Maddison gave what he regarded as his best performance for the club. It came against Manchester City in November 1926 when the Tigers won 3–2 with goals by Bill Cowan, Harry Scott and Billy Taylor. It was reported: 'Maddison's display was heroic. No other word does justice to his brave and really brilliant exhibition.' And Maddison himself reflected:

> The Hull pitch was 'over-ankles' in mud and for long periods I had the Manchester City forwards to play on my own because our defenders couldn't turn round quickly in the muck. The heavy, slippery ball came to me like a cannonball, but that day it was like a cricket ball to me. I caught it and grabbed it with all the ease in the world. Afterwards Jimmy McMullan, the Manchester City skipper, came over and congratulated me on my game.

And in April 1926 Maddison had even scored a goal for the Tigers. Furthermore, it happened in the kind of circumstances that typified his natural buoyancy because he converted a penalty and then saved one! City won 5–2 in a benefit match at Norwich for their captain George Martin. The score was soon 1–1, but midway through the first half the Tigers were awarded a penalty when centre-forward George Whitworth, who would otherwise have gone on to complete a hat-trick, had a goalbound shot handled by Archie Campbell. Maddison went up and scored from the spot, but near the end of the game Norwich were also awarded a penalty after a handling offence. Their goalkeeper Charlie Dennington stepped up to take it, but Maddison promptly turned his drive round the post!

But there were tougher challenges, too, and one of them had occurred in a 3–1 defeat at Stoke in November 1925 when it was quirkily reported: 'The ground was very hard after a week of more frost than snow and was too treacherous for Maddison to run his usual risks.' Maddison himself mused:

> It was the most miserable day of my life. The ground was as hard as iron, it was freezing hard and it had been for days. In the first half our chaps simply swarmed over Stoke and rained shot after shot at them, but then suddenly after about half an hour the Stoke forwards broke away. One of them shot and it was one that I could have caught on a

teaspoon at any other time, but I didn't move until too late. The ball came to my outstretched hand and simply went into the goal. I was frozen. I didn't make my move until too late because my cold limbs wouldn't move as they should have. The ball struck a 'dead log' when it hit my hand. I had practically no feelings in my hands and couldn't have stopped a toffee apple. In the second half the same thing happened. This time, though, the shot was a hard, good one, but I didn't move until too late for the same reason. I preferred the busy days every time.

Curiously, one of City's best post-war goalkeepers Tony Norman would list Sheffield United's Bramall Lane and Oldham Athletic's Boundary Park among his least favourite grounds and Maddison would probably have sympathised with him because he let in seven in a game on both of them during the 1930s. He said:

> The unhappiest ground for me was Boundary Park at Oldham because I always seemed to get it in the neck there. The worst time was one in which in which Oldham won 7–0. They got the ball in the net 10 times altogether, but three of the goals were disallowed for offside. Another time when I went to Oldham the score stood at 5–0 for them at halftime, but I played like a madman in the second half and managed to keep it at five until the end.

But the pluses of his time with the Tigers far outweighed the minuses. Maddison himself withstood challenges from other goalkeepers and also underlined his growing reputation along the way. Paul Bradford said: 'He once kept out Dixie Dean against Everton, who wanted to sign him, but he said that he would go only if they signed the rest of the defence with him.' At the time they comprised the American-born John 'Jock' Gibson, Bell, John Collier, O'Brien and Tommy Bleakley.

The many competitors included Jacob Iceton, who moved on to Fulham, George Wolf, who had spells with Preston North End and Blackpool, Tom Swinburne, who joined Newcastle, and two Scots, Hugh Farquharson, whose unorthodox approach to goalkeeping was thought to have stemmed from understudying Maddison, and Reuben Bennett, who later became a noted member of Liverpool's bootroom fraternity during their post-war glory days. In fact, Farquharson, who later moved on to Dunfermline Athletic, had stood in for Maddison when he had his bout of quinsy and tonsillitis.

But when it came to rivalry for the goalkeeping jersey at Anlaby Road, Maddison was most closely associated with former Yorkshire miner Fred Gibson. They were also good friends and in the end Gibson left City in odd circumstances—when they refused to let Maddison go. Maddison recalled:

> Freddie Gibson got into the side in 1929–30 when I twisted my knee against Cardiff City and stayed in during the one time in my life when I might have had great hopes. It was the season in which Hull broke all the club records by going to the semi-finals of the FA Cup. I was hurt just then, but Freddie was more than a worthy substitute and later went to Middlesbrough for a big fee. But the point of that transfer was that first of all Middlesbrough came in to sign me. But Hull wouldn't part, so 'Boro took the young fellow. I dare say that I could have been transferred several times from Hull, but the directors would never part with me.

Gibson, though, had already received the benefits of his great rival's memorable method of tuition. Maddison explained:

> Freddie was one of the boys I taught with the goal and clothes-line idea. I'd take a rope and tie each end to the bottom of the uprights. That left me a yard or two of slack rope. I'd take the slack and draw it to a point, which represented where the opponent was playing. The length of rope marked the angle. I'd point out to the young goalkeeper that, if he stood at the point of that angle, he could completely block the shot of the opponent. Obviously a goalkeeper can't take a rope out with him in a match and ask the opponent to stand still while he marks out the angle. But this rope business got the young goalkeeper into the way of realising that shots can beat him only if he has failed to realise and effectively block the point of an angle—some angle. It's up to him to weigh up the angle. He can do this, of course, only by continually studying angles. Positional sense in a goalkeeper is merely a matter of realising the angles. A good goalkeeper is distinct from a bad one only by the speed at which he weighs up the angles.

It was also during the latter part of the 1929–30 season that Maddison shared a joint benefit match with fellow defenders Bell and Bleakley—a 3–0 home defeat by Blackpool. But it was a bitter-sweet phase in Maddison's career because he missed out on City's

Cup exploits and was then back in the side for the final three League games when the club were relegated for the first time.

The competition between Maddison and Gibson was to continue for more than two more seasons in the Third Division North. But early in the 1932–33 season Maddison regained his place in the side and soon afterwards Gibson got his move to Middlesbrough. And it meant that Maddison had a major role in City's first promotion campaign when they returned to the Second Division as champions. He played in 34 consecutive League games and his heroism shone through as City clinched promotion at the start of May 1933 with a 2–1 win over York City in their last home game of the season. It was a rough affair at times and Maddison soldiered on despite breaking his left shoulder after just 10 minutes. Not surprisingly, he missed the final game at Rochdale when Edgar Ainsworth, the club's first locally-born England amateur international, made his League debut. But club chairman John Baraclough praised Maddison's stoicism in his speech at a celebration dinner at Hull's Field's Café after promotion, also referring to him as 'our entertainer.'

But further relegation followed in 1935–36 although Maddison missed few games in the Tigers' three seasons back in the Second Division. He was again an ever-present in the club's first campaign back in the Third Division North, during which he turned his big hands to another use on their behalf. Manager David Menzies died in October 1936 and his funeral took place at Hull's Anlaby Road Presbyterian Church, where he had been a member. Menzies' interment took place at Shipley's Nab Wood cemetery on the outskirts of Bradford, the other city with which he had a strong link, but Maddison was one of six City players who carried the coffin at the church service.

In 1937–38, though, the years finally took their toll on Maddison. He had had a few injury setbacks during his long career, once suffering from a bout of lumbago during pre-season training, but this time he was forced to retire after damaging his arm early in 1938. He was top of City's appearances list with 430 in the League when he bowed out in a 1–1 home draw with New Brighton in February 1938. Appropriately, his deputy for the rest of the season, Edward Goodall, also came from the North-East, but Maddison's exit had its irony as City just missed out on promotion in third spot. Just as it was announced in May 1938 that he would not be retained, he played for the reserves in a 4–0 defeat at Doncaster, but he was granted a second benefit game. It was also a 1–1 home draw, it was against Crewe Alexandra and it was the final game of the season. Maddison's teammate Cliff Hubbard took charge of the subscription list opened for the benefit. And it was optimistically announced:

> George Maddison will take his benefit in this match, so everyone will have to pass through the turnstiles. Another big crowd is expected in appreciation of the long and loyal services rendered to Hull City by the popular goalkeeper.

But the reality was that the Crewe game attracted just 4,410 spectators—compared with the 21,756 at their home game only a week earlier when City had lost 1–0 to champions Tranmere Rovers in a potential promotion decider. The club had gone from their highest gate of the season to their lowest in a week and poor Maddison was the innocent victim of fickle fate.

Maddison was released with fellow first-teamers Tom Foster, William Mackay and Ernie Bell and it was said of him:

> The granting of a free transfer terminates a long and valuable connection with Hull City of one of the most popular goalkeepers who have assisted them. No other player—past or present—has served the club for such a lengthy period.

Maddison himself once reflected: 'As a boy, I had no other football ambition but to be a good goalkeeper.' And before he was done, two other goalkeepers benefited from his experience and expertise. One was Billy Bly, City's next long-serving goalkeeper who again came from the North-East. The other was Maddison's own son, George junior.

Maddison senior and Bly were teammates with City for one season—1937–38—but there was an instant rapport between the two. After all, Maddison handed down his first-team jersey to Bly— on his first day at the club for use in a practice match! And Bly, who wore Maddison's jersey for a lengthy spell and was reluctant to part with it even when it became tattered, said: 'He passed on plenty of tips to me, especially with regard to angles. We did all our training together and he was a grand chap.' And when City went to a new ground after the 1939–45 War, Maddison could not stay away and kept a watchful eye on his protégé because in typical style he might regularly be spotted just behind the net of the goal at the Bunker's Hill end at Boothferry Park.

And there was an amazing coincidence about the two Maddisons' careers. Former Northern Ireland international Bill McCracken signed George senior when he was the Tigers' manager and then he also snapped up George junior, who also died young in 1987, when he was in charge at Aldershot—with 24 years in-between. George junior, who had played for City's juniors and then joined Grimsby Town as an amateur, moved to Aldershot, for whom he made two League appearances, after a trial during the summer of 1948 and also had a spell with York City, for whom he appeared in 11 League games. But McCracken must be one of the few managers to have signed two players with the same name who played in the same position!

George senior, who later worked as a plater's helper for local marine engineering firm C.D. Holmes, had made a huge impact on the Tigers' followers with his dynamic disposition, but his family knew him as more of a genial, gentle giant who was easy-going off the pitch, always retained a sense of humour and enjoyed socialising. He lived in Hull's De La Pole Avenue and Spring Bank West before he and his wife Mary settled in the city's Wold Road, an area where City had many clubhouses built. They had three children—Peggy and Mary junior, both of whom were born in Birtley in the 1920s, and George junior, who was born in Hull in 1930—and six grandchildren—Carole, Patricia, Stephen, Jacqueline, Peter and Gary.

Paul Bradford said: 'His grandson Gary said that he liked a drink and a good social life. Apparently he never had a temper or would be angry or aggressive for a big guy who looked intimidating in goal. He would always diffuse a situation instead.' And Carole Bradford recalled:

> He was a lovely bloke who never used to argue with anybody. He loved his garden, where he grew sweet peas and potatoes, and he would always take the family on holiday during the summer when he came out of football. They'd go back to his birthplace of Birtley for one week and there'd always be another week in Scarborough.

There were lots of laughs in Maddison's company, too, because Carole added:

> I can remember that on Christmas Eve he sat me on the gate and told me to look for Father Christmas. He said that he would be coming from the direction of County Road if I kept watching. I would keep watching for quite a while, but he wasn't there, of course, and then my grandfather would tell me: 'You've missed him because you looked the wrong way!' And he always had to watch *Wells Fargo* on a Saturday night before he went out. He and Mary had a black-and-white television with a bad picture, so he would always close the curtains so that he could see it properly!

A social life was equally important to Maddison because Joe Last recalled: 'He would take us with him on the bus from Priory Road to the Eagle on Anlaby Road on a Sunday lunchtime to meet up with former City player Andy Browell.' They never played together, but Browell did eventually work in Hull 'on the buses . . .' And Maddison was socialising to the end because Carole Bradford said:

> He used to go in the Priory pub, but then moved on to Manor Club because there was more singing. He would go in on a Saturday night and they would shout for him to get up and sing. Sometimes he would and sometimes he wouldn't, but that was what he was doing on Whit Monday in 1959 when he collapsed and died.

At the time Manor Club was owned by one-time Hull Kingston Rovers' chairman Wilf Spaven and Maddison had gone on stage in response to requests. He had sung Rovers' theme tune 'When the Red, Red Robin' and 'Carolina in the Morning' and was performing 'Lover, Come back to me' when he suddenly put the hands that had defied so many forwards to his head, collapsed and then died.

But George Maddison, the gregarious goalkeeper, has not exactly been forgotten. Not long ago acclaimed playwright and loyal City supporter Alan Plater made sure of it. After all, he frequently used to show his respect for Tigers heroes by recycling their surnames for characters in his work. Alan's final play, shown by the BBC on television not long after he had passed away in June 2010, was set in his native North-East, starred popular local actors Kevin Whately and Robson Green and was entitled *Joe Maddison's War* . . .

7

CLIFF WOODHEAD

The 1930s began badly for both Hull City and their new full-back Cliff Woodhead. In May 1930 the Tigers were relegated for the first time in their history and Woodhead was signed from Denaby United in his native South Yorkshire. Only weeks after reaching the FA Cup semi-finals for the first time, the Tigers went down with Notts County. They had had a run of only one win in 12 League outings in stark contrast to their Cup exploits and found themselves in the Third Division North, finishing on the same number of points as Bristol City, who had crucially beaten them 1–0 at Anlaby Road in the penultimate game of the campaign.

City retained most of their relegation squad, but they still needed new blood for the new decade and Woodhead, who was born at Darton, near Barnsley, in August 1908, provided it. He had played for Ardsley Athletic in 1928–29, he had had a spell with Dearne Valley Old Boys and he had had trials with two other League clubs, Barnsley and Southport, before Jimmy Lodge, a man of many backroom roles who had been a City full-back himself, spotted him with Denaby. And it was just as well that the Tigers moved in swiftly for his services because Tottenham Hotspur and Sunderland had also been interested in snapping up Woodhead at the time.

In one sense, though, Woodhead at least might have shown Southport what they had been missing when he made his League debut against them at Anlaby Road in December 1930. The Tigers won 5–1 when Woodhead was given his big chance at right-back as a replacement for George Goldsmith, but it turned out to be his only senior game of the 1930–31 season because it was reported: 'His display suggested that his promotion came a little too early.'

Woodhead's full-back partner on his City debut had been the durable Matt Bell, but there was no immediate indication that he would emerge as such a dependable defender in the club's annals as his teammate. As was the case with so many City heroes, he had made an ignominious start and had to go back to his personal football drawing-board.

Woodhead also had to see off competition from two other full-backs called Rodgers. One was 21-year-old Windsor Rodgers, from New Tredegar, who had won an FA Amateur Cup medal with Wycombe Wanderers in 1930–31. He had been signed in August 1931 after a trial, but he never forced his way into City's League team. The other was Arthur Rodgers, who had also joined the Tigers from Denaby.

But Woodhead was still out of favour for the opening game of the 1931–32 season as two other Yorkshiremen, Goldsmith and Arthur Rodgers, both of whom had featured in the Second Division during City's relegation campaign of 1929–30, were given the nod. But Woodhead replaced Goldsmith again for the second game—a 4–1 win at Walsall—and this time he never looked back. It was reported: 'The former Denaby United pair, Rodgers and Woodhead, soon struck up a sound partnership. Woodhead quite justified his promotion and almost brought off a goal with a long-distance shot.' And it was a classic case of 'so near, but so far' because Woodhead never scored a goal in what turned out to be a lengthy League career.

But the Tigers used just the three full-backs in finishing eighth under the new management of Haydn Green in 1931–32 and Woodhead, who was described as 'not heavily-built, but quick in action', made the most appearances. Goldsmith and Rodgers played in 19 and 30 League games respectively, but Woodhead managed 32. The trio played together only once—when Goldsmith played at right-half in a 2–1 win at New Brighton in September 1931—but it was Rodgers who was to leave first.

Both Woodhead and Rodgers had had links with the mining industry because Woodhead had worked briefly at the pithead locally in South Yorkshire and Rodgers had played for Frickley Colliery. But Woodhead was not to be undermined and in September 1932 Rodgers moved to Merthy Tydfil although he later returned to League football in South Yorkshire with Doncaster Rovers. By that time Woodhead and Goldsmith had established themselves as the Tigers' first-choice full-back pairing.

Woodhead, given only an isolated League game by Bill McCracken, the manager who had signed him, benefited more when Green took charge, but his own versatility had also helped him to establish himself because he was equally at home at both right-back and left-back. In his first full season in League football under Green in 1931–32 he had played 21 League games at right-back and 11 at left-back and Woodhead's son Don explained: 'He was naturally right-footed, but it used to annoy him when players were unable to use both feet properly.'

And the full-back partnership of Goldsmith and Woodhead was reliable enough to help the Tigers to promotion for the first time in 1932–33. Rodgers and William Bell briefly deputised for Goldsmith when he missed the start of the season, but Woodhead played in all 42 League games and four FA Cup ties. A lot of the publicity surrounding the promotion campaign concerned the goalscoring exploits of Bill McNaughton, who set a club record of 41 League goals in a season, and Russell Wainscoat, another son of South Yorkshire. City topped the 100 mark in the League, failing to score in only four games, but their defensive record was equally as impressive. They conceded just 45 goals in the Third Division North and only the Second Division champions, Stoke City, had a better record of the 88 League clubs. City could rely on the experience of evergreen goalkeeper George Maddison and former England centre-half Jack Hill, who was to be Green's successor as manager, but Woodhead was the club's only ever-present player that season. Freddie Cowell, later a long-serving youth education officer with City, saw him play and recalled: 'He was a pleasant fellow who played with a smile on his face. He was what was known as a footballing full-back.'

But Woodhead, whose brother Horace, a noted club singer, had died young, found himself embroiled in controversy just as the season was reaching its climax when he married Dorothy Luke at Hull's Bond Street Register Office on April 29, 1933. The trouble was that City were closing in on promotion after winning five games out of six and were due to play at home to Crewe Alexandra on the same day. Woodhead had wanted to keep the occasion secret, but a crowd of about 200 gathered outside to cheer on the couple after two youngsters had tipped them off, but there was a bigger problem surrounding the marriage. Don Woodhead explained:

> The directors wanted dad to put the wedding off to the end of the season because that was the rule in those days. But Dorothy wouldn't budge from April because she'd heard that there was a superstition that May marriages were unlucky!

She did at least insist immediately afterwards that her best wedding present would be for City not to drop any points in their title quest in the afternoon. And she duly got her wish as she watched from the stand when the Tigers, including Woodhead and his best man and long-throw expert Tommy Gardner in their line-up, beat Crewe 3–0. And it was reported: 'The full-backs Goldsmith and Woodhead played strongly and tactfully.'

Three days later City, whose chairman John Baraclough had been told that they would have to kick their way out of the Third Division North, beat struggling York City 2–1 at home to clinch promotion as the defence had to protect Maddison, who had suffered torn shoulder ligaments, and Hill, who had received a black eye. Again it was reported: 'Goldsmith and Woodhead worked like Trojans to prevent Maddison from being more heavily assailed.' At the end of the game the fans invaded the pitch and mobbed the players before they could reach the dressing-room, throwing around the cushions that had been hired by occupants of the grandstand. The players and directors then appeared in front of the stand to acknowledge their supporters. The Tigers lost their final game 3–2 at Rochdale, but still finished two points clear of runners-up Wrexham, whose manager Ernest Blackburn took charge at Anlaby Road in late 1936.

Woodhead and Maddison, in fact, became close friends and they and their families socialised a lot together, often at Hull's Walton Club. The Woodheads then lived relatively close by in De La Pole Avenue, but there was a notable occasion on which the two players were on different wavelengths on the pitch. During the 1930s City's defence often found themselves up against former internationals such as Tom 'Pongo' Waring, Fred Tilson and William 'Ginger' Richardson and in one instance a plan backfired, according to Don Woodhead. He said:

> There was a famous one-time England centre-forward who always used to clout goalkeepers and this time it had happened twice to George Maddison, who then told my dad to keep out of the way the next time it looked likely to happen. But dad forgot what he'd been told and came across to tackle with the result that Maddison well and truly flattened both him and the centre-forward!

Woodhead, though, suffered few injuries although his fitness got him into trouble on one occasion. His son Don said:

> One of the other players was feeling really down because he was short of money at Christmas time. As a result, my dad feigned injury for the first game of the festive programme so that the other lad could play. When dad then declared himself fit soon afterwards, the club realised what he'd done and he got the biggest telling-off of his career!

But Woodhead was otherwise a firm fixture in City's side and his absences were few because he missed only 32 League games out of a possible 336 in eight seasons after the not-so-splendid isolation of his debut. At one point he missed only two out of 168 in a four-season period. On one of those occasions there was a strange sequel. In April 1934 Woodhead returned after missing his only League game of the season and played in a 1–0 defeat at home to Preston North End. Fans protested about the referee, the Anlaby Road ground was closed for 14 days and City started 1934–35 with two away games.

By the time that the 1939–45 War ended his League career Woodhead had made 305 League appearances for the Tigers, which still leaves him joint 14th with post-war left-winger Ian Butler in the club's all-time list. And there were quirks that affected both the beginning and the end of his career and in one case he was prevented from finishing higher up the club's appearances list. In both instances the circumstances surrounded League games that ultimately meant nothing.

His second chance in the first team came after a game at the old Wigan Borough club in September 1931 that the Tigers lost 3–1. It was the second fixture of the season after City had opened it with a 1–0 win at home to Halifax Town, but a month after the trip to Wigan—a match refereed by Arthur Kingscott, the controversial official who had been in charge of City's FA Cup semi-final exit in 1930—they resigned from the League and it was expunged from the records. But in those two opening games there was a question-mark against Goldsmith's form and the fact that the one at Wigan had gone ahead confirmed the views of City's management. As a result, Green gave Woodhead another chance in the original third game at Walsall and it was a defining occurrence in his fledgling career.

But if that instance worked to Woodhead's advantage, then the opposite occurred at the end of his career. Two more games were deleted from the records, but this time Woodhead had played in them. They were two draws—2–2 at home to Lincoln City and 1–1 at Southport—before the 1939–40 League competition was abandoned when war broke out. Woodhead accordingly finished on 305 in the League although he continued to play for the club regularly in unofficial wartime fixtures.

Another setback in Woodhead's career was relegation from the Second Division in 1935–36 when City abandoned their traditional colours of amber and black for one disastrous campaign. They sported ultramarine and white colours instead with Woodhead and centre-forward Jack Acquroff making most appearances in them, both missing only one League game that season. As City stumbled towards relegation, it was said at one stage: 'In defence it is a pity that Woodhead's consistent and valiant resistance continues to count for so little.' The stark fact that season, though, was that the Tigers had the joint-worst defensive record of conceding 111 goals in the League—the same as Third Division South strugglers Newport County.

City began the 1936–37 season promisingly, but they faded as Woodhead missed much of the second half of the season and finished fifth. They changed back to their amber-and-black colours and they changed managers regularly in 1936. Haydn Green's successor, Jack Hill, resigned midway through the relegation season, David Menzies returned for a second spell in charge only to die after the side had been unbeaten in their opening nine League games and Ernest Blackburn, whose Wrexham had finished as runners-up to City in their 1932–33 promotion campaign, replaced him.

Woodhead missed only four games in 1937–38 and one in 1938–39 when City finished third and seventh respectively. He was also involved in January 1938 when they set a club record by beating Southport 10–1 at home and a year later when they went one better by defeating Carlisle United 11–1 at Anlaby Road. And in April 1939 Woodhead had a benefit match in a curious reciprocal arrangement. The Tigers travelled to Scotland to face Queen of the South for Willie Savage's benefit and won 3–1. Five days later the Doonhamers repaid the compliment for Woodhead's benefit in what arguably became City's last official game at Anlaby Road before their move to Boothferry Park. The game attracted a crowd of 4,000 and this time Queen of the South won 3–2.

But soon afterwards the 1939–45 War ended Woodhead's one-club League career. At first he played in wartime football for the Tigers. It comprised 18 games in the North-East Regional League and five in the Football League War Cup in 1939–40—all at right-back. Then there were 22 in the North Regional League and four in the Football League War Cup in 1940–41. His last game of any kind for City was a wartime fixture in April 1941 when they lost 8–0 at home to Middlesbrough as former England international George Camsell made his first appearance of the year for them and scored five times. Woodhead also played some wartime football for York City and served in the Royal Navy even though he was unable to swim!

Woodhead, in fact, had hardly been paid fortunes during his lengthy career with the Tigers. When he finally made his bow in Second Division football in 1933–34 following his ever-present record on the road to promotion, his wage was £6 a week with £1 extra if he played in the League team and bonuses. And the weekly amount dropped to £4. 10s. during the close season! He got a weekly rise to £6. 10s. in 1935–36—although it reverted to £6 immediately after relegation—and his summer pay went up to £5 between 1935 and 1937. But his weekly pay was then cut in the two full seasons immediately before the 1939–45 War—to £5 during them and £4 during the summers.

When hostilities ended, Woodhead moved on. In August 1946 he joined Goole Town when it was reported that his arrival was greeted with 'general satisfaction in the town's football circles.' He had joined a Goole side who won only one of their first eight Yorkshire League games and indeed he made his debut in a 4–0 defeat at Ossett Town. But it was reported: 'Cliff Woodhead made an outstanding debut for Goole.' And it was added that his 'responsibility for defeat was negligible.' One of his teammates at Goole was inside-forward Norman Anderson, with whom he had played some early wartime football with the Tigers. And his colleagues also included Goole's pre-war captain and defender Harry Clapham, whose grandson Jamie has played League football regularly.

Woodhead was also given a taste of management, but his stay at Goole was short-lived—apparently because of interference by their secretary Luke Phillipson. Don Woodhead said:

> He didn't stay long at Goole. They made him player-manager, but in those days the club secretary picked the team, so dad told him: 'That's my job.' But he did it again, so my dad told him: 'You can pick the team all the time.' They talked him into going back, but he finally finished with them two more games in. The secretary picked the team for the second match, so dad put his boots in his bag and was off.

Woodhead went to work on the railway after leaving Goole, but eventually an opportunity arose for him to return to the Tigers, who had moved into their new Boothferry Park home. Don Woodhead said:

> He got a job breaking up railway wagons at the Springhead yard in Hull. It was known as wielding the big hammer, but he got appendicitis and was lucky to be still alive, so he decided to stop that job and Hull City gave him the chance to join the ground staff and coach the juniors. He would also help with painting the grandstands as well as training the youngsters. He loved it although he got only about £8 a week, so he went to work as a barman for the club's old

centre-forward George 'Spud' Murphy, who was licensee at the Priory, so that he could supplement his wages and carry on his football work.'

Woodhead also went on a course at Lilleshall to get his coaching qualifications and became a success with City because one of his promising youngsters, David Coates, who later became a member of the club's 1958–59 promotion-winning side, recalled:

> I think that Cliff came from an era when full-backs were hard men who booted the ball a long way. But he didn't have to be hard with us as a youth team because we were successful. Under him we won the Northern Intermediate League and their league cup in the same season when we beat Leeds United in the final in 1953. It was on the same day that Blackpool beat Bolton Wanderers in the FA Cup at Wembley in what became known as the Matthews final.

His other young guns from the early 1950s also respected him because Bob Dennison said: 'Apparently he was a good, solid full-back. He was always around and was a super bloke—one of the best. He was a really nice chap.' Brian Bulless added: 'Cliff was a lovely fellow. He was easy-going and helpful. If we had any problems, he would try to solve them for us.' And Benny Bridges recalled:

> I think that all the lads liked him. We knew what he had achieved as a player, so everything that he said was gospel to us. When you're 16 or 17 and you met people such as Cliff, you believed that whatever they said was right and didn't question it.

Bridges, though, also had a stranger memory of Woodhead:

> I can remember that in one game I took my shirt off at halftime and wore it inside out for a few moments. I then took it off to change it back for the second half and Cliff wouldn't let me. I think he must have been superstitious!

And when young forward Dave Fraser joined the Tigers as an amateur in 1953 after moving from his native Scotland, his father famously informed Woodhead: 'You're his dad now!' But there was a further instance of the respect that he earned from City's youngsters because Don Woodhead said: 'At one of the juniors' away matches he was given a leather wallet that had £25 in it. The team had clubbed together for him, so it showed how highly people thought about him.'

While on the coaching staff, Woodhead also had to repair footballs and he retained his leather-stitching set as a memento. But his links with City eventually ended became he was deemed to be surplus to requirements despite producing plenty of promising youngsters. The first team struggled, finally being relegated in 1955–56, and Don Woodhead said:

> They told him that they were cutting down on staff and wages. Obviously he was disappointed because they wouldn't have been saving a hell of a lot. But he said: 'I'm glad I'm going and not Jimmy Lodge because he's a lot older than I am.' He believed that he had a better chance than Jimmy of getting another job, but he was still heart-broken. He made an excuse for not continuing, but he still used to go and watch them.

This time Woodhead, whose two sons, Cliff junior, who emigrated to Australia at one stage, and Don, both settled in North Yorkshire, made the most of the barman skills that he had learned under Murphy and became a publican. He had about 20 years as a licensee in Hull, running the Mermaid, the Bonny Boat, the Priory, where his old teammate George Maddison was a regular customer, and the St George. And while working for Hull Brewery, Woodhead emulated Maddison in one sense because he played in a friendly game in which he went in goal!

Woodhead ultimately moved to Bransholme, a huge new housing complex on the outskirts of Hull, and was a widower when he died at home in June 1985 after suffering from pneumonia. Fittingly, his funeral directors were Shepherd and Sons, a firm once headed by Arthur Shepherd, who had had a spell as the Tigers' chairman during Woodhead's playing years.

Don Woodhead reflected on his father:

> He was a very modest bloke. You would hear more about his playing career from other people rather than from him. As far as I'm concerned, you couldn't meet a nicer bloke even though I'm his son. I never heard anyone say a bad word about him. He was friendly, but not a pushy type. He lived for football and always wanted to improve himself. And he obviously enjoyed himself at Hull City.

He was one of their most loyal servants and an obituary notice substantiated Don's opinion because it described Woodhead as 'one of nature's gentlemen.'

8

BILLY BLY

There was a dark, devilish humour underlying goalkeeper Billy Bly's assessment of his lengthy Football League career, all of which he spent with Hull City, when he once observed: 'I love the game. Nobody twisted my arm to make me play.' Bly remains the longest-serving player in the club's history, but his record would have been far more impressive if it had not been for two factors—he lost much of his early career to the ravages of the 1939–45 War and he also missed out because of a series of serious injuries, the most significant of which was a broken arm, that would have destroyed the morale of a lesser man.

Bly, who was only 5ft 9in tall, played in an era when goalkeepers' attitudes were envisaged as veering somewhere between the daring and the foolhardy and they were not the protected species of the modern game. Nowadays goalkeepers are expected to cut big, imposing figures: in Bly's day they were smaller, expected to be nimble, supple, lithe and brave and faced greater injury risks. In blunt terms it was the age of 'the kamikaze 'keeper.' Bly himself said: 'They say that all goalkeepers are daft, but it's not much use standing on the goal-line and hoping for the best when you see a forward charging through.'

And Bernard Fisher, who was one of Bly's goalkeeping rivals at City and also a close friend, said:

It was claimed that Tony Norman was the club's best goalkeeper based on clean sheets and playing in a club-record 226 consecutive League games, but he never had the battering that Billy had when forwards were quite happy to put the man and the ball into the back of the net. Billy was also the best goalkeeper we'd ever seen when going down at a forward's feet in a one-to-one situation.

It was barely surprising, therefore, that Bly's two best-known nicknames were 'the India-rubber man' because of his agility and elasticity and 'the brittle-boned hero' because of the many injuries that blighted his career. Chris Chilton, whose own lengthy City career was just beginning as Bly was reaching the end of his, said:

> He showed me how he would put his back and heels up against a wall and then touch his toes. He asked me if I could do it and I reckoned it was nearly impossible. If you try it, you've no chance because you'd fall over. You can't get down, but he was that supple. He was unbelievable for his age. He wasn't very big, but he was fearless apparently when he came out to forwards. He was around a long while and must have been a great goalkeeper.

Another long-serving teammate Brian Bulless added: 'He was very agile and just dived from one post right across to the other so easily. He was a wonderful fellow and a brilliant goalkeeper even though he was injury-prone.' In addition, there often seemed to be a black sense of occasion surrounding some of Bly's many injuries.

For example, there was the opening of Boothferry Park immediately after the 1939–45 War. The venue hosted its first League game against Lincoln City in August 1946 when the Tigers had their highest-ever home League attendance of 25,586. But Bly was stretchered off after a collision with Lincoln's Harry Parr and full-back Arthur Watson took over from him in goal. Between them they kept a clean sheet in a goalless draw and Bly was at least fit to play against Crewe Alexandra two days later.

In February 1949 promotion-chasing City entertained Manchester United in the quarter-finals of the FA Cup in front of what remains the club's record home gate—55,019—and lost 1–0 to a controversial goal. But towards halftime the injury jinx struck again because it was written: 'The advancing Bly missed the ball as he dived amid a forest of attackers. He was injured and lay prostrate for a while. Bly had obviously been shaken badly and, although he resumed, he was nursing his head for some time.'

In March 1954 an injury cost Bly dearly on a personal basis when City beat Falkirk 7–1 at home in a relatively-meaningless friendly. Initially he damaged his elbow in a collision with Falkirk's centre-forward Angus Plumb, but then later in the first half he broke a bone and ultimately missed the rest of the season. His son Roy explained: 'He went up towards the crossbar to make a save and the force of the ball snapped his wrist against it.' As a result, wing-half Trevor Porteous replaced Bly until regular goalkeeper Tommy Forgan came on as a substitute at halftime. But what made matters much worse was the fact that Bly had just been called up for England B's squad to meet West Germany B in a representative match in Gelsenkirchen.

The English squad included Bly's former City teammate Don Revie, Fulham star Johnny Haynes and Roger Byrne and Duncan Edwards, two of Manchester United's Busby Babes, but Roy Bly said:

> City's manager Bob Jackson made my dad play even though it was just a friendly. Dad refused to play at first and argued that, if he were injured, he would lose more than the £3 fee which players were given for friendlies at that time. Afterwards he said that he wanted to see chairman Harold Needler and he did after Jackson had given him only 30 shillings as his fee because he had played in less than half the game! It was the only time that dad was given a sniff of playing for his country. He was normally a very easy-going person, but I gather he was very annoyed on this occasion.

Bly was also still recovering from a broken nose that he had received in a League game at Blackburn a few weeks earlier and two years after the friendly fiasco he was again injured at Ewood Park. It happened in a 2–0 defeat on Good Friday and this time the timing had another ironic twist because Bernard Fisher had to rearrange his wedding plans at 24 hours' notice.

Fisher had intended to get married in his home city of York on the Easter Saturday at 10am and then stay in the area to play for City's reserves at Bootham Crescent later on. Instead he had to dash from the wedding reception to play for the first team in Bly's place at Boothferry Park! Fisher explained:

> We drew 2–2 at home to Fulham and Johnny Haynes scored their goals. I'd expected to be in the reserves at York, but I was called up for the first team because Billy had broken his ankle. As a result, I married and then had to catch a train to Hull and a taxi to Boothferry Park with my wife. We arrived half-an-hour before the kick-off! I then remember playing in the return game against Blackburn on the Easter Monday and we lost 3–0. A voice from the crowd shouted to me: 'That's what married life does for you!'

Bly had numerous other injuries on less-auspicious occasions. In October 1946 Bly broke his thumb at Tranmere and returned for the FA Cup first-round tie at home to New Brighton the following month. But he first underwent a curious fitness test because on the day before the tie he faced a series of shots from Harold Meens and Arthur Taylor, who were said to be 'two of the club's strongest kickers.' In October 1950 Bly broke his wrist just before halftime in a goalless draw at Chesterfield and missed the rest of the season. Future England manager Don Revie went in goal—as he had done a week earlier when Joe Robinson hurt his arm in a 3–1 home defeat to Leicester City. And in January 1952 Bly injured his shoulder in a 5–0 home win over Coventry City, causing him to miss a 2–0 win at Manchester United in the FA Cup. Robinson stepped in when Bly failed another intriguing fitness test because he could not hit a punchball rigged up by coach George Lax without feeling pain.

And it was not as if Bly failed to take precautions to look after himself because teammate Bob Dennison said:

> The taps on our bath in the dressing-room were like hosepipes and the water was about 3ft high so that it was just under your chin when you sat down in it. The water from the hot tap was scalding, but after a game Billy would sit right underneath it and let it run over him. Everybody else would flinch because they couldn't stand it, but Billy was nearly always fit to play the following week even though he had a lot of injuries during his career.

And his son Roy added: 'I was soon aware of how he used to suffer a lot of injuries, but he never complained and he never talked about pain. He said that they were just a part of his job and would just give us a wink and a smile.'

Bly, who was born in the Walker area of Newcastle in May 1920, certainly had longevity on his side in terms of his career. The youngest of eight children, he was a first-teamer with the Tigers from 1939 to 1960, finishing fifth in the club's all-time appearances list with 403 in the League. And after spanning four decades in League football, he then played on into his 40s, mostly notably helping out non-League Weymouth in an emergency.

In addition, Bly made an impact during the 1939–45 War when his burgeoning League career was put on hold. He helped the 86th Regiment of the Honourable Artillery Company to become the champion team of the British Army of the Rhine under the guidance of future British Prime Minister Edward Heath and received a warm tribute from England international Tommy Lawton, who wrote:

> There is a such a shortage of real first-flight goalkeepers that I know that many club managers would willingly make a long trip under almost any circumstances to secure the signature of one who fills the bill. Now is the time for them to start moving because I have seen a goalkeeper who is a natural in the last few days—Billy Bly. I don't know just where, when and how he can be fixed up because he is serving with our occupation troops in Germany. But I saw him pull the game out of the fire for his team when they met a Swiss XI who showed only four changes from the one who met a full England team at Stamford Bridge.

And during the conflict Bly played in the same team as Bert Williams and Ted Ditchburn, both of whom became England goalkeepers, and yet took preference over them. Again he was unluckily foiled in his international ambition and Roy Bly explained:

> During the War the servicemen received passes to go on home leave for so many hours and would return for short visits. But Stanley Rous, from the FA, had mentioned to my father that he was in the forefront of English goalkeepers and it would be only a matter of time before he would be selected for the national side. On one occasion my dad was granted a home-leave pass for 48 hours and he was asked to guest for a football club, which professional players often did at that time. He had guested himself for Lincoln City, Dumbarton and Hamilton Academicals, but this time he refused because he wanted to go to Newcastle to see my mum Dorothy. As a result, he felt very strongly that Rous put the boot into his England chances.

Bly, in fact, had not expected to be a goalkeeper. He had also been a full-back and a half-back at school in the North-East and once said of goalkeeping: 'I decided that it was too cold a job for me!' He also had a frail build and at one stage he had to stop playing because of his weak ankles. As a result, he joined Walker Boys' Club and played for them as a centre-forward and winger, but it was back to goalkeeping when he moved on to Walker Celtic. This time he established a reputation and City, whose early-1920s goalkeeper Arthur Briggs had also played for Celtic, invited him for a trial during the summer of 1937.

As Bly embarked on his career, he was lucky to encounter a goalkeeper who was reaching the end of his career—George Maddison. Bly joked that Maddison's booming presence and the size of his hands were enough to frighten him from thinking of soccer as a living! But Maddison told Bly's parents William and Annie: 'Leave him alone! I'll look after him.'

And Bly kept a clean sheet on his League debut in a 2–0 win at Rotherham—perversely on April Fools' Day in 1938—and played in the final eight League games of the season, displacing the established John Ellis. But Jack Curnow appeared in the only two League games of the aborted 1939–40 season and Bly's only first-team appearance for City in 1939–40—at Curnow's expense—was at Hartlepools United in the wartime North-East Regional League. He made 16 more wartime appearances for City in 1940–41, but did not reappear for the club until League football resumed in 1946. The Tigers had retained the basis of their first-team squad when they readjusted to life after the 1914–18 War. But this time it was different because only Bly, Harold Meens and brothers-in-law Dai Davies and Ernie Bell played League football for the club both before and after the conflict.

Bly cemented the reputation that he had established for himself in wartime football and became City's first-choice goalkeeper, fitness permitting. But the arrival of Raich Carter as player-manager took the club on to a higher plain as the Tigers won the Third Division North title in his first full season in charge in 1948–49. Bly kept 20 clean sheets in his 38 League games and was one of the stars of the FA Cup run to the quarter-finals, gaining recognition for his part in the 2–1 giantkilling win at Blackburn in the third round in January 1949 because it was written: 'Between Blackburn and success lay Billy Bly, who saved at all angles when they were not at fault with their marksmanship. It was Bly's brilliance that contributed more to Blackburn's undoing than did anything else.'

He was a popular figure and the fans insisted that he should address them after the final home of the season against Doncaster Rovers when promotion had been clinched. And he was even mentioned in a supporters' song from the 1940s, which was performed to the tune of 'Sioux City Sue':

> I took my wife to a football match to see Hull City play,
> We waited for a trolley bus for nearly half a day,
> And when we got to Boothferry Park, the crowds were rolling in,
> The bus conductor said to me: 'Do you think that they will win?'
> Shoot, City, shoot! Shoot, City, shoot!
> The grass is green, the ball is brown,
> And we got in for half-a-crown,
> Shoot, City, shoot! Shoot, City, shoot!
> There ain't a guy as spry
> As our goalie Billy Bly.

And his goalkeeping arguably reached its peak in a 2–0 FA Cup fifth-round replay defeat at Tottenham Hotspur in February 1954 when it was written: 'The defiant Bly's performance was really epic. The acrobatic and daring Billy defied all-comers with his wonderful anticipation and positioning.' And John McAdam wrote in the *Daily Express*:

> As long as they talk football Tottenham way, they'll talk not so much about how their side knocked Hull out of the FA Cup as of how goalkeeper Billy Bly defied them. It was an inspired piece of goalkeeping that deserved a much better fate. Bly saved long shots and short, point-blank shots and high ones and screamers along the ground. The crowd knew well that they were in the presence of greatness. At the end they rose to him as one man and gave him a personal ovation all the way off the field. Well they might. Billy Bly is one of the unluckiest goalkeepers in the business. He has broken almost every bone available, but there he was with superb confidence, tipping the ball over the bar and round the post, diving at onrushing feet and positioning himself like a master. Spurs might have won by at least 4–0 but for him and I wish to see nothing better than his performance. What will be told for a long time is

the tale of the greatness of Bly.

It summed up Bly's prowess and he was duly City's guest when they again met Tottenham in the FA Cup in 1981.

Bly's stock remained consistently high and teammate Andy Davidson said:

> There were goalkeepers behind him when he was in the Forces who later played for England, but they couldn't have laced his boots. He was the greatest goalkeeper I saw and could bounce about like a rubber ball. He had everything—he was like an agile cat. He frightened everyone to death at times because he would shout: 'I'm coming out to stop it.' And he would give you an earful if you were in the six-yard box. He'd shout: 'What are you doing here? Get out! I don't need you.' Billy was the best goalkeeper I played with or against.

And City commentator Keith Martin wrote of him:

> Bly was arguably one of the last, seasoned exponents of the old-time game: their talents had matured under a war, under privation and under the bondage of a maximum wage. Supremely orthodox, his technique was carefully groomed on a basis of good sense and courage. He positioned himself correctly, made his catches cleanly and got his body behind the ball at all times. Agility was the final adornment to his mastery of the fundamentals. Bly also turned the daring dive at the feet of an onrushing forward into something of a personal art and a hallmark.

His goalkeeping colleague Bernard Fisher, who also played international handball at Hull's Costello Stadium with Bly in their spare time, added:

> Billy never double-fisted a ball when he went to punch it. His argument was that you should catch it if you could get two fists to it. We trained with the other players for running and five-a-side games, but, as goalkeepers, we did various other exercises, including using a punch ball like boxers for timing. But no specialist training was given other than that. You learned by watching others and from your own mistakes. In my case it was difficult to establish myself in the first team while Billy was around. We were always the best of friends, but I got into the first team only when he was injured.

And another teammate Len Round recalled:

I remember that Billy always seemed to get the ball when he dived down to get it off a player's feet and I didn't. Billy told me I was going out too fast, we would practise and talk about it and it made me a better goalkeeper.

Bly was also a determined character who liked to do things his way because Fisher reflected:

One day Billy went out just after the rest of us to train round the Boothferry Park track. We were opposite the players' entrance when Billy came out and trainer Angus McLean shouted to him: 'Run the other way!' That meant him going left to right, but Billy replied: 'I've run round the other way round the track for 20 years, so I'm not changing now.' A right argument took place and Billy trained by himself for a few weeks until it all settled down.

And Roy Bly admitted:

Dad had his routines and could be set in his ways. I remember sometimes waving to him in the mornings when he would walk to Boothferry Park with neighbours such as Ken Harrison, Harold Meens, Denis Durham and Andy Conway. There were few cars on the roads in those days, but eventually dad bought a black Morris with handles facing the wrong way on the doors and foot platforms at the bottom of them on the outside. But my earliest memory of understanding what his job was came in 1958 when I was asked if I wanted to go to football to see him play. But my only thought was about going to Saturday pictures at the Carlton or Priory cinemas and that meant that my mum couldn't go to see dad play for City! I was still not interested in football until I went to a new school and we were told that there would be a practice at the end of the day. I rushed home and told my dad, who had just arrived home from training, so he went straight out that lunchtime and bought me a pair of boots. That was the kind of man he was. Then he taught me how to break them in by standing them in a bucket of water to stretch the leather and mould them to the shape of the feet because he had learned the trade of cobbling when he'd been in the Army.

Bly, in fact, could turn his goalkeeping hands to all kinds of things. Roy Bly added:

He could also do a bit of joinery and once made me a football rattle. And then, of course, he painted it amber and black. Dad also used to sketch things and do life drawings. He crayoned things such as postboxes and bananas on charcoal sheets of paper. I have always wondered why he didn't do something with his talent, but in those days it was almost frowned upon to be artistic and in the end he devoted his energies to his football. But when he worked at Everthorpe Borstal later in life, he would copy the badges of football teams and stencil them on to tobacco tins. A prison warder once got my dad to recreate the Manchester United badge on to his son's bedroom. And dad also painted the ceiling in what was the nearest thing to the warders' mess. It had been old and dull, but dad made it colourful. He would also take inmates with him and pass on his skills to them. It was his way of showing them a trade and proving that there was something for them outside the four walls of a prison.

Bly's injuries meant that he was never an ever-present during any of his many seasons with City, but he missed only one League game in his second promotion season—in 1958–59 in the newly-formed deregionalised Third Division. And when the club released him in April 1960 after clocking up 403 League games for them, there was a public outcry with the columns of the local Press being assailed with correspondence from angry fans. City would not even let him make a farewell appearance in the final game of the season at home to Ipswich Town, which was meaningless because they had already been relegated, although the besieged board later admitted that they made a mistake about it. Bly was told to play in the reserves at Lincoln City instead, but he kept his customary dignity, saying: 'I would have liked to have completed next season because I intended retiring then anyway.'

His last League game was in a 1–0 defeat at Bristol Rovers in late March 1960 and it left him in second place in the club's all-time League appearances list. He remains fifth and since his debut a total of 13 other goalkeepers—Cyril Hannaby, Joe Carter, Peter Atkinson, Alex Corbett, Joe Robinson, John Savage, Tommy Forgan, David Teece, Ron Capewell, Bernard Fisher, Mauro Rintanen, Len Round and Barry Lord—had rivalled him in the League.

Bly soon guested for Bridlington Town in a 2–1 win over the Green Howards in a charity match when autograph hunters besieged him and City's directors finally offered him a testimonial match. And chairman Harold Needler, who insisted that they could not afford to let Bly play on, claimed in a damage-limitation exercise: 'There has never been a wrong word between us and Billy in all his 23 years' long service. The lives of football-club directors would have been made much easier if only we had had 11 Billy Blys.' But Bly's treatment was a public-relations gaffe—especially when it became known that he had been told of his departure in a curt, 33-word letter from manager Bob Brocklebank—and local wood-carver Cyril Hirst helped a group of youngsters from Hull's Hardwick Street area to make a foot-high 'Oscar' to present to him with a note, saying: 'This is a small token of our appreciation of your wonderful service to Hull City in particular and football in general.'

But even his testimonial match in October 1961 seemed fated. City would not provide a side for it, so it was between an ex-Tigers' team and an All-Stars' XI and it also coincided with a polio outbreak in Hull. And then the original date clashed with a testimonial match at Bolton for former England hero Nat Lofthouse, who had retired as a player earlier that year. Some leading players found that they were double-booked, so Bly had to put his game back by three days and he and Fisher had to go to Bolton in pouring rain to negotiate with them. The outcome was a crowd of 5,387 and it raised just £600 for him.

Yet even though Bly was less than a month away from his 40th birthday when City told him that he was being released, his passion for playing remained undiminished. He played for local singer Ronnie Hilton's Showbiz XI, but a better offer was to come along because he joined Weymouth, who were then in the Premier Division of the Southern League, during the autumn of 1961 when their manager, former Republic of Ireland international Frank O'Farrell, needed a goalkeeper in an injury crisis. O'Farrell, who later took charge of Manchester United, had played for Preston North End under City's new manager Cliff Britton, who recommended Bly to him.

Bly took on a new lease of life and helped Weymouth, whose squad already included Ken Bryan, who came from Hedon to the east of Hull, to the FA Cup fourth round, in which they were drawn at Second Division Preston, who eventually won 2–0 at the second attempt. It had been a special tie for both O'Farrell against his old club and also for Bly because it threw up one of the strangest incidents of his lengthy career. The first meeting had to be abandoned because of fog and O'Farrell recalled:

> After 13 minutes the referee blew his whistle, called us together and said: 'Look, it's very bad, so we'll go off the pitch for a while.' All the players went into the drying-room to keep warm until such time that it had improved. But all of a sudden somebody noticed that Billy wasn't with us. Somebody said: 'Where's Billy Bly? He must be still out on the park.' Somebody else suggested that someone had better go out and look for him. He found Billy still in the goalmouth. When he came in, I asked him: 'Billy, what were you doing out there?' We've all been inside for a few minutes.' He said: 'I didn't know. I thought you had them under pressure up the other end!'

And the twilight of his career continued to throw up the kind of quirks of fate that had so often dogged him when he joined Hull Brunswick in the Yorkshire League. While playing for them against Bridlington Trinity, David Crawford was on the mark against him after just 15 seconds of the game before a Brunswick player had touched the ball and Bly admitted: 'That's the quickest goal I've ever had scored against me.' He was also a founder member of the Ex-Tigers' Association for former City players and soon afterwards stayed in local football by helping out Mike Rawding as part of North Ferriby United's management team for five years from 1972. It was an arrangement that eventually ensured that his name would never be forgotten because United and Hull City play each other for the Billy Bly Memorial Trophy during every pre-season build-up.

At the same time Bly had had to maintain a working life outside football and he had given it some consideration towards the end of his career with the Tigers because he opened a sweets and confectionery shop close to Boothferry Park. And the move enlivened the club's training sessions because teammate Mike Brown recalled:

> I remember Billy bringing in a little case to training every morning. It was stacked and contained everything from cigarettes to Mars Bars. We'd play five-a-side games for a Mars Bar a man in training and batter each other. The losers had to pay out and you'd kill for a Mars Bar!

Bly then had a spell as an estate agent and later spent 10 years as a painter and decorator at Everthorpe Borstal, nearly 20 miles west of

Hull. He died at the age of 61 in March 1982, but he had always been in demand and had remained well-liked. He would, for example, accept invitations to attend the annual produce show in the East Riding village of North Frodingham and at the peak of his fame he gave a goalkeeping coaching session at a garden party at the home of City director Bob Metcalfe, who had become the Sheriff of Hull in May 1952. Metcalfe, in fact, left the board soon after Bly's shoddy treatment at the end of his playing career with them.

Bly's longevity was rarely in question. There was interest in him from the top flight when he first established himself in the team in the immediate post-war years and Grimsby Town made an audacious inquiry about him during the autumn of 1950 when he was unusually dropped by City. It happened for a game at Boothferry Park against the Mariners, who were trying to replace their goalkeeper Wilf Chisholm, but the Tigers would not let Bly go even though he missed most of the 1950–51 season.

Typically, Bly himself also placed loyalty high on his list of priorities because he was invited to a local presentation evening 15 years after leaving the Tigers and told the audience about the principles that had punctuated his life and approach to football and made him so popular: 'When a player starts to slide after holding a first-team place, he often wants to leave his club, but I think the sign of a good sportsman is when he sticks by them and tries to fight his way back.'

9

RAICH CARTER

Portraits of Raich Carter in football terms tend to show him as an imposing, imperious figure. Hull City's record appearances holder Andy Davidson was only a youngster when Sunderland-born Carter joined the club as player-coach in March 1948 and they never played for the first team together, but he observed: 'Raich had wonderful ability and was one of the all-time greats. He hardly used the right foot and he hardly ever headed the ball, but he still ran the games. In fact, he refereed them!' And the renowned playwright Alan Plater, who was a staunch City supporter and also originated from the North-East, reflected: 'He was the greatest of his kind and he knew it. He reinvented the game as he went along. He didn't just play it: he presided over it.'

But there was a different image of Carter when he was away from the bright floodlights of football because his second wife, Pat, said:

> There was a public figure and a private one. The telephone was always ringing with people asking him for his opinions, but at home he was the opposite of what he had to be as a footballer. He was quiet, witty and very easy to live with.

And their daughter, Jane, added:

> He was very sensitive. He was a kind, soft man who would give away his money to tramps and help other footballers. Football was all a stage act for him because he was performing once he got on to the

field. Everybody liked to talk about football with him and I think he missed it when he wasn't directly involved in it.

And Carter, who was born in the Hendon area of Sunderland in December 1913, did not always have things all his own way in football. His father Bob had played for the old Burslem Port Vale, Fulham and Southampton before running the Ocean Queen public-house in Sunderland's dockland, but Raich, who had attended Hendon Boys' School and played locally for Whitburn St Mary's and Esh Winning, was rejected by Leicester City as a youngster when their manager Willie Orr, a former Scottish international, told him: 'You're too small to play football. You should go home and build yourself up physically. Get some brawn and weight on you and gain some experience of the game!' Carter later admitted: 'It shook me rigid.' He joined Sunderland as an amateur and then they gave him a £10 signing-on fee to turn professional when Huddersfield Town offered him a trial.

Carter, who felt that he had to prove that he was not a cissy because his full name was Horatio, then trained as an electrician, but maintained towards the end of his playing career: 'I knew that I did not want to go back to any form of electrical engineering or indeed take up any job outside football.' He had cast aside most aspects of his apprenticeship although he would apparently go round switching lights off when he was at home! The habit then caused consternation during his City days when he was invited to switch on the seaside lights at Withernsea!

Carter shrugged off the setback at Leicester to establish himself at Sunderland, for whom he scored 119 times in 245 League games, and then Derby County, winning the FA Cup with them both. He scored in the 1936–37 final when Sunderland beat Preston North End 3–1 and then he was in the Derby side who beat Charlton Athletic 4–1 after extra time in 1945–46. His wife Pat reflected:

> Sunderland was close to his heart because it was where he played as a kid. He was always excited about the time he played for Sunderland because he started just after the dark days of the Depression. He always respected how the supporters raised the money to get to games, so he felt that the players had to give performances in return.

At the same time Carter, who became an auxiliary fireman, joined the RAF and was then a physical-training instructor during the 1939–45 War, turned away from his beginnings in the Ocean Queen because Pat added:

> He didn't like pubs because he could see the sawdust and spittoons from his bedroom. Pubs represented a life when you didn't work. He had that willpower and didn't drink, gamble or smoke. He never smoked and had only the occasional drink because he was dedicated.

There was another anomaly, though, because Carter became a tobacconist in Hull towards the end of his League career!

Carter, who knew tennis icon Dan Maskell from their time together at Loughborough Rehabilitation Centre during the 1939–45 War and played county cricket for Derbyshire three times in 1946, surprisingly won just 13 England caps for someone whose supreme status in the game galvanised the East Riding when he joined the Tigers. He made his debut for them in a 1–1 draw at home to York City in early April 1948, having been given special permission to play by the Football League because he was a late-season signing, and the gate was 32,466: the attendance at the previous home game against Tranmere Rovers had been just 13,588. Carter recalled:

> There was a lunch for the players at the Station Hotel in Hull to give me the chance of meeting them. From the start I made a point of trying to be friendly with the boys and make things easy. Football teams always welcome new members, but I was a bit concerned about all the publicity that had accompanied my transfer. I wondered whether it might have made the boys feel a bit antagonistic towards me. I did not want them to feel that I was putting them in the shade nor did I want there to be any suggestion that I had a superiority complex and was looking down my nose at them.

But his move to Boothferry Park from Derby, for whom he had scored 34 goals in 63 League appearances, had hardly been clear-cut because there had also been interest in him from Nottingham Forest, Notts County and Leeds United. At the end of March 1948 Derby entertained Liverpool and Carter was omitted. He recalled: 'As soon as I arrived, I was surrounded by the seven Hull City directors and rushed off to the Derby boardroom. I said: "What again? The Seven

Dwarfs after Snow White?" That gag clinched it.' He immediately signed in a £6,000 deal during halftime!

But Carter admitted that he had had mixed feelings about his destiny. County's offer had been lucrative, but they wanted him only as a player. There was a snag about the length of contract with Leeds because they had offered him only a three-year deal when he wanted one for five years, while Forest and City were offering Carter the job of assistant manager with a view to stepping up. He said:

> I was very impressed by the interview with the Hull directors, who were all young to the game and so obviously eager and keen to go places. I realised, too, that it was a good opportunity to gain experience in managership as Major Frank Buckley's assistant. I had no doubts that working for Hull City was going to be all right, but I was a bit uncertain whether I was doing the right thing in going into the Third Division. But set off against my reluctance to play in the Third Division was the fact that Major Buckley was a much older man than Nottingham Forest manager Billy Walker and the managership of Hull was the one more likely to become vacant first.

Carter did not have to wait too long. Buckley had had grievances with the club as far back as October 1947, but he resigned two days after Carter's debut because of a dispute about 'points of policy.' His resignation was due to take effect from early May 1948 immediately after the season had ended, but Leeds immediately stepped in for his services. Carter himself had other priorities even though he was Buckley's obvious successor. He had been chosen as a reserve for England for their international against Scotland at Hampden Park on April 10: ironically, Stan Mortensen, who was to become a City player, scored in England's 2–0 win and, more significantly, Neil Franklin, whom Carter was to bring to Boothferry Park in a club-record £22,500 deal in February 1951, was also in their line-up. Carter had also been selected to captain the Football League against the League of Ireland at Preston in what turned out to be his final representative appearance for an English team a few days later.

But on April 23 City's board held a three-hour meeting, after which it was announced that Carter had been appointed as their new player-manager. He admitted: 'I never expected that promotion would come so soon. My aim is to foster the game and improve the standard of football. You cannot command success on the field: you must strive to attain it.' And it came as no surprise when his own promotion soon led to promotion for the club.

Carter soon moved into the transfer market, signing his former Sunderland colleague Eddie Burbanks, but he was largely happy with the squad he had inherited from Buckley because he said:

> My immediate impression was that there was plenty of good material, but it was not all being used to the best advantage and I decided first of all to find out what positions the various members of the team really liked to play in. There were players who seemed to have the ability if only they could be found the right niches and encouraged along the right lines. All my life I had played First Division football and I made up my mind that I wanted Hull City to try to do the same no matter what style opponents might adopt. Occasionally class might be caught on the wrong foot by bulldozing tactics, but in the long run it was class that paid. I was fortunate in not only having team spirit, but an unparalleled keenness and enthusiasm from the directors right the way down through the players to the lowliest member of staff. The players were on tiptoe to better themselves and go places. All I had to do was to show them what I wanted and how to play good football— and they went and did it.

But Carter, who signed Danish international Viggo Jensen and then Bill Price, Joe Robinson and Ernie Shepherd during the 1948–49 season, was well aware of the increased expectancy that had come with his elevation because he said:

> Probably I was the only one who had no ideas about winning promotion. I had been given such a completely free hand that I knew the responsibility for success or failure must be with me. The board's attitude throughout had been: 'Okay, Raich, if that's what you want, you have it.' My boats were burned. I had no excuses or way out if Hull were to flop badly under my managership. Personally I was content to pray that the club should do well: the championship could take care of itself. I was quite philosophical about that.

The outcome, though, was sensational despite Carter's caution. City set a League record by winning their opening nine League games of 1948–49 although he missed a penalty in one of them at home to Accrington Stanley. The record had been jointly held by Arsenal,

Everton and Sheffield United and lasted until Tottenham Hotspur won their first 11 games in 1960–61. The Football League would not allow City's board to mark the feat by giving mementoes to the players, but Carter reflected:

> As we won one match after another and the style of play we had adopted proved to be well-founded, the players' confidence in the team and themselves became more and more assured. In addition, the £2 bonuses coming in regularly were undoubtedly great incentives to put everything they had into their play.

The Tigers also established another League record because they were undefeated away from home in 13 Third Division North games until mid-February 1949 when then they lost 4–2 at Bradford City. By then, though, they had taken three points out of four against close rivals Rotherham United, who had only two full-time professionals because most of their players were miners, during the Christmas period and embarked on what developed into a thrilling FA Cup run. The Millers, in fact, were on their way to finishing as runners-up in the Third Division North for the third successive season and Carter mused:

> The Christmas success encouraged further the belief in Hull that we were heading for the championship of the Third Division North. It did seem to me, though, that the people of Hull were primarily concerned about what Rotherham were doing, which was putting the cart before the horse. Personally I was very much more concerned about what my own team were doing.

But the FA Cup run took over early in 1949. It had started relatively quietly with wins over Accrington Stanley and Reading, but then three giantkilling episodes in away ties followed. The Tigers defeated Second Division sides Blackburn Rovers 2–1 and Grimsby Town 3–2 and then won 2–0 at First Division Stoke City. And Carter said:

> The outstanding game was the one with Stoke, but I also have a vivid memory of my goal against Grimsby, where rivalry was outstandingly keen. That game was more than a match between two local clubs: it was symbolic of the rivalry existing between the country's two chief fishing ports. We were awarded a free-kick about 20 yards out. I feinted to centre the ball, but instead hit it with all the force I possessed and it sped straight and true inside the post. When we went to Stoke, I was not caring very much whether we won or lost. All that

concerned me was that we should not be annihilated. Before the match I said to the boys: 'Have a good game. Lots of people have come from Hull to watch us and we don't want them to be disappointed. Just try your best!' From the kick-off we did everything right. Even I was surprised about the way in which we settled down at once to good, constructive football, moving the ball rapidly with accurate passes. It was one of the great thrills of my career to have seen the way my boys played football that day.

The Tigers earned themselves a home tie against FA Cup holders Manchester United in the quarter-finals and it attracted the highest home gate in the club's history—55,019—but they lost 1–0 to a controversial goal by England international Stan Pearson because it was claimed that the ball had gone out of play before Jimmy Delaney set it up. Carter himself put the defeat in a wider perspective because he said:

It was a dry, sunny day and the ground was not ideal for good football. I thought to myself: 'Whoever scores first will win this match.' I don't think Manchester United looked any better than City. We were holding our own and I was satisfied. It was not until 10 minutes from time that United scored the only goal of the game. I don't think that anyone on our side was really sorry and I personally was relieved.

Carter was concerned about the fixture pile-up caused by the Cup run and added:

We started off not minding whether we won or lost our ties as long as we put up a good show. But the boys were playing so well together that it looked as if they would never go out. As a manager, I appreciated the fact that our run in the Cup was not only helping the club financially, but also bringing us a lot of useful publicity. But I was scared stiff that it was going to be at the expense of our promotion to the Second Division. The Cup successes also brought in their wake an accumulation of postponed League games, which had to be fitted in towards the end of the season. Those matches were going to be of vital importance in deciding the issue between Rotherham and ourselves and I did not see how I could expect the boys to cope with such a heavy programme and play so much football without tiring. In addition, grounds would then be hard and dry and bare of grass—less conducive to the class football that I had tried to impart to the team and more liable to cause injuries. And if my hair had not already turned grey of its own accord, I should not have been at all surprised if those weeks of the 1949 cup ties had not turned it so!

At the start of the season I didn't give promotion a serious thought, but at this stage I was seriously worried. Following our sensational Cup progress and the fact of our games in hand on Rotherham, everyone was taking it for granted that our promotion was assured. But I was too consciously aware that it was very easy to slip up although promotion might be in sight. And the reaction was going to be colossal if we were to slip at that stage. There was no more relieved man in Hull than I when we finally put the issue beyond doubt. For the first time in my life I faced a season in the Second Division. Enthusiastic supporters began talking of emulating Charlton Athletic's example in 1936 and going straight through to the First Division in two seasons. My answer to that kind of talk was that I should be quite happy if we finished the season third from the bottom. I was only too conscious of the fact that four out of the last five clubs promoted—Stockport County, Tranmere Rovers, Doncaster Rovers and Lincoln City—lasted only one season in the Second Division.

Carter's approach, though, had inspired his players because centre-half Harold Meens added:

Major Frank Buckley, who was a strict disciplinarian, had got together the nucleus of the side. But then Raich and Eddie Burbanks came as players and it developed from there. As a manager, Raich promoted team spirit in the side. He involved the players and their wives in everything and it was as if the club were a family concern. We used to play for one another and, if a player was having an off-day, then we would do our best to keep the ball away from him. Our defensive record was the best that City ever had because we had only 28 goals scored against us in a full League season. I was really proud to be a member of that particular side.

Football writer Sidney Gibbon added: 'When Raich Carter came to Hull, he brought with him two qualities that even a £25,000 transfer fee could not buy—the ability to transmit some of his own mastery of a football to others and, maybe all-important, the gift of team spirit.' And fellow soccer writer Peter Morris summed up Carter's influence:

The club had ambitions, a livewire chairman and a crowd potential never fully realised. Carter made a few changes here and a few switches there, took on the mastermind role on and off the field and got Hull into the Second Division at the first attempt. It was strange to see him in an amber shirt, but Hull didn't care and they made him a civic hero.

Carter missed the last game of City's title-winning season because of an ankle injury. Ironically, it was at Carlisle, where he had made his first appearance for Sunderland's reserves as a 17-year-old. The Tigers then began 1949–50 well and were second after a 3–0 win in the fog at Luton during the autumn, but fell away and won only one of their last 15 League games to finish seventh. In 1950–51 they were inconsistent and finished 10th. The momentum had been lost and in the early summer of 1951 Carter's wife Rose, with whom he had had a daughter called Jennifer, died in Hull at the age of 38. She had suffered from rheumatic fever in childhood and had been poorly for a long time.

City did not start the 1951–52 season too well and trouble was brewing. And Carter, who then lived on Anlaby High Road in Hull, sensationally resigned by letter on September 5, 1951, but chairman Harold Needler was in Norway and the board did not meet until the following week. They then issued a statement: 'The directors considered a letter from player-manager Raich Carter, tendering his resignation to take effect immediately. The board unanimously accepted his resignation.' But they would not elaborate on it, so Carter explained that it was 'because of a disagreement on matters of a general nature in the conduct of the team's affairs.' He added in a statement of his own: 'I have been pleased that the club have been so successful during my sojourn in Hull and I have made many friends from whom I shall be sorry to part. At the moment I have no plans for the immediate future.' He refused to change his mind and he was still registered as a player, but the following month he was asked not to train at Boothferry Park. Carter later recalled: 'I had a couple of good years under Harold Needler, but then we fell out and I departed.'

The Tigers remained managerless, but the club invited him to a board meeting on November 27 'with the intention of clearing up a misunderstanding.' It was then announced: 'Differences between Carter and the club have been resolved.' Carter, who had gone into business locally as a tobacconist and sweet confectioner two weeks earlier, said: 'I am returning as a player and hope that my efforts will assist the club to do better.' City had gone 12 League games without a win during his absence, taking just two points, but they suddenly won 2–0 at home to Carter's former Derby colleague Peter Doherty's Doncaster Rovers on his return after a heel injury on December 8.

City remained inconsistent even though they earned revenge with a 2–0 win at Manchester United in the FA Cup, but there was a revival and the return game against fellow strugglers Doncaster for the final game of the 1951–52 season set the seal on Carter's League career. Fittingly, he scored the only goal of it after 78 minutes and it was reported: 'Carter worked hard to be on the winning team, showed some satisfying touches and fine scheming and it was fitting that he should score.' It secured safety as City finished 18th, but it was the start of a series of disappointing campaigns when they finished in the bottom half of the Second Division and failed to capitalise on the impetus created by Carter's 1948–49 title-winning squad.

He then made his last City appearance two days after the League season had ended and appropriately it was against Sunderland, who included internationals Willie Watson, Trevor Ford and Len Shackleton, in a 2–2 draw in the East Riding Invitation Trophy at Boothferry Park. The fixture attracted a crowd of 29,274 and it was written of Carter: 'The clever flicks and pushes were there. So were the famous left-foot shots. He bowed out with a typical game.' At the end there was a pitch invasion as fans assembled in front of the directors' box, cheered for 15 minutes and chanted: 'We want Raich.' He did not reappear and it was left to Hull's Lord Mayor, Ralph Smith, to tell the throng that Carter was already in the bath!

Carter had made just 136 League appearances for City, scoring 57 goals, but his effect on the club was durable. He was awarded a civic testimonial and the Tigers' board offered him life membership of the club after they had met towards the end of April 1952. The following month City Supporters' Club gave him an inscribed silver tea service at a civic fund presentation evening at Hull City Hall and Carter said: 'I have enjoyed playing football in Hull and I am glad that I came.

Football clubs have their ups and downs. We have had our downs this season, but we have come up trumps.'

But Carter's playing days were not over because he joined Cork Athletic in January 1953 and was rewarded with an Irish cup-winners' medal with them at the age of 39. He reflected: 'I never had a major injury and I was lucky that nature prematurely greyed my hair, which, I suppose, made me stand out.' He did not stay long with Cork, though, because his next job in English management beckoned as he took charge at Leeds: ironically he succeeded Buckley again! And United went up to the First Division with a 4–1 win over the Tigers, who went down, in April 1956. Carter reflected: 'I know just what a struggle it was for Hull City to get into the Second Division and it seems rather strange that we should become sure of promotion against my old club.' He was at Elland Road from May 1953 until the summer of 1958 and observed:

> I say what I think and that often gets up directors' backs. I may not be the most tactful fellow, but I don't see why I should take a charm course to get back into soccer. Anybody can be a 'yes man' and hold his job if he is lucky. Raich Carter is not built that way.

Carter had married Pat Dixon, who had worked for the Tigers, in January 1955 and they decided to return to East Yorkshire. He concentrated on his newsagency and stationery shop on Hull's Anlaby Road and insisted that he was finished with football, saying: 'It is not going to be easy to turn my back on soccer, but I intend to do so and make my business a success. Once I get settled down in Hull, that is that. I have nothing but happy memories of the city.' But in October 1959 he was linked with a return to Boothferry Park in a coaching role. And he turned down the manager's job at Barrow before taking over at Mansfield Town, where this time he replaced former England international, long-throw specialist and ex-Tiger Sam Weaver. He stayed with the Stags, with whom he nurtured future City hero Ken Wagstaff's career, from February 1960 to January 1963 before taking over at Middlesbrough. He remained at Ayresome Park until February 1966 when his career in management finished. And he later said: 'It's far from easy being a manager. The pressure remains even when you go home.' In August 1967 Carter took a job as the head buyer for the sports centre at Hull and East Riding Co-operative Society's store in Hull's city centre, but his contract was terminated after 16 months.

Carter continued to watch City and remained in demand. His wife Pat said: 'He was a great family man, but he wouldn't let his family get in the way of his job. People often asked him if he could remember such-and-such a goal and they were always amazed that he knew in detail how he scored them all.' In October 1988 Carter and Bobby Gurney, a fellow goalscorer for Sunderland in the 1937 FA Cup final, briefly teamed up at Boothferry Park. City drew 0–0 with Sunderland and the only time that the ball ended up in the back of the net that day was when Carter and Gurney kicked off from the centre-spot, passed it from one to the other and it was planted into the South Stand goal as part of the pre-match entertainment!

Carter, whose son was also named Raich, died at home in Willerby to the west of Hull in early October 1994, but he has never been forgotten. He had already featured on a rare and rarely-used postage stamp for the Republic of Equatorial Guinea, a Spanish colony, in odd circumstances when eight top players were pictured in a set to commemorate the 1974 World Cup. Philatelists believe that it was part of a trend by Eastern European countries in particular to use poorer colonies for money-making ventures with stamps. A more enduring tribute came with the opening of the Raich Carter Sports Centre in his native Hendon in October 2001. And the Tigers faced Sunderland in the first game at their Kingston Communications Stadium in December 2002 for the Raich Carter Trophy.

Carter was once described as having 'an intense will to win so sharply in contrast with his finely-chiselled features, pale face and slight physique' and the accolades that have survived him are many. His England colleague Stan Matthews once said: 'He was a silver-haired genius with the golden touch in his boots. He was a football artist with perfect ball control and could outwit any defence. He was perhaps the finest tactician that the game has ever known.' And former Sunderland player Willie Watson, who represented England at football and cricket, said: 'Raich carried empty space around with him like an umbrella!' David Coates, who came from Silksworth in the North-East, was brought to City by Carter and later played for him at Mansfield, reflected:

> Raich had a wicked sense of humour and the ability to make a point firmly, but also humorously. He always coated his criticism with a touch of humour and he was always very generous with the people he played with. Raich was easily the most outstanding personality I have met in the game. He was outstanding to look at because, even though he was not all that tall, he gave the impression of being a big man. He had an aura about him and he knew it.

In fact, Carter himself once admitted: 'I used to be arrogant, but I've matured and grown more tolerant. Now I'm just conceited!' And one other football job that Carter took at the end of his career was when he became a member of the pools panel who would predict the results of postponements. He was still achieving what he had once been deemed to do best—presiding over the game . . .

10

VIGGO JENSEN

During the autumn of 1948 Hull City were linked with a possible move for Denmark's international left-half Ivor Jensen, but nothing ever came of the rumours that had originated from sources in Copenhagen. Jensen had recently represented Denmark at the Olympic Games in London and in a goalless draw against England in Copenhagen, but, whatever the possible accuracy of the speculation, the Tigers remained unperturbed. After all, they had signed another Danish international, Viggo Jensen, from EFB Esbjerg two days earlier. Maybe something was lost in the translation because City's manager Raich Carter said of Ivor: 'I know nothing about this Jensen.'

Viggo Jensen, though, was to establish himself as a significant part of City folklore after moving to Boothferry Park in amazing circumstances. He, too, had played for Denmark at the Olympics and then faced England, who included his future City teammate Neil Franklin, in the first international between the two countries soon afterwards, but then he suddenly travelled across the North Sea as part of a trade delegation with the specific aim of joining the Tigers during the trip. And Jensen's arrival as an amateur at least captured the public imagination, especially because it came days after City's player-manager Raich Carter had signed teenager Paddy Sowden from the more prosaic Bacup Borough!

The initial seeds for Jensen's move were sown at the Olympics when there was a meeting between a covert City convert and Dr

Andreas Handler, from Randers. Carter described the man of mystery involved in the negotiations simply as 'a good friend of Hull City, who is not a member of the board.' Anyway Dr Handler told Jensen of the Tigers' achievements and ambitions. And Jensen, who was keen to play in England, was suitably impressed, so Dr Handler wrote to the club. But Carter said: 'On hearing this, we told him that we could not make any approach to Jensen unless he had a clearance certificate from his own club.'

But Jensen remained undeterred and duly set sail for England in late October on the SS Alexandra. But the weekend journey of the trade delegation, which fittingly coincided with the inaugural meeting of Hull Junior Chamber of Commerce as the city slowly got on to its feet again after the 1939–45 War, literally did not go smoothly because the departure of the SS Alexandra, a butter-boat, from Esbjerg was delayed for 24 hours because of gales in the North Sea. It eventually docked at Grimsby at 9.30am on October 25 and the delegation stayed there overnight, but just before noon the following day Jensen arrived at Hull's Minerva Pier, accompanied by his employer, Holger Lauridsen, from Esbjerg, and interpreter Albert Neelsen. Carter explained: 'The next development occurred when Mr Lauridsen brought Jensen over and asked if Hull City would sign him as an amateur.'

Jensen, then a married man with a three-year-old son, was employed in the fishing industry and was supposed to be 'coming to Hull on business.' It looked increasingly that his mission was more football-orientated because Danish sources insisted that he might make contact with City as a priority of his visit. Officially Jensen had come to the area for a three-week stay and would need a permit from the Ministry of Labour if it were extended, but he soon 'approached the Tigers at Boothferry Park.' He was said to speak 'a little English,' but talks were conducted with Neelsen's help. City's directors, meanwhile, had agreed to meet on the night of Jensen's arrival, but he signed as an amateur before the board meeting after the necessary papers had gone through. And Carter added: 'We have been satisfied that he has received his clearance credentials from EFB Esbjerg and his signing has followed.'

Jensen himself added:

I wish to thank the directors of Hull City for their kindness and I hope I will be a big success. In coming to England, I am following in the footsteps of Nils Middelboe, who played for Chelsea for many years, and my only hope is that I shall meet with similar success. I trust that I shall be an ambassador for Danish football and that I am able to help in cementing friendship between my country and England.

The comparison with Middelboe was apposite because he had ended up in English football with the Casuals, Newcastle United and finally Chelsea just before the 1914–18 War after also coming to prominence in the Olympic Games—when Denmark were the beaten finalists in the tournaments in London in 1908 and Stockholm in 1912.

The Tigers' next task was to fix up Jensen, who had been born at Skagen in Denmark in March 1921, with a job outside football. But it was easy enough because a lot of Danish fishermen operated out of Hull and he was soon promised a job as a representative with a firm of fishing-vessel owners. Jensen then suddenly found himself thrust into football and social matters. He trained with his new teammates for the first time on the day after he had signed and then went golfing with them at Hessle. It was a social occasion involving lunch and tea, but City, who were by then at the top of the Third Division North table, suffered a rare defeat—because Hessle won the golf tournament! Jensen also met local firemen at White City Social Club in Hull on a night out with teammates soon after signing, but he did not join in with the darts, snooker and table-tennis. He just stayed long enough for the hosts to point to the fire in the club as a means of indicating to him what their job was!

The next question surrounded Jensen's eligibility to make his City debut straightaway and it was still in doubt as they built up towards their home game against New Brighton during the first weekend following his arrival. It was reported that the Tigers were 'awaiting news from the Football League that the credentials of Jensen have been accepted.' But everything was sorted out in time and he made an immediate impact. He was given the No. 8 shirt in place of Scottish wartime international Willie Buchan, playing as an inside-forward for the first time since he had appeared for Jutland against Copenhagen back home. And he still needed an interpreter to explain his intended role for the Tigers to him, but he remained relaxed and started the move from which Norman Moore opened the scoring after 15 minutes. He was also on the mark himself in a 4–1 triumph and was described afterwards as 'a magnetic, new draw.' He then scored in his next two games, too—a 2–0 victory at Chester and a 5–1 home win over Southport.

Jensen soon followed up his goalscoring start in the League when he was on the mark with a penalty, as he had been against Southport, on his FA Cup debut in a 3–1 win at home to Accrington Stanley in the first round. Player-manager Carter also scored in all four games and, although Jensen missed a penalty in the FA Cup against Reading, City had discovered just what a force they were going to be that season. They went on to reach the FA Cup quarter-finals in which they lost 1–0 at home to Manchester United in front of the biggest home gate in their history—55,109. Jensen, in fact, had bravely played on with an ankle injury for most of the 2–0 win at First Division Stoke City in the fifth round. The Tigers were still setting the pace in the League as well and Jensen maintained his momentum three weeks before the cup tie against United by registering a hat-trick in a 6–0 win at home to Halifax Town. And he had to come from behind to do it! He scored with a header after just two minutes, but then Buchan, by now restored to the inside-left berth, added two of his own, one of them coming from the penalty spot. Buchan then missed another penalty before Jensen overtook him to complete his hat-trick.

Neither the Tigers nor Jensen, who had won 15 international caps for Denmark, looked back that season. The team, who gained promotion by pipping Rotherham United for the title by three points, were the Third Division North's top scorers with 93 goals and only Notts County, who finished in a mid-table position in the Third Division South, managed more throughout the country. And even though Jensen had still been back home in Denmark for the first 13 League games of the campaign, he finished as City's joint second-highest goalscorer in 1948–49 with 14 from 27 outings—the same as Carter—as Norman Moore topped the charts with 22. It was hardly surprising, therefore, when Jensen received a special mention from Carter at the club's celebration dinner at Hull's Royal Station Hotel and a goodwill message from the burgomaster of Esbjerg.

And it did not take Jensen long to adapt to Second Division football. In 1949–50 Jensen set a club record, since surpassed by striker Les Mutrie in 1982, by scoring in seven successive League games on his way to becoming the second-highest goalscorer behind Carter with 12 in the League that season. Eight goals came in the record-breaking run, which stretched from a 4–2 home win over Plymouth Argyle in mid-September 1949 to a 1–0 home win over Leeds United towards the end of the following month. Bizarrely, the only double came in a 6–2 defeat at Sheffield Wednesday in the second game of the sequence—in a season in which City had a poor defensive record. He then scored against Grimsby Town, Queen's Park Rangers, Preston North End and Swansea Town, as the Tigers took seven points out of a possible eight. And it was said of the 2–1 win at Swansea: 'It was no innovation to find Jensen doing the damage.' But the game almost ended Jensen's hopes of continuing his run because he injured a foot and some ribs and was doubtful for the next game at home to Leeds. But he resumed training and was passed fit on the Friday before the game against a United side boasting their 17-year-old sensation John Charles. Adding further spice to the clash was the fact that former City manager Major Frank Buckley was then in charge at Elland Road although he missed the occasion to go scouting. Jensen duly scored the only goal of the game in the 65th minute, which left him as City's joint leading goalscorer with Carter on nine so far. But, more significantly, it was the first time that two foreign players had been the top marksmen with English clubs because German Alous Eisentrager, the prisoner-of-war who had stayed on to play for Bristol City, was also on nine.

Jensen, who played at inside-right for the duration of his scoring sequence, was way off Arthur Chandler's 16-game scoring record with Leicester City in 1924–25, but there was an ironic twist to his feat with the Tigers. While Jensen was setting his club record, Carter was desperate to increase the club's forward strength! He tried to sign future England international 'Wee' Ernie Taylor from Newcastle United, whose manager, ex-Tiger George Martin, would not let him go. And he was also interested in Leicester City's Don Revie, who was also a target for Arsenal, Manchester City, Derby County, Burnley, Fulham and Cardiff City. Jensen's run ended with a 5–0 defeat at Southampton and the following week he played his first League game for the Tigers in the No. 9 shirt after Revie had been signed and included at inside-right when he made his debut at home to Coventry City.

And in February 1950 Jensen was also on target in front of the biggest gate ever for a League game in Hull. A total of 50,103 fans packed Boothferry Park for a promotion battle between City and Sheffield Wednesday, who took the lead through Oscar Fox after 46 minutes. But Jensen, who turned professional later in the year, headed an 80th-minute equaliser from Eddie Burbanks' cross in a game watched by former England full-back Ernie Blenkinsop, who had played for both clubs. It also signalled the peak of the Tigers' League fortunes during Jensen's stay in England.

City won only one of their last 15 League games in 1949–50 as their initial prospects of a second successive promotion diminished dramatically. But it still served to underline just what a versatile acquisition Jensen had been. When he joined the Tigers, he was classified as a former Danish international full-back and it was said that he had played in every position with the exception of goalkeeper and on the wings. And he was to maintain his footballing flexibility at Boothferry Park. In his first season with City he had appeared at inside-right apart from in a League game at Southport in which he operated at right-back and a cup tie at Reading when he played at centre-forward. But in the 1949–50 season he wore six different amber-and-black shirts—8, 9, 2, 4, 10 and 6—in order.

The most ironic aspect of it all, though, was that Jensen was then to go on and establish himself in a seventh position on a regular basis. During the 1950–51 and 1951–52 seasons he alternated between left-back and right-half for the most part and he began 1952–53 with a productive stint at inside-left that brought him eight goals in the first 13 League games. Then in 1953–54 he had a spell at left-half, but he rarely missed games and played in more and more of them at left-back.

Jensen himself said:

> I'm not a full-back, but Denmark played me there in the Olympic Games because they were so strong at right-half. I've played at half-back since I was so high, but I like playing at inside-forward as well because you can play football there. But I don't know why they play me at centre-forward.

Fellow City full-back Bob Dennison added:

Viggo was just a brainy, intelligent footballer. He was a touch player who could play just as well at inside-forward as he could at full-back. He didn't have a bad left foot, but he was naturally right-footed. And he thought that it helped him when he settled in at left-back. His view was that you could look down the line only if you were left-footed at left-back. But he thought that, if you were a right-footed left-back, then you could bring the ball inside, see the rest of the pitch and have a much better picture of what was on.

And the long-serving Andy Davidson, who also fitted into a variety of positions with the Tigers before becoming a regular full-back, added:

Viggo was a terrific player because he could play anywhere. I believe that he twice faced Stan Matthews and played him out of the games. He was a proper athlete who could do somersaults without touching the floor. He was a natural.

Bit by bit Jensen integrated himself into East Yorkshire life and the hearts of the City fans. Initially he had struggled to speak English—a situation which was apparently not helped on one occasion early into his stay with the Tigers. At first he was afforded accommodation at the club's hostel near the city centre and was supposedly taught some useful English words by his new teammates. But one particular adjective was not as polite as they had led him to believe and he used it when he was served with one of his first meals in England at the hostel. Unfortunately, he put the word—a seven-letter expletive—in front of 'thank you' much to his landlady's horror as she arrived at the table with his meal!

But one teammate, centre-forward George King, helped him to learn English and became a close friend. And later into his City career Jensen apparently made the most of his linguistic abilities because Davidson added:

Viggo didn't speak much English when he arrived, but it didn't take him long to learn it. And it didn't stop him from taking the mickey out of referees. If he'd done something wrong in a game, he would just say: 'Ja?' back to them and then they'd reply: 'Never mind then!' In fact, he spoke better English than a lot of people, but the referees didn't know it!

Jensen, in fact, admitted that he was able to speak better English than to write it, but further evidence of how much he had also tried to show his versatility off the pitch occurred in October 1954. Hull Watch and Licensing Committee gave him permission to sell hot dogs from a mobile canteen at an authorised street trader's stand at the junction of the city's Hessle Road and Rosamund Street. But on home match days he also took the canteen to Boothferry Park, where he sold Danish hot dogs on the forecourt at the entrance to the ground. The chief constable had told the committee that it was a continental idea, but no-one wanted to turn down Jensen because of his hero status in the city. And Dennison recalled:

> It was basically a hamburger and hot-dog stall. City bought the house next to the car-park at Boothferry Park for the secretary Cyril Lee, but it had a spiral staircase and he had a wooden leg! And the club let Viggo have his stall next to the house on match days. But he was always playing, so I don't know who ran it. Maybe his wife did.

In early 1954 Jensen had received a benefit cheque of £750 from City soon after completing five years with the club. Fittingly, the award arrived at a time when he had increased the club's coffers by about £8,000 when he converted a last-minute penalty—which he himself had won against future England World Cup-winning manager Alf Ramsey—against Tottenham Hotspur in the FA Cup fifth round to earn them a replay, which they lost 2–0 at White Hart Lane four days later in front of an attendance of 52,936. But the 1–1 draw at Boothferry Park attracted a crowd of 46,839 for what was City's first all-ticket game for four years and they had to play with 10 men after Ken Harrison had injured his knee badly after just three minutes. England international Eddie Baily gave Spurs the lead, but then Jensen came to the Tigers' rescue. And he said of the first meeting:

> It had been decided before the game that I should take any penalty-kicks. I remember running round with the ball and all the Tottenham players flocking around the referee in a wild sort of protest. At last the ball was placed on the spot, but then it was kicked away. I placed the ball on the spot again and a Tottenham player came up and whispered to me: 'You'll never score.' But luckily I did.

He must certainly have understood English by then, but he was still able to ignore it when the situation arose . . .

As the 1956–57 season unfolded, Jensen decided that he would return home to Denmark and City Supporters' Club decided to open a testimonial fund for him with the board's support. Jensen blotted his copybook on a rare occasion when he missed a penalty in his final away game at Chesterfield and he then bowed out for City in a 2–0 home win over Chester in the rain in November 1956. It had initially been hoped that he would appear in the following Saturday's FA Cup tie at home to Gateshead because he had 'last-minute jobs to do,' but it was not to be. His departure came 10 days later after the clash with Chester, but it was marked by a dance in his honour at Hull City Hall when chairman Harold Needler sent a cable of good wishes from Toronto. And teammate David Coates recalled: 'They did a do for him and had a massive whipround because he was so highly popular.' Jensen was bought a mini-piano, which had a silver plaque attached to it with the inscription: 'Presented to Viggo Jensen by Hull City AFC Supporters' Club in appreciation of his services to the club as a player and a gentleman.' It came from the proceeds of his testimonial fund and it was presented to him by City Supporters' Club president Norman Shenker. In addition, the long-serving Billy Bly presented Jensen with a clock at a social function at City Supporters' Club's headquarters three days after his final appearance. Bill Bradbury joked that it would save him from being late for work in the future and Jensen replied that he knew that English people, especially students, were always treated well in Denmark. He added: 'Now I can go back to Denmark and tell them it is exactly the same in England.'

Curiously, Jensen, who also spoke of his 'eight happy years' in Hull, finished his stay in a similar way to how it had started. His first social evening in Yorkshire had included darts, snooker and table-tennis soon after his arrival: the function with the supporters just before his departure included darts, snooker and dominoes! And much later Jensen again reflected:

> I had so many wonderful adventures, but one of the things which I shall always remember and which impressed me so much during the first few years at Boothferry Park were the 30,000, 40,000 or 45,000 crowds. I cannot say more than I would do it all over again if I could

go back to 1948. I would like to have played First Division football, but that was not to be. Eight years are a long time, but they passed too quickly.

The Great Dane had made 308 League appearances for the Tigers, his record left him 13th in the club's all-time appearances list and he had been an ever-present during the 1951–52 and 1952–53 seasons, playing in 119 successive Second Division games at one stage. He is also joint 21st with Brian Marwood in City's goalscoring charts with 51 in the League, more than half of them coming in his first two seasons with the club when he featured more prominently in the forward-line. But he still chipped in with goals in the No. 3 shirt and was a contemporary of Jack Brownsword, another goalscoring full-back who built his reputation as a penalty king with Scunthorpe United after playing briefly for the Tigers after the 1939–45 War.

Jensen, who died in late November 2005, had a successful coaching stint back at his old club EFB Esbjerg when he went back to Denmark, but he still kept in touch with some of the friends he had made in East Yorkshire. He even returned to the area for a reunion during the mid-1970s when he played for the ex-Tigers at Ideal Standard's ground, which much later became City's youth headquarters, in central Hull. Jensen's original arrival at Boothferry Park had hardly been conventional, but it paid dividends because he quickly and consistently won the hearts and minds of his City colleagues and supporters as an ambassador for Denmark.

Bob Dennison added: 'Viggo was a smashing bloke and I enjoyed playing alongside him as a full-back because he was always willing to help out. He would tell young players not to listen to the crowd.' Another teammate Brian Bulless also summed up his attributes as a person when he said: 'Viggo was a lovely fellow who was helpful with his advice on positional play. If he didn't think you were doing the right thing, he'd tell you what to do.' And wing-half Jimmy Greenhalgh, who played alongside Jensen in his first season in English football in 1948–49 when the Tigers won promotion and reached the FA Cup quarter-finals, said:

I was a working-class player who would never be classed as a great one. But Viggo Jensen opened the door to skills we'd never heard of and I have abiding memories of the range of his ability. For example, he was the first bloke to pull a ball down on his instep. We hadn't seen that kind of technical ability before.

Jensen was always courteous and polite, but, above all, his footballing finesse was never in doubt, though, and it was once written of him:

> He is certainly one of the greatest bargains ever to step on to an English football ground. The fans on the terraces admire his superb mastery and the magnificent physical fitness that carries him full speed throughout 90 minutes of the hardest game. He is fearless, but fair and he can play anywhere with equal facility—the hallmark of a great footballer.

11

ANDY 'JOCK' DAVIDSON

Andy Davidson is a classic example of someone who had to defy the odds to become a hero and achieve legendary status. He went on to play in more League games—520—than anyone else in Hull City's history, but his success and longevity had to be achieved the hard way. He was frequently labelled as 'a tough-tackling Scot,' but he had to show immense resilience to establish himself in the first team in the first place. After all, he nearly did not play any senior football for the Tigers because he was plagued by homesickness when he first saw the dereliction of war-torn Hull. And when he was finally persuaded to return to the club, he had to battle back from three broken legs to become a first-team regular.

Davidson, who was born in the Scottish village of Douglas Water in the Lanarkshire coalfield in July 1932 and had an elder sister Ella and elder brother Craig, first came to Hull in 1947, but kept returning to Scotland. On one occasion City's manager Major Frank Buckley went to Scotland to persuade him to return, but his brother Craig, a lorrydriver who had played for the club himself as a winger, eventually tipped the scales. Craig Davidson played 18 League games under Buckley in 1946–47, a further four early the following season and Andy said:

> My brother was a long-distance lorrydriver and came to Boothferry Park to ask for a trial. He had played for Cambuslang Rangers in

Scotland and was a better player than I was, but he wasn't so interested in football. He was naturally two-footed, but he got injured, needed six operations and never played again. And Newcastle United had offered £15,000 for him two weeks before it first happened.

Craig, who had sought a trial when he stopped over with a consignment for Hull's docks, also recommended Andy to City and initially they shared digs. But Andy became homesick when Craig, who also had a trial with Crystal Palace, left the club. Andy, who had played for his local Scottish side Douglas Water Thistle, said:

In 1947 Anlaby Road in Hull was rubble and there were stories about people who had spent every night for six weeks in air-raid shelters at the bottom of their gardens. It had been a rough time for the Hull people. I came from a mining village in Scotland, where there was no such thing as a war. Douglas Water was very sheltered. I never went out of the village, so it was a big change to come to such a big place.

I didn't particularly want to leave home, but big brother said: 'Come to England' and in our family what big brother said went. But I could not understand half of what the people in Hull said and I'm sure they didn't know what I was saying. I had no friends of my own age, so back home I went. Douglas Water was a village with a pit. It was close to another village called Ringside and they were spread over about 20 square miles with a total population of about 700. Coming to a big city such as Hull was a big move and I went back home three times. I wouldn't have stayed in Hull if my brother hadn't brought me back.

Douglas Water was a typical coalmining village of about 500 people, but they had two football sides. Every mining community did in those days. I'd been down a coalmine and the lads took the cage down to the bottom quickly for a joke, so I decided that I wasn't going down there again. I was working on the railway back home, but my brother told Hull City about me and I was offered a trial. I said to him: 'Where's Hull?' He said that it was a city near the east coast of England. I replied: 'Well, let it stay there!' Anlaby Road had been flattened by the bombing. I went back home because I'd never seen such a big place. I even borrowed the landlord's son's bike to go back home! But the landlord made it easy for me and looked after me well. And Ted Tarrant, who was a hell of a player, was one of the lads who looked after me well, too. The size of Hull was a shock when I first came to it, but in the end I never wanted to leave.

Stan Dixon, a defender who had played for City in the late 1920s, also helped because he managed four cinemas in the East Riding and Andy added: 'Stan used to let us get into his cinemas free because he knew us.' Craig also returned to Yorkshire to play for Scarborough in 1948 and the brothers eventually settled in the East Riding. Above all, it gave Andy the chance to be part of the family's footballing heritage. His cousin, Jimmy Davidson, was to win eight caps as a defender for Scotland while with Partick Thistle in 1954–55, and his father Tom's cousin was Bill Shankly. Andy said: 'We all grew up together and Bill made his name with a side called Glenbuck Cherrypickers. Eventually he was capped by Scotland, but he was never picked as often as he should have been.' But Tom Davidson always kept his distance because Andy added:

> When I turned professional at 16, they said: 'You can have £5 a week.' That was money that my dad hadn't seen in the coalmines. He was a very quiet fellow who would never watch me play—even in my local side. He'd walk away and then come back to ask how I'd played. He walked out of the Best Stand at Hull City because he couldn't stand it in case I did something wrong.

But family feelings were equally as forceful in formulating the young Davidson's football façade because he said: 'I'd always wanted to play for Celtic, but my grandfather, who was a mason, never spoke to me for 10 months when I talked to Rangers and didn't join them!'

Davidson's early career was not helped by his view of Buckley, City's first post-war manager, because he recalled:

> He was very ruthless. His career had been in the Army and I'm not sure that he knew all that much about football. He would have about 300 trialists down on Tuesdays and they would all get no more than 15 to 30 minutes in which to prove themselves. He was a good talker, but he would teach you how to go over the ball. They would take the old sleepers from the railway, put a ball against them and you had to tackle. Sometimes you'd finish off running with blood.

But Davidson was able to find more allies as he adjusted to life in East Yorkshire and inside-forward Frank McGorrighan was one. Davidson recalled:

> Frank was a lovely man and a natural comedian. When Major Buckley

came into the dressing-room, it would go quiet apart from Frank, who was never worried about him and would carry on chattering away as if nothing had happened. Frank's favourite trick was to try to 'nutmeg' opposition players. Sometimes he would run round the other side of them after doing it and sometimes he just wouldn't bother. I told him that I wanted to start doing it, but he said that I was too young to try it and needed to grow a bit!

Later on Davidson also became close to City's youngest-ever captain Johnny Neal, who would forge a notable career as a manager, because he said: 'I was the best man at his wedding. He was a good pal because we'd been in digs together. He was a hell of a sprinter. He was a flier who could do 100 yards in 10 seconds.'

And Davidson gradually developed a single-mindedness, which was typified by the occasion in February 1949 when City controversially lost 1–0 to Manchester United in the FA Cup quarter-finals in front of a record crowd of 55,019: 'I'd been playing at Doncaster that afternoon, we'd won 3–1 and I was too chuffed to worry about the first team losing!' His focus also enabled him to recover from the injury setbacks early in his career because he added:

> I was written about as some kind of miracle man, but I didn't see it that way. Football was my life and I couldn't see myself turning to anything else, so I set out with one purpose after each accident—to get fit to play again. There were times when I had to fight a lone battle to get fit and watch the rest of the lads kicking a ball around. I daren't join in, but I had to show that those who said that I was finished were wrong.

The first break—to his right leg—was in a public pre-season practice game in 1950. He then went into the RAF at Finningley, near Doncaster, and then got a luckier break—in the first team. But in his 11th League game—a 3–0 defeat at Swansea in January 1953—he broke his left leg. And he made only two more League appearances during the following two seasons because he made a comeback in the A team in November 1953 after being advised not to play again for a year and broke the same leg again. Davidson typically blamed himself for returning too soon.

But he had at least had a taste of first-team action even though there was little to suggest that he would become such a firm fixture in the side. His League debut came at centre-forward in a 2–0 defeat at Blackburn in September 1952 and he scored in the return game at Boothferry Park a week later. He was then switched to centre-half, where he played when City became FA Cup giantkillers in January 1953 by beating First Division Charlton Athletic 3–1 at home, and it was reported: 'The hero of the game was a young man of 20 who had already been at Boothferry Park for six years—centre-half Andrew Davidson.'

And as Davidson finally became a first-team regular, he played in what he regarded as his favourite game for the club—even though it was only a friendly! In October 1955 City were debatably given the chance to entertain top Hungarian side Vasas when Wolverhampton Wanderers pulled out of a tour game against them and he recalled:

> We were right down on our luck and yet we had one of our greatest victories. There was an uproar when we were given the game because we were at the foot of the Second Division and had taken only three points from 12 games. Vasas had annihilated big clubs, so the papers went berserk when we got to play them. The Press slammed the match on the grounds that we had no chance and British football would be a laughing-stock after the certain slaughter. But the lads, stung by all the criticism, played like heroes, beat Vasas 3–1 and Bill Bradbury, who had just joined us from Birmingham City and could have gone on to bigger clubs, got a hat-trick. Vasas thought they were playing a little club, but Bill tore them apart. To be fair, we outplayed them and the win was no fluke. And it tasted all the sweeter because we upheld British soccer prestige.

Davidson, who acquired a love of boxing, played mainly at right-back or wing-half for the rest of his career although there were occasions when he briefly resumed the centre-forward role. And he knew his preference as he underlined his reputation as an uncompromising hard man because he said:

> I had always played a left-half from being captain of the under-14s back home at the age of 11. I think that it all started when Frank Harrison got injured and I never got away from being at right-back after that, but I hated it. I hated playing at right-back because I didn't think that I was getting into the game enough, so I used to say to opposition wingers from the start that they had one of two choices—

the cottage hospital or the infirmary. I would then point out that the food was better at the cottage hospital, but that the surgeons were better at the infirmary! Funnily enough they nearly always seemed to settle for playing at left-back instead of on the left-wing after that! But I was sent off only twice in my career and one occasion was the first game of the season at Coventry after we'd been promoted in 1966 when Bobby Gould made a personal remark to me, so I retaliated. When it came to the return game at Boothferry Park, Bobby came up to me before the start and apologised for what he'd said. I still told him about his choice of hospitals and he went as white as a shroud!

I was frightened of nobody. Other players from other clubs never bothered me. It didn't matter to me—I just hated losing. I would never shake hands with an opposition player when we lost. But if we'd won, I'd even shake hands with the referee and linesmen. But when I look back, it was stupid. In the 1960s team we had players who wouldn't look after themselves, so I would have to do it. I never said: 'I played well.' If the side won, that was what mattered.

Davidson's teammates appreciated his commitment, too, because Chris Chilton, his successor as captain, said:

Nowadays Andy would have been caught on camera all the time because he nailed that many! I had to go back with the centre-half when the opposition went up for a corner-kick. If the centre-half had been dishing it out a bit, Andy would say to me: 'All right, leave him to me. I've got him. You just fill in that area.' The ball would go in, somebody might head it out at the near post and it might not even have got into the centre of the goal. It would be cleared out and everybody would push out, but you'd look back and there would be the centre-half laid out flat in the penalty area. Andy had gone past him and chinned him!

If you were involved in City's team—as I was from 17—and you had the right attitude, Andy would take you under his wing and he'd protect you. He was like a mother hen. He wouldn't suffer conmen or anyone who was flash in the pan. You had to do it in training and especially in games because he would threaten his own players in the dressing-room if need be. I learned a lot from him in that respect. You had respect for him because he meant it when he put that black-and-amber shirt on.

Before a home game Andy's sleeves would be rolled up, we would be up and at them and he would be really geeing the players up. Then

John 'Jackie' Smith, Hull City's prolific marksman from their early years

Tommy Bleakley, Hull City's long-serving defender of the 1920s

Matt 'Ginger' Bell, Hull City's long-serving captain and full-back of the 1920s

Full-back and long-serving backroom man Jimmy Lodge in his younger days with Hull City

Hull City legends Jimmy Lodge (left) and Cliff Woodhead (centre) sit back and listen as Jack Hill makes a point. Hill made 11 appearances for England as a half-back and was with the Tigers as a player and manager before the 1939–45 War and as a scout after it

Bert 'Paddy' Mills, Hull City's prolific goalscorer who had two spells with the club

George 'Geordie' Maddison, Hull City's goalkeeping character from the North-East

Cliff Woodhead, Hull City's long-serving full-back of the 1930s who later joined the club's coaching staff

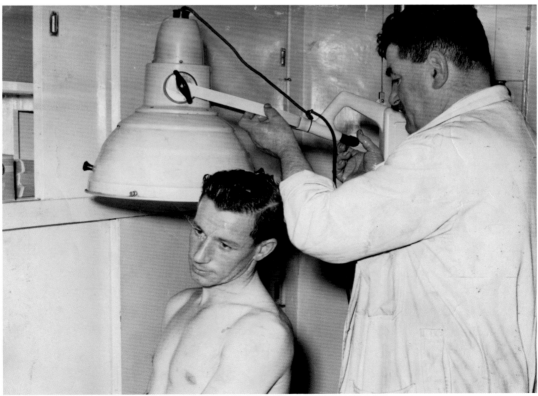

Injury-plagued Hull City goalkeeper Billy Bly (left) receives treatment from the legendary Jimmy Lodge during the 1952–53 season. Lodge served the Tigers in a variety of roles in two spells with the club, including player, coach, trainer, masseur and physiotherapist, until his death in 1971

Billy Bly nurses a broken nose after picking up one of his many injuries during his yeoman service with Hull City when they lost 3–1 at Blackburn Rovers in January 1954

Billy Bly behind the counter of his confectionery shop just down the road from Hull City's old Boothferry Park ground

Hull City's England international inside-forward Raich Carter soon after joining them towards the end of his illustrious career. He led them to the Third Division North title in 1948–49 in his first full season as player-manager

Hull City's popular 'silver-haired' genius Raich Carter leads them out at Boothferry Park

Hull City's popular utility player Viggo Jensen pictured soon after his arrival at Boothferry Park from his native Denmark during the autumn of 1948

Hull City's versatile Danish international Viggo Jensen tests his throw-in technique

Andy Davidson, who overcame a series of serious injuries during his Hull City career, is helped home by fellow legend Doug Clarke (left) and the prolific Bill Bradbury after being hurt during a 2–0 defeat at Swindon Town in the early part of the 1958–59 promotion season

Hull City's record appearances maker Andy Davidson during his early days with the club in the late 1940s

Tough Scottish defender Andy Davidson in action towards the end of his long Hull City playing career in a 4–0 win over Heart of Midlothian in a pre-season friendly in August 1967

The versatile Brian Bulless uses his cultured left foot during Hull City's 2–0 home win over Hartlepools United in March 1957 in which he scored

Doug Clarke in action in his days when he was still an inside-forward in Hull City's 2–0 home win over Hartlepools United during the 1956–57 campaign in which he was on the mark. He was on his way to his best return of League goals in a season—18—during his time with the club and finished as joint top goalscorer with Bill Bradbury

Hull City's all-time record marksman Chris Chilton (left) sneaks in after being set up by Billy Wilkinson (right) for one of his four goals in their 7–0 win over Barnsley in October 1964 under the new Boothferry Park floodlights

Chris Chilton typically hangs in the air to beat a group of Sunderland defenders and complete his last League hat-trick for Hull City in a 4–0 home win in January 1971

Master finisher Ken Wagstaff scores the first of his two goals in Hull City's 3–2 home defeat against Sheffield United in January 1970

Ken Wagstaff beat Orient's goalkeeper Ray Goddard for Hull City's third goal in a 5–2 home win in April 1971

Ken Houghton heads Hull City's winner in a 2–1 success at home to Millwall in January 1970

Hull City's Ken Houghton, who had spells with the club as both a player and manager, eludes some close marking to beat ex-Tiger Les Green to score his side's second goal in a 2–2 home draw against Derby County. The goal came in April 1970 in the testimonial match for the long-serving Jimmy Lodge

Garreth Roberts beats Sheffield Wednesday goalkeeper Bob Bolder to score the first of his two Football League Cup goals for Hull City in a 2–1 first-round home defeat in August 1979. Watching Roberts, the middle of the three City players, are his teammates Trevor Phillips (left) and Keith Edwards

Hull City's diminutive captain Garreth Roberts scores with a rare header in Hull City's 3–0 home win over Preston North End in April 1984

Hull City's long-serving Welsh international goalkeeper Tony Norman in action

Hull City's popular goalkeeper Tony Norman, who has battled to overcome serious illness since his playing career ended, relaxes with a pint at Robin Hood's Bay in North Yorkshire after completing Alfred Wainwright's coast-to-coast walk on behalf of the Children's Heart Federation in 2005

Brian Horton (right) during his first spell with Hull City as a manager and player with his assistant and long-time friend Dennis Booth. The durable Horton led the Tigers to promotion in his first season in a managerial role in 1984–85

Brian Horton in coaching mode during his second spell with Hull City when he was their assistant manager

Dean Windass, who had three spells as a player with Hull City, in celebratory mood

A signed copy of Dean Windass striking his historic Wembley winner for Hull City against Bristol City in May 2008

a buzzer or a bell would go in the dressing-room, which was the referee telling the players to go out. We'd go into the tunnel, Duggie Clarke liked to run out last and I might be just in front of him. But we used to stop in the tunnel and I used to ask what was happening because I was impatient with nerves and wanted to get out on to the pitch and into the fresh air. I was then told that it was Andy welcoming the opposition. 'I thought: 'What a nice gesture that is! I wouldn't have thought that of Andy!' Eventually I got up near the front and sometimes I might even go out after Andy. And then, of course, I realised what was going on. His welcoming committee to every player in the opposition was: 'I'm going to break your legs.' He would be threatening all of them and you could see any young players in the opposition team go white. But he said it to everybody and he wound them up, even the experienced, seasoned professionals. In hindsight, I thought that Andy stirred them up that much—especially the defenders—that they wanted to kick hell out of me because they couldn't get to him! He was unbelievable.

Dennis Butler, who was Davidson's full-back partner for much of the 1960s, added:

I can remember one game at Plymouth when Nicky Jennings started on the left-wing for them. And it was an occasion when Andy tried to talk a player out of the game by telling him early on: 'You can make up your mind, but you and the ball won't both be going past me!'

And winger Mike Bowering, a teammate in City's 1958–59 promotion side, recalled:

Andy once told me when we were playing Chesterfield that they had a full-back who could be easily wound up if I said a few things to him, so I started to make some personal comments about his family as a joke. All of a sudden it was as if he had steam coming out of his ears and I suddenly thought that I might be in mortal danger. Fortunately Andy realised what was happening and ran 40 yards across the pitch from where he'd been playing to outside-left where I was and sorted the full-back out for me!

Davidson still had his own injury worries, notably when he missed 20 successive League games after damaging his knee at Swindon during the 1958–59 promotion season, but then he played in the next 140. In 1961–62 he missed three League games before embarking on another run that included three seasons with an ever-present record. He made 177 consecutive League appearances until January 1966, by which time he was captaining the Tigers on their way to the Third Division championship under manager Cliff Britton.

The combative Davidson even had a bottle flung at him from the crowd at Grimsby in April 1966 as City closed in on the title, but he and Britton had a mutual respect at that time. Davidson said:

> Cliff had a photographic memory and would go through every player individually from one to 11 to assess their performances. I used to listen to him and think: 'You've got me right, but surely you couldn't do the same for the other 10.' But he did. If I'd made one mistake, he'd nail me for it on a Tuesday morning when he went through everybody's performances. He never forgot anything from the 90 minutes of a match and was a great tactician. He was unbelievable. He knew the game from back to front. He'd watch a match, talk for hours and hours about it and never forget a thing. He knew every ball that had been passed and you couldn't bamboozle him.

Britton responded:

> Perhaps one of the biggest surprises for many people has been the form shown by our captain, Andy Davidson. He was written off by many critics even before the season started, but I don't think he has had a better season—not while I have been in Hull anyway. He and Dennis Butler are as good a pair of full-backs as could be found in the division.

Davidson's enjoyment of his time under Britton finally erased the memories of his struggle to come to terms with Buckley's regime. But City failed to build on their momentum from 1966 and Davidson's playing career was coming to an end. He reflected:

> Cliff Britton had one weakness—he was too loyal. We lost 5–4 at Ipswich when we looked as if it we'd carry on where we'd left off after promotion and do well in the Second Division. But Cliff brought in kids who had had no experience in the first team. He didn't seem to want to bring experienced players to the club and it was probably because he was too loyal to everyone—the first team, the reserves and the juniors. We weren't capable of going any higher, but Cliff wanted to give people a chance. Buckley was the opposite.

At one stage Davidson had a spell of 11 seasons during which he only once failed to make 40 League appearances, but the end finally came 11 minutes into City's 3–2 win at Aston Villa in November 1967 because of persistent Achilles tendon trouble. He also chipped in with 18 League goals for the club, but he announced his retirement as a player in July 1968 and joined the backroom staff, insisting:

> I cannot grumble. It was a wonderful 20 years and City were my life. I had a couple of offers when I came out of the Forces because Newcastle United and Sheffield Wednesday were after me, but I had no inclination to go to either of them. But I gave half of my life away when I stopped as a player. I couldn't accept it, but the good old days were over. I was never interested in coaching, but City sent me on a course and I was more of a nuisance on it, but they passed me. But it wasn't the same as playing. I would get frustrated with players who had everything, but weren't the least bit interested in winning. And they don't think that you're trying to help them. Some of the characters were out of order and I got to the point when I wasn't bothered any more.

He had had a testimonial match on April Fools' Day 1969—amazingly, the day that future club hero Dean Windass was born—and Ken Wagstaff scored twice when City beat reigning League champions Manchester City 2–0 in front of a 13,027 crowd. It brought in £2,512 and was preceded by the singing of 'Auld Lang Syne'! Davidson eventually became City's assistant manager in late September 1974 and did everything from coaching to scouting at various times. Not surprisingly, he was as driven as ever, as he proved in January 1977 when the Tigers lost 2–1 at Luton and he was involved in disputes with the match officials and home fans. He needed a police escort down the tunnel at the end and later underlined his typical motivation and passion when he admitted: 'I can't help getting involved and I've told myself a hundred times that I shouldn't, but I've got to learn to be a lot more sensible about it. I did let myself get involved, but how do you change what is human nature?'

The final curtain came down on his time with the club in December 1979 when he was sacked with manager Ken Houghton and coach Wilf McGuinness after a 7–2 defeat at Brentford. Davidson reflected:

Hull City were the biggest part of my working life, so I took it hard. I was only scouting for them at the time, but they made their decision and I had to go. It hurt at the time, but I bought a fish business and earned more from it than I ever did from playing football. I'd love to know what happened with all the money that went into Hull City in the 1960s. There were big crowds, but the players weren't all that well paid.

The final twist came when he found that one of the customers listed on his fish round was Bob Chapman, the chairman who had sacked him, and he claimed in typical fashion: 'I did the only thing I could do with the fish—I stuck it through the letter-box!'

In the end Davidson fitted in to life in East Yorkshire contentedly after his initial doubts, enjoying rugby league and becoming a close friend of the code's local legend Johnny Whiteley. He recalled: 'On one occasion when I was suspended I went to see Hull FC in a rugby-league game at the Boulevard instead of watching City, so the club fined me!'

And all along he retained his Scottish accent and pride. The accent, though, landed him in trouble in the build-up to a match at Plymouth in the 1970s when he was on the coaching staff. The City party were ordering their light pre-match meals in their hotel when Davidson was approached by a waiter who looked and sounded like the character Manuel in *Fawlty Towers*, which was then topical. Davidson told him in his best Scottish brogue that he wanted a Spanish omelette and the waiter duly disappeared with the order. He returned a few minutes later with an omelette that Davidson refused to eat because he was convinced that it had mould on it. Davidson asked what it was supposed to be and the waiter replied: 'It's your spinach omelette, sir!'

Davidson, whose cousin Jimmy's last game for Scotland was in a 7–2 defeat by England at Wembley, also had his native pride put to the test. City's former secretary Malcolm 'Mac' Stone recalled:

Wilf McGuinness and Andy Davidson were great characters when they were on the coaching staff. One night at the end of a season Andy had a party, but we were under strict orders not to mention that England had beaten Scotland at Hampden Park earlier in the day because he was so upset by the result. Wilf, who is one of the funniest people I've ever met, turned up in an old raincoat and, when he took it off, he had his England blazer and tie underneath. He was persuaded to take them off for fear of upsetting Andy, but underneath them he was wearing his old England No. 6 shirt! I told him: 'Get that off!' But Wilf was a great guy.

Everything in Davidson's background was moulded by a sense of single-minded steel which insisted that, as a leader and loyal, one-club man, all that he ever wanted was the best for the Tigers during his long stay with them. He reflected:

I'd left a small mining village in Scotland to come to a city that had been bombed to hell during the War. I ran home three times, but then I loved the place once I'd settled in Hull and never wanted to leave it again. At the start I was just a lad leaving school, but I made a lot of friends and I took Hull City as my club. In turn, the club became very personal to me.

12

BRIAN BULLESS

Brian Bulless has earned himself a reputation as an easy-going, unobtrusive person who has often shunned the limelight and never liked a fuss. As one of nature's gentlemen, therefore, he was acting entirely out of character when he dramatically burst on to the Football League scene with Hull City as a teenager in April 1953. Not only did he score on his first-team debut, but his winner against the Tigers' fellow strugglers Southampton at Boothferry Park three games from the end of a tortuous season also went a long way to preserving their Second Division status after a battle against relegation.

Bulless, who was born in Hull in September 1933, was doing his National Service when he was given his League baptism as City faced an injury crisis. Left-wingers Brian Cripsey and Eddie Burbanks had groin problems, the versatile future Republic of Ireland international Fionan Fagan had an ankle injury and another winger Ken Harrison was sidelined by knee trouble, so Bulless was given his big chance at outside-left in what was described as 'the most critical match ever at Boothferry Park.' He had scored 13 times in 19 Midland League games from the wing for the Tigers in 1952–53 and duly obliged with the only goal of the Southampton game after 51 minutes with a left-footed shot. Barnsley were isolated at the bottom of the table and it was a question as to who would go down with them. As it was, the Tigers finished 18th, Southampton were relegated and it was written of Bulless:

He rendered his club a wonderful service. He has ability and an instinct to fight and his heart is in the game. He was once far enough back in defence to concede a corner and he does not hesitate to go fighting for the ball. The signs are that he can give good service to City.

Bulless, who had joined the RAF as an 18-year-old, recalled:

I was stationed at Warton, near Blackpool, when I played my first game, but I came home most weekends. On this occasion there was a call to the camp to say that the club wanted me to play against Southampton. I had a warrant officer who was hated in the camp because he was a bit firm, but he loved football, so he let me come home on leave with a special pass to play. It was a relegation game, but it was a dream debut for me. Johnny Linaker, who was on the right-wing, took a corner, I more or less swung my foot at it as it came into the penalty area and the ball flew in. Another time it might have gone over Bunker's Hill! I can remember that Peter Sillett, who went on to play for England, was in the Southampton team, but it was a story-book start for me. We just scraped through and survived and in the last match of the season we went to Sheffield United, who had just got promotion as champions, and won 2–0. I wouldn't say that I felt under any pressure at the time, but I lived in town and walked from Charles Street to Boothferry Park to calm my nerves before that first game.

Bulless was, in fact, brought up to be a city gent in all respects because Charles Street was close to his birthplace in central Hull. His parents Arthur and Charlotte had five children and he was the youngest, following in the footsteps of brothers Bob and Michael and sisters Betty and Edie. Brian, who attended Blundell Street School and then Clifton Street Senior School close to Hull's city centre, was actually born in Francis Street, which was a significant factor in his early football education.

Youngsters from the city centre would regularly take each other on at football when they reached their early teens and Bulless explained:

The lads from one street would challenge those from the others in the area. There were odd times when we would catch a bus to find a field on which to play, but I was actually from Francis Street West and it was Francis Street East that got badly bombed, so that's where we used to play—on the sites of buildings that had been flattened. I suppose that the Germans may have done us a favour in that respect! But we would arrange matches against other streets on light nights or sometimes during the day when there were dark nights. And we would often get good crowds because the regulars from the pubs around the area would come down as spectators until it was opening time. It used to be good and it was where I got started in football.

Anyway the unconventional development of Bulless's skills paid dividends, especially for his refined left foot. It was one of his great strengths and he said: 'I had a good left foot and a bit of speed and I wasn't afraid to go into a tackle. Using my left foot was natural from kicking my first football at school.' His ability also earned him recognition with Hull City Boys, for whom his penchant for scoring crucial goals was soon evident. After all, Bob Dennison, later a teammate with the Tigers, recalled: 'I played alongside Brian for City Boys although he was a year to the month younger than I was. We reached the Yorkshire Schools' Cup final against Rotherham and won 1–0 with Brian scoring the goal.'

Bulless went on to sign for the Tigers as an amateur in August 1949, turning professional in October 1950: 'I started in City Juniors, progressed to the A team and then got into the reserves.' He then moved on to make his goalscoring League debut at outside-left—a position that he did not always relish. But he wore the No. 11 shirt exclusively in the early days and reflected:

> Eddie Burbanks left and then it was between three of us—'Paddy' Fagan, Brian Cripsey and me—for the outside-left position. I'd always been on the wing when I was at school and when I played for City Boys. And I was on the wing for most of the time I played for City Juniors, but then I would play in other positions because of emergencies. At one stage I was moved to inside-left when Wilf Mannion was out of the side for a short time. I also played at left-back, but in the end I think I preferred the old wing-half role. My favourite position was left-half because I always wanted to be in the game all the time. I felt as if I were out of the game too much on the wing and I always wanted to be involved in it, which I could be at wing-half.

Bulless was also typically down-to-earth about his different roles as his career flourished slowly because he added:

> There weren't so many left-sided players in the game, my other foot was only for standing on and I didn't care where they played me as long as I was in the team. I never had an opinion in those days. As long as I was on the teamsheet when it went up, that was all that mattered. I was happy as long as I was playing. If I got chosen, that suited me.

He was in and out of the side during the 1953–54 season, but he made the most of one opportunity to underline his reputation for chipping in with essential goals. It came in a fourth-round FA Cup replay at home to Second Division promotion hopefuls Blackburn Rovers in February 1954 and helped to set up a lucrative tie with Tottenham Hotspur at Boothferry Park that went to a replay before City went out after two dramatic encounters. A group of 70 volunteers had cleared snow off the pitch in wheelbarrows and handcarts and Bulless took advantage by opening the scoring after 29 minutes. Alf Ackerman, who had set him up for his goal, made it 2–0 after 67 minutes before former England B international Tommy Briggs managed a consolation effort for Blackburn in the last minute. Oddly enough, Bulless scored only one other goal that season—in the next away League game nine days later when he and Ackerman were again on the mark together in a 2–2 draw at Brentford.

Bulless's naturally-philosophical approach stemmed from the fact that it took him a long while to become a first-team regular despite the impact that he made on his League debut because he said: 'I wasn't a regular from that moment on. I just filled in if there were any injuries.' But the switch inside from outside-left in place of Mannion, the former England international, towards the end of the 1954–55 season soon brought him another vital goal. City were again close to the relegation zone in the Second Division because the goals had largely dried up even though they had started the campaign promisingly. They entertained fellow strugglers Doncaster Rovers in April 1955 and Bulless opened the scoring after 14 minutes. It ended 1–1 after Doncaster's 16-year-old protégé Alick Jeffrey had equalised 11 minutes later, but the Tigers made life difficult for themselves by taking only one point from their last four games. They finally finished 19th, but Bulless's goal against Doncaster was their only one during the poor run.

This time, though, it was the prelude to Bulless finally becoming a first-team regular. He had made a total of only 32 League appearances in his first three seasons in League football: in 1955–56 alone he then played in 36 League games and never looked back. The major disappointment, though, was that the Tigers were finally relegated to the Third Division North and Bulless reflected:

> There was a lot of unrest among the senior players for some reason. I think I was aware of it. I was only a youngster, so I kept quiet in the background, but I could hear what was going on. In my opinion we had a lot of bad luck. Time after time we'd come off and wonder how we'd been beaten. But we weren't good enough. It was as simple as that.

But in 1956–57 he missed only one of City's 46 League games and scored nine goals, which was to be his best tally in a season. And in mid-March 1957 it included the only hat-trick of his League career when the Tigers beat Barrow 3–0 at home. Playing at inside-left, he scored after 18, 53 and 87 minutes, while Bill Bradbury missed a penalty before his third. Bulless said:

> That's one game that always sticks in my memory. I think we won quite comfortably. I played against some great players such as John Charles and Denis Law, but I also played with a few of them, such as Wilf Mannion, Stan Mortensen and Neil Franklin. At the time City had some good players without the success to go with them.

It prompted a transfer request in October 1957 when Bulless said: 'I have no quarrel with the club. City have treated me very well indeed, but I feel I am not making the progress I could. I feel that you can get in a rut by staying in one place too long.' Two months later he was linked with a move to Leeds United after their manager Raich Carter had watched the Tigers in an FA Cup replay at Barnsley, but he said: 'Brian was one of the youngsters I signed, but I have no special plans regarding him.' And City's manager Bob Brocklebank said: 'The suggestion was made some time ago, but I turned it down because we do not want to let any of our players go if we can possibly avoid it and, of course, we turned down Brian's transfer request.'

Bulless accordingly stayed on to pursue his one-club League career and it was far from humdrum for him by Good Friday in 1958. That was when he played his part in a bit of club history as City beat Oldham Athletic 9–0 in what was to be their biggest win at Boothferry Park and Bulless recalled:

> Bill Bradbury and Colin Smith got hat-tricks and the rest of the forward-line—Doug Clarke, Brian Cripsey and I—all scored once. I remember that David Teece, who had played for City, was in goal for Oldham and that we seemed to score every time we attacked. It was a day when everything went right.

Everything went even better in 1958–59 because the Tigers were promoted as the runners-up to Plymouth Argyle in the new, deregionalised Third Division. Bulless damaged a knee and a bilious attack almost scuppered his comeback after he had missed 13 League games, but he still figured at left-back, left-half, inside-left and outside-left during the campaign. And it was a season that started slowly with only one win in the first seven League games, ending in a 6–1 defeat at Southampton. Bulless reflected:

> There was a bit of unrest in the early part of the season although I can't really remember what caused it. We scored goals regularly, thanks in the main to Bill Bradbury and Colin Smith although they got good support from some of the others. All-round we may not have been a great side, but we had a lot of team spirit and that was very important to us.

In fact, he had again asked for a move early in the season. This time the request was granted although Brocklebank said: 'Bulless is not being awkward about the transfer.'

In the end the camaraderie among the squad prevailed. The disaster at the Dell was followed by four successive wins and the momentum grew. City twice won six League games in a row and Bulless added:

> It was unbelievable, but everybody went everywhere together as a gang and I think that it gave us an extra ingredient. We got hammered at Southampton, but it might have geed us up and we pulled our fingers out because we then went on a hell of a run, especially at home. We maybe surprised ourselves, but there were

some strong characters, such as Andy Davidson and Bill Bradbury, in that side. Andy was a 100 per cent player in every game and he set an example for everybody in the team. There was once a game at Chesterfield, who had a rough-looking character in their side. He was calling people names and riling them, so Andy ran right across the pitch to sort him out! Bill was a great fellow, but he was probably too outspoken and wasn't frightened to open his mouth when he thought he was right. Sometimes he was right and sometimes he was wrong, but it didn't bother him. He was also a hell of a good player and his goals speak for themselves.

The mercurial Bradbury set a post-war club record of 30 League goals in a season and in September 1959 he was Bulless's best man when he married Jean Winson. And the club houses close to Boothferry Park give another clue to the comradeship that culminated in a glorious campaign in 1958–59: the Bullesses, in fact, continued to live in one of them until 2011. It even led to a football transfer market with a difference because Bulless explained:

> A lot of the players lived near each other in the club houses in those days, but I was the only one to buy mine. Bill was a good friend and I eventually moved into what had been his club house when he was transferred from City. It was then transferred to me, but I applied to the club to buy it from them when I had to finish playing and they agreed to the sale.

And even though Bradbury and Smith, who scored 26 goals, were prolific in 1958–59, Bulless again popped up with a key goal for City near the end of the season. He scored just twice during the campaign, but the second one was in a 2–0 home win over Bury when the Tigers clinched promotion in the penultimate game of the season. He settled City's nerves by scoring when Colin Smith won Doug Clarke's corner and later his close pal Bradbury was also on the mark. And Bulless recalled: 'All I know about my promotion-winning goal against Bury was that I was only a few yards out, but the ball went in and that was the main thing.'

It was then a question of City trying to pip Plymouth for the title in their last game. They were at Wrexham, but suffered their second hammering of the season as they went down 5–1. And the repercussions were to spill over into the following season because

Bulless said:

> We went to Wrexham and were beaten 5–1 when we needed just one point to be champions. After the game words were said when Stan Kershaw, one of the directors, came into the dressing-room. He said that the directors weren't too pleased even though we'd got promotion, but what was said didn't please the lads. We were singing in the bath afterwards because we'd done our job and got promotion, but then it all upset us.

Bulless returned to Second Division football in 1959–60 and was ever-present for the only time in his career. No-one else played in all 42 League games, but the Tigers still went straight back down, finishing in 21st place. They won only two of their first 15 League games and had another poor run when they won only one in 12. City gave themselves a ray of hope by remaining undefeated in their last seven games when the emerging Dave King scored five times. But goals had previously been a problem: manager Bob Brocklebank had tried to solve the problem by signing experienced forwards Jackie Sewell, the former England international who had once been the most expensive player in the country, Ralph Gubbins and Roy Shiner in quick succession, but Bradbury left for Bury during the second half of the season and Bulless failed to score for the only time in his first 10 seasons as a first-team player at Boothferry Park.

Sewell at least enjoyed the environment because he once said: 'I liked the place and the lads in the dressing-room were super blokes, especially "Jock" Davidson, Brian Bulless and Doug Clarke.' Bulless, though, was left to rue the second relegation season of his City career and reflected:

> We felt we weren't getting the run of the ball and we weren't confident. It was a long struggle and some of the lads left. We had a good squad although we got relegated. It sounds silly, but it didn't bother us because of the team spirit. We still put the effort in.

And the topsy-turvy nature of the Tigers' fortunes in those days made Bulless well aware of the vagaries of footballing life because he added:

> Everything goes against you in a relegation season. But in a promotion season it's the opposite. Everything just seemed to come

off. In 1958–59 I had some niggling injuries, but everyone and everything seemed to be in the right place at the right time.

Bulless continued to be a first-team regular in a variety of roles on the left in City's first two seasons back in the Third Division, but stomach and knee injuries started to take their toll on him and he played in only 21 League games in 1962–63. The end of his illustrious, one-club League career came in October 1963 and he finished it in his last two games where he had started it—on the left-wing. But he was soon forced to see a specialist because of a knee-ligament problem and eventually left during the summer of 1964, having made 326 League appearances to leave him 11th in the club's all-time appearances list. He had also chipped in with a total of 30 League goals. But he was always typically self-effacing about his career and once insisted: 'I always considered myself lucky to have played with and against some great players.'

Bulless did make a brief excursion into non-League football with Hull Brunswick, but admitted: 'I had a couple of games, but wasn't really bothered.' He then went to work as a labourer for major Hull company Reckitt's—not all that far from where he had been born and brought up. And Bulless's commitment on the pitch should never be underestimated just because of his image as an unassuming nice guy. As City won 2–0 at Doncaster in the run-in to promotion in 1958–59, it was reported that Bulless was 'always eager to wander to where the fight was thickest.' And in early November 1956 he had wandered even further in a 3–1 defeat at Chesterfield as he raced back to cover near the end. He landed in the crowd after cartwheeling over a concrete wall and received a badly-bruised thigh, a sprained wrist and abrasions and cuts to both knees. Three days later manager City's manager Bob Brocklebank received a letter from Chesterfield Supporters' Club representative Charles Scott to ask about Bulless's welfare, but, more significantly, he was ruled out of the following week's home game against Chester and it ultimately robbed him of an ever-present record for the 1956–57 season.

And Bulless did return to Boothferry Park when he was awarded a testimonial match in 1965 although he did not play in it. Again Bulless was his usual unassuming self because he said of it: 'The spectators don't want to see me. They want to see the players I am getting together.' City beat an All-Star XI 9–8, the game attracted a crowd of 6,329 on a wet night and it appropriately took place in April in view of some of his goalscoring exploits. The All-Stars included England internationals Ray Wood and Ron Flowers, ex-Tigers Jack Brownsword and Bill Harris, who had played for Wales, and former Hull schoolboy Alex Dawson, who had gone on to play for Manchester United. Dawson scored four times, but there was evidence of Ken Wagstaff's emerging hero status as a marksman with the Tigers, who had just missed out on promotion from the Third Division, because he had his No. 8 shirt ripped from his back when the fans invaded the pitch at the end.

Bulless had had his ups and downs with the Tigers and there were occasions when he attracted interest from elsewhere and might have moved on. And his long-standing teammate Bob Dennison observed:

> I think that Leeds United wanted to buy Brian as a left-winger, but he wouldn't go because he didn't like playing there and he wanted to play at inside-left. And he was always a big family man and I don't think that he would have wanted to go away from home.

Ultimately Bulless would probably agree because he has always said: 'My family keep me going.' After all, he said of his notable goalscoring League debut for City as a 19-year-old: 'I was pleased for my parents.' And the family connection has continued with the club because his teenage grandson Jack has developed through the Tigers' youth set-up. Whether he will have the same poise of his grandfather's left foot remains to be seen, but Brian insisted: 'It's not a bad 'un'!'

And Bulless's loyalty as a person and versatility as a player always made him highly-respected. His 1960s teammate John McSeveney said: 'It was a treat to play with Brian. He could pass the ball and play little one-twos, which always allowed you to play a bit in your own areas. He was peerless and a Rolls-Royce of a footballer.' And Chris Chilton, who also played in the same forward-line in the same era, added:

> Brian had everything apart from probably a right foot, but he'd be worth his weight in gold today. He had pace, he could tackle, he could head the ball, he had strength, his left 'peg' was special and I learned a lot from playing alongside him. They talk about the best players ever at Hull City, such as the Raich Carters and Ken Wagstaffs of the world, but Brian must be in the top five. What a marvellous footballer he was!

13

DOUG CLARKE

There may be a football maxim that a player may earn himself a chance to move to a club if he is impressive against them. And that is just what Doug Clarke did when he sealed a switch to Hull City. In April 1955 Clarke scored a hat-trick for Bury against the Tigers, who then signed him in a £2,000 deal the following November. Quite simply, he beat them and then he joined them!

And Clarke, who was born in Bolton in January 1934, made his mark emphatically at Boothferry Park because he went on to make 368 League appearances for the Tigers. It left him joint ninth in the club's all-time appearances list—ironically on a par with defender Tommy Bleakley, who also came from the Bolton area. And Clarke is also joint eighth in the Tigers' list of all-time League goalscorers: again there is an intriguing coincidence because he is level with Ken Houghton on 79. The two of them never played together for the first team because Houghton arrived in early 1965 and Clarke left later in the year. But Clarke was noted for his ferocious shooting and Houghton was his natural successor with City because he, too, was known for his powerful shot.

Clarke recalled:

My son once introduced himself to someone in London and, when the fellow found out about the Hull link and that I was his dad, he complained that I'd injured him on Bunker's Hill with one of my shots! They used to say that it was just a natural asset. I just knew that I could hit a ball hard. Bernard Fisher, one of the goalkeepers at Hull, hated facing me in training. When we had shooting practice, he would say to me: 'Oh, it's you again. I'd better watch out for my fingers!'

Clarke had started his career with Bolton Wanderers as an amateur and then joined Darwen before moving on to Bury, with whom his brother Alan also had a brief spell, in February 1952. Then came the defining Good Friday hat-trick at Gigg Lane in a 4–1 win for a Bury side who included future City centre-half Norman Neilson and former England half-back Henry Cockburn. It was a month after Bob Brocklebank had taken over as City's manager as they struggled against relegation and Clarke scored three times in the opening 36 minutes, once with the aid of a deflection. The Tigers won for the first time under Brocklebank in the return fixture on the Easter Monday and subsequently stayed in the Second Division, but he was well aware of Clarke's capabilities and made his move the following season. Clarke, who scored 15 times in 37 League appearances for Bury, himself said of his hat-trick: 'I can't reflect on it as much as I'd like to, but I do remember that I'd just started in the first team after being in the Army.'

City were again involved in a relegation scrap in 1955–56 after winning only one of their opening 15 League games and it was then that Brocklebank acted swiftly as Clarke became the third forward to be signed in quick succession. Bill Bradbury, who ironically was to leave the Tigers for Bury, arrived from Brocklebank's old club Birmingham City in a £4,000 deal in October 1955. The following month former England centre-forward Stan Mortensen agreed to join City from Blackpool in a £2,000 deal, saying: 'I have chosen Hull chiefly because they are in a desperate position. I love a fight and there is one for City this season.' But Brocklebank also claimed to have put in an offer, which he described as substantial, for another inside-forward and the following day Clarke was duly snapped up. He recalled:

I got a shock really because I was the last person to know what was happening. Bury just told me that I might be moving in a day or so because Bob Brocklebank had been in touch from Hull City and they had accepted his offer. You couldn't say 'no' in those days because the club pulled all the strings. You would get only one-year contracts, so everything was in their favour. I just accepted it, but it was one of the best moves of my career and one of the best things I ever did because I enjoyed it all the time I was at Hull and made some loyal friends.

Brocklebank then made extensive changes to his forward-line for the next game at home to West Ham United and both Clarke and Mortensen scored on their debuts in a 3–1 win. Bradbury put the Tigers in front after nine minutes and then Clarke was on the mark in the 33rd minute, scoring from six yards following a corner from John Neal. And it was written of Clarke's performance at inside-right: 'He fitted quietly, but skilfully into all the plans in a manner that promised some more-than-useful work.' And Clarke himself pointed out: 'I was back in Hull nearly 50 years later in November 2009 when City were again at home to West Ham, but this time they were in the top flight.'

The attendance for the West Ham game in 1955 was a little more than 10,000 higher than it had been for the previous home game a fortnight earlier: in fact, it was the biggest of the season at Boothferry Park—24,050—but the Tigers still struggled and were relegated. And when Clarke scored in the final game of the season— a 3–2 home win over Stoke City—the gate was down to just 5,232. But the new inside-forward trio of Clarke, Mortensen and Bradbury scored 23 of City's 53 League goals that season even though they had missed the start of it: the problem that led to relegation was that the defence kept only four clean sheets—three of them away—in the 42 League games.

And in January 1956 Clarke had scored his first away goal for City when they were knocked out of the FA Cup at the third-round stage after two tussles with First Division Aston Villa. He also rates it as his most memorable as he was able 'to hammer in a shot which Keith Jones had no chance of saving' after eight minutes, but Jackie Sewell, who was later to become one of Clarke's City teammates, set up the equaliser a minute before halftime and Villa won the replay 2–1 at Boothferry Park after snow and ice had been cleared off the pitch. Clarke recalled:

> I was really pleased with my goal at Villa. It was a good result for us, we played well and we nearly won it. But Peter McParland scored the

equaliser and he went on to get both goals for Villa in the final the following season when they beat Manchester United.

And Clarke, whose brother Alan had signed for the Tigers while visiting him on leave from his National Service duties and was then called up with goalkeeper Bernard Fisher in an emergency during the Suez crisis, further cemented his reputation with the Tigers in the Third Division North in 1956–57 when they finished eighth and he finished as the joint leading League goalscorer with Bradbury on 18. The following season he added a further 16 League goals—three behind Bradbury, who was the top marksman—as City finished fifth and there were some landmarks—both personal and collective.

In September 1957 Clarke went one better than his hat-trick for Bury when he scored four in a game for the Tigers as they beat Halifax Town 4–2 at Boothferry Park. Clarke opened the scoring after just 50 seconds, added a second before halftime and completed his hat-trick after 56 minutes with a typically-powerful shot from 30 yards. Bradbury also scored for City, but Clarke added his fourth with 'another sizzling drive' after 75 minutes. Halifax, to be fair, had been handicapped by an injury to full-back Bert Ferguson in those pre-substitute days, but the ironic aspect of Clarke's haul was that City had scored only one goal in total in their opening four games of the season. And he recalled:

> I can basically remember the occasion because I won an award as Sportsman of the Week from a publication which, I think, was called *The Sporting Record*. One of the editors contacted me to congratulate me and presented me with an inscribed Ronson cigarette lighter. But I didn't smoke and I lost it! I'd probably have got a Porsche nowadays!

And there was another comparison between then and now that has sprung to Clarke's mind because he added:

> When you scored a goal in those days, you got a pat on the back and a handshake from your teammates. But things change and I think that footballers are now expected to do a double somersault with tuck whenever they score. If I'd tried that after scoring four in a game, I'd have been knackered!

In March 1958 Clarke had a transfer request rejected when Newcastle United showed an interest in him. But the following month the

Tigers registered what was to be their biggest League win at Boothferry Park—9–0 over Oldham Athletic. In addition, all five members of the forward-line—Clarke, Bradbury, Colin Smith, Brian Bulless and Brian Cripsey—were on the mark. Bradbury and Smith recorded hat-tricks and Clarke recalled: 'I can remember that we spent the last few minutes desperately trying to get a 10th.' Ironically, ex-Tiger David Teece, another Lancastrian, was in goal for Oldham that day and on the way to the game he had read his horoscope, which read: 'An adventurous day which does not turn out as well as you might suppose . . .'

By this time things were not turning out as Clarke might have supposed, too, because he was switched from inside-right to outside-right on a regular basis during the latter part of the season. He first took over the No. 7 shirt from Welsh winger Johnny Stephens and was to spend most of the rest of his City career wearing it. Clarke said:

> I'd been an inside-forward for six years of my career since starting out at Bury. But Bob Brocklebank said that he wanted to try me out as a right-winger. I didn't mind and said that I would have a go. And I soon discovered that you had a bit more room and freedom out on the wing. We played the old W formation in those days and I knew that I could cross a ball fairly accurately, but they told me that I had a bit of speed. I never thought that I was quick, but it turned out that I was! And the fans on the railway side of the ground at Boothferry Park gave me a lot of encouragement. They'd roar me on and blow me down the wing!

And it paid dividends in 1958–59—the first season of the deregionalised Third Division—when he helped them to promotion as the runners-up to Plymouth Argyle, scoring 12 goals in 45 League games. He missed only the early-season goalless draw at home to Swindon Town and finished third in the goalscoring list behind Bradbury, who set a club post-war record 30 in a season, and Smith.

The Tigers were the Third Division's top goalscorers with 90 that season and Clarke served up another of his Easter treats in front of their biggest gate of the season of 24,156 when they drew 3–3 with close rivals Norwich City, who had reached the FA Cup semi-finals. Clarke scored twice—after four and 35 minutes—and it was his second goal that was memorable because he said: 'I can remember taking a penalty against Norwich during our promotion season and hitting the ball so hard and straight at the goalkeeper Sandy Kennon that it nearly took him into the net before I followed it up!' Oddly enough, he would probably not have taken the penalty in the first place if Bradbury had not still been groggy after being injured.

The promotion season had not started well and City had won only one of their opening seven League games by the time that they lost 6–1 at Southampton, but then everything gelled and Clarke recalled:

> About half that team were just taken out of local soccer, but we all got on together. There were no cliques and everybody mixed in. That's what you should do, but that team weren't all that brilliant as individuals. It was just that that season we pulled together to work for each other. If you saw the make-up of the team as individual players, you would ask: 'How did they do it?' There were good, local lads such as Colin Smith, Les Collinson and Mike Bowering, but we were all in it together as a team. We stuck together and would go out together on a night after matches. There was nothing else that made us successful.

Apparently there was also a tough side to the squad, too, because Clarke added:

> We were once playing cards on a train journey to a game in London when Andy Davidson suddenly asked Mike Bowering if he had the seen some rabbit droppings on an embankment as we went past. Mike naturally thought he was joking because we were going at about 80 miles an hour, but Andy was serious and an argument developed. Mike laughed about it later, but at one point it looked as if it might end up in a fight because Andy's eyes were protruding like organ stops!

Clarke scored just three times in 34 League games in the Second Division in 1959–60 as City went straight back down, but he continued to be a regular fixture in the side. He scored 10 times in the League in 1960–61, including another Easter special with two in a 2–2 draw at home to Chesterfield, in Brocklebank's final season in charge, but then the goals gradually dried up. The regular appearances carried on, though, and he was an ever-present in 1961–62, just as he had been in 1957–58. It changed for him only when manager Cliff Britton started to splash out on forwards midway through the 1964–65 season. On Boxing Day 1964 he scored in what was to be his last away game for the club when they won 3–0 at Port Vale and he played in the return fixture two days later when the Tigers triumphed 4–0. But that was it: there were newcomers on the block.

But Clarke insisted:

> I really enjoyed my time in Hull and it's not the dead-end place that a lot of people say it is. I probably gave City my best years. I loved Hull as my second home because I have some great memories and I made some great friendships. There were some good social occasions such as going out into villages such as Beeford and playing darts. I enjoyed my life in Hull and really got into it outside football because I was happy in the company of the people.

Clarke moved on to Torquay United during the summer of 1965 after spending 10 years with the Tigers, who never offered him a testimonial. The club instead gave him a loyalty cheque after five years' service—and then a watch for helping the reserves to win the North Regional League title in 1964–65 instead! The first team just missed out on promotion that season although they made sure in 1965–66 when Clarke helped himself to further success of his own as Torquay, for whom he scored 21 goals in 119 League games, went up from the Fourth Division. He contributed 11 League goals in his first season with them and stayed at Plainmoor until the summer of 1968 when he joined Bath City. The following year he moved on to Bridgwater Town and in 1972 he rejoined Torquay as a player and reserve coach.

Four years later the indefatigable Clarke turned out for Bodmin in the South-Western League when he was in his 40s—and was promptly sent off for the first time in his career! He recalled:

> I don't think that I'd even had a booking in my life. It was in a game at St Austell by the seaside, there were only about 60 people there and one of their players had a go at one of ours, so I swore, but the referee was just behind me and heard me. I told him that I hadn't sworn at him, but he sent me off. I went to an FA hearing and said that I had used bad language, but that I was just saying it to myself, so the sending-off was quashed.

But Clarke's spell at Bodmin also brought back memories of another controversy. It stemmed from his days with the Tigers when they were involved in an FA Cup marathon with Darlington in the second round in 1960–61. It stretched to four replays after an initial 1–1 draw at Feethams that ended in chaos. City were leading with a goal from Dudley Price when Darlington's left-winger Bobby Baxter floated over a last-minute cross that seemed to drop over the bar, but referee Jim Parkinson signalled a goal. He insisted that the ball had gone under the bar and then through a hole in the net and awarded an equaliser. It was 1–1 again in the first replay at Boothferry Park and there were three more at Leeds, Doncaster and Middlesbrough, where the Tigers finally won 3–0. Clarke was on the mark as City earned themselves a third-round tie at home to his home-town club Bolton, who won 1–0 to add to their elimination of them in the inaugural Football League Cup earlier in the season. But the manager who brought Clarke out of his retirement to play for Bodmin was the same Bobby Baxter, who had also been one of his teammates at Torquay. And Clarke said:

> We've since had a laugh about the goal that should never have been and I've told him that we had to play five games and for an extra seven hours all because of him when we should have got through in the first place. I've also told him that he's always miserable and the only time that he smiles is when he thinks about that cup tie at Darlington!

Clarke also became involved in a carpet business and settled in Devon, as did Bob Brocklebank, the manager who had brought him to Boothferry Park. Clarke described Brocklebank as 'a gentleman and a nice bloke,' while he himself was viewed as a great character as well as an exceptional player during his City days. Clarke, who has a brother known as Venn Tracey and is a stand-up comedian and character actor, invited imaginative stories that became apocryphal and yet better with each telling. One famous one was that he once encouraged his City teammates to join him for greyhound racing at Hull's Craven Park, where he had received a hot tip about a certain dog. The story goes that the players then bet heavily on the dog concerned and were then stunned when it died during the race, but Clarke always insisted: 'I probably wished it had, but it didn't!'

Tales were also told about Clarke's alleged delicate nature because his 1960s teammate Chris Chilton said: 'Doug was frightened to death of needles and they used to have flu jabs in those days. Everybody had to have them, but he used to run away because he was petrified!' And other colleagues Andy Davidson and John McSeveney told of an occasion when a City party came across a serious road accident in the Midlands while they were travelling to an away game and the sight of it made Clarke ill. He admitted:

> We were on our way to Swindon and the accident involved a motor-bike. I could take knocks as a player, but it was just the sight of it that made me feel sick. Who wouldn't be afraid when that kind of thing happens?

But McSeveney added:

> Doug's mentality changed when he got on to the field. He was robust and was up and at them. He was a cheery fellow and a strong player. He usually played on the opposite wing to me and I would say to him: 'I'll see you at the far post, Duggie.' It meant that I knew that I would get a good supply from him. I scored a lot of goals from the left-wing and my trick was being there when the ball came over. Doug might shoot across the penalty box and I'd be waiting at the far post to score. I got the glory and Clarkey got nothing!

In addition, Bob Dennison and Brian Bulless, both of whom played against Clarke when he scored his hat-trick for Bury against City, were well aware of his shooting capacity. Dennison said: 'Doug was a good-hearted, solid player. He was strong and fast with a hell of a shot.' And Bulless, who was renowned for his left foot and once lived nearly opposite Clarke near Boothferry Park, added:

> I had a lot of good times with Doug. He was a good lad and a good right-winger and he cracked in a few goals because he had a hell of a right foot. Maybe we had a good balance between us, but we certainly tried our best.

Ironically, Ken Houghton not only succeeded Clarke as the Tigers' powerful hot shot, but also later gave a trial to his son Stuart, who stayed with goalkeeping hero Billy Bly at the same time as future England winger Brian Marwood, when he took charge at Boothferry Park. And Clarke's trademark has apparently lived on in his family because he has remained optimistic that his teenage grand-daughter Antonia Cord will earn herself a place in the Great Britain team for the 2012 Olympic Games in London. She has attended Millfield School, which has a top reputation for sport in the West Country, and done well in bobsleigh tournaments. But she is also a dab hand at shooting! And Clarke added:

> I have fond memories of going up to Lissett in the East Riding to see some friends on a farm during my days with City and practising the other kind of shooting there. Bobsleighing would be far too dangerous for me, but, if the grand-daughter shoots as well as I used to at football, then she won't go far wrong!

14

CHRIS CHILTON

It apparently did not take long for Hull City's manager Bob Brocklebank to recognise the latent talent that 16-year-old Chris Chilton displayed when he took part in a major trial organised by the club at their old Anlaby Road ground. Chilton, who had been born in the Holderness village of Sproatley in June 1943, had had a season in rural senior football with Bilton before writing to the Tigers for a trial, whose format turned out to be a match that lasted almost three hours with youngsters often playing for 20-minute periods as decisions were made about their potential. And Brocklebank later recalled:

> Chilton was one of about 80 lads we had down for a trial. There were four games going and I told our secretary John Adamson to sign him up after only 10 minutes of watching him. I hustled him round to his parents and obtained their permission for him to sign.

Chilton, the fourth of five children, had sought the trial with the backing of his father Albert and Bilton's captain Eric Grubb. He recalled:

> I wrote in with my dad's help, but I think that Eric had contacted City beforehand and spoken to Bob Brocklebank just to say: 'I've got a young lad who's been playing for Bilton in the Church League. I think that you ought to have a look at him. Will you give him a trial?' I think the reply was: 'Tell him to write in.' They'd had the first period of the trial game and I still hadn't been on. But in the second period one of the forwards got hurt and I went on. I came off at the end of the game, they asked

me my name, they made contact with my mam and dad and they said they'd like me to be a ground-staff lad. I was 16 and I'd already put in a request to go to Hull Art College because I fancied doing something in design or whatever. I'd been accepted, but I said 'yes' to the idea of £3 a week with City.

Chilton joined the Tigers' ground staff in the summer of 1959 and went on to become the greatest goalscorer in the club's history with 193 in the League. He twice scored four goals in home games—against Wrexham in October 1983 and Barnsley under the club's new floodlights in October 1964, the first coming after just 12 seconds—he also recorded nine further hat-tricks and he reached double figures in terms of League goals in nine full seasons out of 11. And Chilton achieved his feat in 415 League games, putting him fourth in the club's all-time appearances list.

But the making of a marksman in an East Riding backwater was not easy. Chilton, who had elder brothers John and Ralph and sisters Ann and Susie, said:

It was quite a tough upbringing. I can remember as a kid that there was still rationing and we used to have oil lamps, but all the kids had an involvement in football as they grew up. The entrance between the bottom pub, the Constable Arms, and the shop on the corner was the goal and there was one little outside light.

And if anybody in the village got a football for Christmas, then they had more friends than anyone else. We would never get a ball because we couldn't afford one, so we would go to the local butcher and ask for a pig's bladder to make one. There was a slaughter-house in the butcher's shop in Sproatley and, if they'd killed a couple of pigs, then we'd ask for a bladder. They'd be out of shape and we had to blow them up. It was tough, but you could blow them up quite hard although, if they went on to a nail or a spike or something, then that was it. It was finished, so we reverted to using rags in an old sock. When I did eventually acquire a ball, I used to go up to the police-station in the village. There used to be a clear wall with no windows and no doors that joined on to this field and I'd go there on my own for ages and practise shooting and passing against the wall.

Chilton attended Sproatley Primary School and then South Holderness School in Preston, where he first played competitive football. He recalled:

I would go home from school on a night-time and take all the fluff off a worn-out tennis ball, leaving just the rubber. I'd go into my bedroom and I used to head it against the wall. It took me months to master it. When I first started, I was that bad that I couldn't even hit the wall. But gradually I got better, I'd head it lots of times and I'd set myself a target all the time. I used to come out of my bedroom with my forehead or even my nose red raw from heading this ball, but I'd do it for an hour. But even with a tennis ball you've got to have the weight right and the angle right because once you go off line, you've had it. I did repetitions all the time against my bedroom wall. It was a bungalow and in that bedroom there were two single beds and a wardrobe, so I would estimate that I had about three square yards in which to operate, so it did wonders for my accuracy. Eventually I reached 20 a couple of times and I thought that wasn't bad.

Then there was the practice as a teenager that nurtured his stamina because Chilton added:

We used to run everywhere and a day out for us was to get a big tractor inner-tube from the rear wheel, get it blown up with a foot pump, mend any punctures with a bit of rubber and glue and then bowl it all the way to the seaside at Aldbrough. We'd take a ball with us if someone had one and we used to run the six miles from Sproatley, but we had no qualms about it. You all had to take turns with bowling this big tyre. It was massive, but then we'd go into the sea with it. We used to have competitions as to who could get from the top of the cliff to the bottom the quickest. We used to pick a spot where you could run down, but it was still steep and you used to hit the sand at the bottom at about 40 miles an hour. You couldn't control yourself: you'd just run down and hit the sand. It helped my running power, though.

Chilton also drew inspiration in different ways from his parents Albert, a security officer at BP Chemicals' Saltend base, and Jean. He said:

My dad was a really good footballer apparently, but he was also a quality sprinter and our house was full of trophies he had won with his sprinting. He was a really powerful runner and I've still got a set of silver coffee spoons that he won. And in that last year before I went to City, my mum worked all through the potato-picking season. She went out her way and bought me a pair of boots with her earnings.

Obviously I'd tended to have the old hand-me-downs from my two brothers, but these were the best boots I ever had. They were more modern and I treated them as if they were the crown jewels.

Chilton also had plenty of heading practice in his early days at Boothferry Park because he recalled:

They used to have 'a hangman's noose' at the North Stand end. It was ash in those days, there was a big wrought-iron fence and they used to bring out this noose with a ball on it like a scaffold. They used to have me practising my heading on it and I got quite good at it because the timing had to be right. Sometimes they used to put me through rapid repetitions because I used to have to climb and head the ball and run to a mark when I landed. I then had to turn round, set off straightaway, judge the flight of the ball because it was still swinging and head it again. Sometimes I'd stutter, climb and miss the ball completely because it was going away from me as I was jumping up. But gradually you got used to it, it improved my timing and I used to do it all the time.

Chilton, in fact, found a general lack of orthodoxy during his development with City because he said:

Some of the training methods were odd, to say the least. It was a case of the senior players coming out of the dressing-room, walking round the track four times with a racing newspaper and then asking Johnny Mahon, the trainer, whether they were going have a game of five-a-side or not. They used to tell him what was happening! But you were just naturally fit. The club had an A team then as well as the first team, reserves and juniors and they had about 40-odd professionals, but I wasn't aware of the competition. I was involved and, when you're a youngster, you don't really think: 'Right, I'm going to be a first-team player.' Some might do, but I didn't. I just thought: 'I'm here, so I'll just give it my best shot and see what happens.'

Chilton did enough to be given his League debut at Colchester on the opening day of the 1960–61 season, but City lost 4–0. He recalled:

I got three kicks in that game—two up the backside and one on the back of the head—and that was it! I can't remember all that much about the game, but I know we had a really young forward-line and that there was a little bit of resentment in the dressing-room from senior professionals.

But two days later Brocklebank made three changes for a home game against Newport County, bringing in the extra experience of Brian Bulless, Jackie Sewell and Doug Clarke, and Chilton scored his first senior goal:

> It was 5–1 to us, it was pouring with rain and I scored with a diving header at the clock end, as we used to call the North Stand then. Mind you, Newport had gone a bit by then. I remember diving in, connecting with this header and sliding right into the crash barrier round the track because it was that wet. I launched myself at the ball and just kept going, but, when I landed, all I could remember was the railing coming at me.

His 82nd-minute goal was one of three in the last 10 minutes and Newport included winger John McSeveney, who was to join the Tigers during July 1961 when Cliff Britton replaced Brocklebank as manager. And McSeveney insisted: 'Cliff built the team round Chillo. He was unselfish and he was scoring goals on his own before Ken Wagstaff came, but you always need different types of players in teams.'

Chilton scored his first hat-trick against Queen's Park Rangers in his first season in League football and had added two more before his four against Wrexham, for which he did not prepare properly in Hull because he admitted:

> I was out the night before—clubbing it. I went into Cumberland Club off Wincolmlee to play darts and snooker. For some reason it was some celebration and I thought to myself: 'I'm going to go. The club won't know.' I didn't go anywhere else, but I had a real skinful. Then I went out on the Saturday and knocked in four!

But later in the 1963–64 season things did not work out so well for Chilton and McSeveney. Chilton explained:

> As a ground-staff lad, I'd signed on for £3 a week and I used to give my mum £2 10s. of it for board. And I had to find my bus fares out of the remaining 10 shillings as well as a bag of chips or a chip butty on a dinner-time. But when I signed professional and got into the first team, I got a signing-on fee, which was tremendous really. It was £20 in a lump sum, but it was taxed and I got £13 6s. 8d. And they put my wages up to £5 a week as a professional with another £3 if I got into the first team, another £4 for a win and £2 for a draw. Later on there

were crowd incentives and bonus structures and in one game against Bournemouth in 1964 we lost 4–3 at home and missed two penalties. I missed the first one when I shot over the bar and then John McSeveney missed the other, but it would have guaranteed us a £100 bonus if we'd won. It was a lot of money then, but I blew it and John blew it, so we weren't very popular . . .

But Chilton flourished during 1964–65, having his best haul of 27 League goals in a season even though he failed to score in the opening 11 Third Division games and had a transfer request granted. But reinforcements to the forward-line were imminent as manager Cliff Britton took advantage of chairman Harold Needler's generosity with the £40,000 signings of Ken Wagstaff, Ian Butler and Ken Houghton in quick succession. But a return of one point out of six during the Easter programme ruined City's promotion hopes and Chilton reflected: 'We played well and things just didn't go for us. We were creating chances, but they didn't stick and we didn't get the rewards.'

But the Tigers made no mistake as they won the Third Division title in 1965–66 with Chilton contributing 25 of the team's 109 League goals. They also reached the FA Cup quarter-finals and promotion was secured on a Friday evening in May in Britton's home city with a 2–1 win at Bristol Rovers. Chilton, who scored City's second goal, said:

After the game all the lads went out and finished up going their different ways, but Waggy and I went into a little nightclub in Bristol. It wasn't too plush, there were gambling tables and I remember telling him: 'I'm not gambling or anything because I've got only a few quid on me and I'd rather have a drink.' Straightaway Wag went across to the tables, we had a drink and in about half-an-hour we hadn't a penny between us, so we left the club and walked back to the hotel. It was about two o'clock in the morning, we couldn't get a taxi because we had no money and I can remember us going down the main street singing 'Molly Malone'. We were swinging and singing our heads off because we realised then that we had achieved something. In fact, it was probably the first thing that either of us had achieved in football.

Chilton, who was linked with a £65,000 move to Leeds United in September 1967, continued to score regularly at Second Division level and also took over as captain when the long-serving Andy Davidson announced his retirement in 1968. Chilton recalled:

> The only way in which it interfered with anything was when the players sent me in for a discussion about a bonus or a pay rise. They were all there after one training session and I was sent in to see Cliff Britton because I was the captain. He dealt with that side of things and, when I came out three hours later, they'd all cleared off. Cliff got on to his tiddlywinks, his board and his coins, I had three hours' football conversation and never really got round to discussing the pay rise!

City failed in their promotion push under new player-manager Terry Neill in 1970–71, but again reached the FA Cup quarter-finals and Chilton chipped in with 21 League goals. He had a purple patch in mid-season with 11 goals in nine League games, but then there was a largely barren spell in the second half of the season. He then had a crowd of 28,350 for his testimonial match against a full-strength Leeds United side when he and Wagstaff both scored hat-tricks—the only time it happened in the same game—in a 7–6 win. The duo then toured Australia with an FA representative squad during the summer of 1971 and yet some cracks were appearing. Chilton was jaded, his mother Jean was seriously ill and he missed a pre-season tour to Scandinavia. In addition, he did not see eye to eye with new assistant manager Tommy Docherty, so he played in just the two opening League games of 1971–72 before being sold.

Chilton attracted attention from numerous top-flight clubs and finally opted for Coventry City in preference to Chelsea and Leicester City, joining them in a £92,000 deal at the end of August 1971. And an incident at the height of the negotiations at Boothferry Park made up his mind to move because he recalled:

> I walked down North Road into the ground and, as I went through the entrance, I didn't make a beeline for the boardroom because I was still thinking. The next thing I heard was a director shouting behind me: 'Ken! Ken!' I looked over my shoulder and the director was walking towards me. He said: 'Don't you think it would be better if you went to Chelsea?' I said: 'I don't really know. Why is that?' He said: 'They've offered £100,000.' But I replied: 'Seeing that I'm not Ken, you might be mixing me up with somebody else.' He said: 'Oh, sorry. Did I call you Ken?' I said: 'Yes—twice.' That to me was an absolute insult. I didn't

really want to leave. Until that director spoke to me as he did, it was still an option to stay with the club because I was confused. But when somebody had spoken to me in those terms and didn't know my name even though I'd been there for 12 years, where did I stand? I thought I was a person: they thought I was a commodity.

Chilton had a brief spell in the First Division with Coventry, scoring three times in 27 League games, amid rumours that City had sold him because he had a back problem. Early in his career he had had to play in a corset, but he insisted:

> I know what kind of medical examination I went through when I joined Coventry. I didn't know that there were that many things that they needed to do! I was X-rayed and examined by specialists and doctors, who checked everything.

A back injury did end his League career at Coventry, but Chilton added:

> It was during pre-season training after my first season. One of the training sessions involved 'doggies' and they had balls that you had to sit on at every particular point at which you turned round before coming back to base. You had to sit on each ball three times. I was okay and managing fine, but then I got to one ball, went down to sit on it and didn't get up. Fatigue had set in and I was in agony. All the strain had gone into my lower back. I went through hell to try to get fit again, but it was the start of the end.

Chilton returned to East Yorkshire to play briefly for Bridlington Town, whose manager John Thompson he had known for a long time. But early in 1974 Scarborough refused to meet Town's asking price of £1,000 plus a player for Chilton and then former Wales and Arsenal defender Wally Barnes, who had become a football commentator, contacted him. Chilton recalled:

> He said: 'Would you like to go to South Africa?' I told him that he must be joking, but he said: 'I can offer you the chance to go to a club called Highlands Park in Johannesburg for a month and everything has been paid for you. We'll give you a retainer while you're there to keep you going. See what you think, but there are return tickets for the pair of you if you don't like it.' They offered more money than I had ever earned at Hull City. Yet this was semi-professional football. But we did the treble in my first season with Highlands Park and they couldn't believe it. We won the championship, the Coca Cola Cup and the

league cup. Eventually I took over as player-manager after three seasons and we won the treble again.

At one stage Chilton was voted Player of the Year in South Africa, but factors, such as the political unrest, made him decide to return home. And he went back to City as youth coach in February 1978 following a call from his former teammate Ken Houghton, who had become the club's caretaker manager. It came at a good time because Chilton recalled:

> I became a coalman for my mate, Dave Fallowfield, in East Hull. He was a family friend and he said: 'Do you want to come and help me for a week?' I said I would because I'd come back from South Africa feeling fit and strong. As it was, I lasted a day! I was absolutely knackered, it was snowing and I was aching in places where I didn't know it was possible to ache. Houghy rang on the same day. He was obviously looking for someone, but he got a qualified coalman! He said that he wanted me to come and look after the youngsters and the reserves, so the coalman was transferred quickly! One day as a coalman was enough for me, but Houghy must have got word that I was back in town and the juniors won the Northern Intermediate League that season although it was only a little bit to do with me.

Houghton stayed as City's manager until he was fired in December 1979 and Chilton became caretaker manager, but he said:

> It didn't last long and I didn't harbour any thoughts of becoming the manager of the club on a longer-term basis because it was still a learning process for me. I wasn't ready for it by any stretch of the imagination. It was a different ball game from South Africa, where it was only semi-professional.

Former Wales manager Mike Smith became Houghton's successor, but Chilton even donned City's amber and black again at the age of 37, coming on as a substitute for the reserves in a 3–2 win at Notts County in October 1980. He even scored the winner following a corner two minutes from the end, while he also played alongside a young centre-forward called Billy Whitehurst, who was on trial from Mexborough Town. Chilton recalled:

> I was in charge of the reserves, but I played at left-back! We weren't sure what Billy had to offer, but he was at the ground, so we said we'd play

him upfront in the No. 9 shirt. Anyway this big guy was a bit like a rhinoceros let loose in a paddock. But he had the assets of pace and strength. The edges were as rough as a badger's backside, but there was just something about him.

But in February 1982 City went into receivership, Smith, his assistant Cyril Lea and commercial manager Gordon Dimbleby were sacked, the players became available on free transfers and Chilton and youth development officer Bobby Brown were put in temporary charge. Chilton reflected:

> I can remember us playing away, winning one of the first games we had in that situation, and the players started singing in the bath afterwards: 'On the dole, on the dole, on the dole . . .' and 'We won't get paid . . .' But the players stuck to it and all of a sudden we'd won six games out of seven, so something had happened to give the players a confidence about what they were doing.

Brown also left eventually, but Chilton said: 'I wanted to stay at the club, but I was not keen on the manager's job because there was too much going on.' As it was, Scarborough entrepreneur Don Robinson took control of City, bringing in Colin Appleton as the new manager during the summer of 1982. Chilton said:

> I didn't know Colin personally, but I knew of him. Colin was introduced and we had a good day at the ground to discuss things. But I hit it off with him straightaway because I thought: 'What a football guy he is!' All he talked about was football and I thought how knowledgeable he was. What he didn't know about football wasn't worth knowing.

The new brooms swept to City to promotion straightaway and Chilton reflected:

> They were still hard times because there was no money and no luxuries or anything of that kind and the players had to take salary cuts because of what had happened. People perhaps wouldn't believe some of the things that went on from a travelling point of view because of the financial state of the club. Going to a place such as Blackpool came into the category of a journey on the morning of the match—with Colin and I actually cooking toast and honey to serve to the players as the pre-match meal on the coach! All that stands out is the overall atmosphere. Being involved was superb, especially to see the success of the players because most of them had been through receivership the season before.

Appleton dramatically resigned after a 2–0 win at Burnley at the end of 1983–84 when the Tigers narrowly missed out on a second successive promotion. And Chilton said:

> I hadn't a clue about it and it was one of the biggest shocks I had in the game. The whole night was an absolute heartache. It had been a heartache before the players had got off the pitch because they knew they'd missed promotion. The news about Colin just made it a sort of double whammy. I was probably as low as I'd ever been in football.

This time Chilton was keen to become manager. But he was overlooked as Brian Horton was appointed as player-manager and he admitted: 'It was a kick in the teeth, but I didn't dwell on it. I just accepted it because Don Robinson had said to me that I would still be with the club as the No. 2.'

Horton and Chilton piloted City to promotion to the Second Division in 1984–85, but there was an end-of-season reshuffle. Horton opted to promote Dennis Booth to assistant manager and relegate Chilton, who explained:

> He said that he still wanted me to look after the kids, but that to me was not acceptable. I remember going up into the seats in the South Stand and I sat there just looking out across Boothferry because I knew that that was the end. I was absolutely heart-broken.

Chilton found that his third promotion season with City—one as a player and two as a coach—had a hollow ring about it. And he said:

> In the end I resigned technically. I got a small settlement, but I was just so disappointed that I didn't even want to take it any further. I became so disillusioned with football, so I made the decision then that that was it and I would move away from it. I got a job as a representative for a mortar company, but it wasn't my forte.

But John Thompson, who had signed him for Bridlington Town, was manager of North Ferriby United by then and asked Chilton to be his assistant. Chilton said: 'It wasn't the same as being in League football, but it was pleasurable because I knew a lot of people at Ferriby.' Then in the spring of 1987 Chilton returned to League management when former City defender Peter Daniel, who had taken over as Lincoln City's caretaker manager, needed an assistant. But Lincoln tumbled out of the Football League and Chilton recalled:

I must say that I was disappointed with some of the players in terms of their commitment towards saving the sinking ship because it was non-existent with some of them. They were the more senior players as well, but we tried to make the best of a bad job in a way.

But there was another twist in 1989 when Appleton had a second spell in charge at Boothferry Park and needed an assistant to succeed Tom Wilson. Chilton recollected:

The call came and Colin rang me. He needed some assistance because there were cliques among the players and he was having problems with discipline. It sounds as if I were a hitman! We decided to have a meeting and he said he would see me the following afternoon in the car-park of the Blacksmiths' Arms at Coniston. He felt he wasn't getting the support he needed, so he wanted some help. I said: 'Obviously we'll have to come to some financial agreement.' I put something to him and he said he would speak to the chairman about it.

But City lost 2–0 at home to Brighton and Hove Albion, Don Robinson resigned as chairman and was replaced by Richard Chetham and Appleton was fired before anything could be finalised with Chilton, who reflected:

Colin was having discussions with Don Robinson and he'd said that he was pretty sure that everything would be all right. But that weekend the chairman resigned, Richard Chetham took over and then sacked Colin. But it gave me a boost anyway because Colin recognised me for what I was. It was disappointing because I loved the football club. There were times when I felt I wanted to leave, but when I did leave, I didn't want to—both as a player and in management.

But Chilton had many memorable moments with the Tigers, especially as a player, and his strike partner Ken Wagstaff said shortly before their prolific partnership ended in 1971:

He's a rarity—a big man with pace and all-round skills. He's good in the air and will run for everything, but his main quality is bravery. Our partnership came naturally. We hit it off the first time we played together. Chris flicked a ball over and I ran on to it and scored. And we've just gone on from there. We always seem to know where each other is and we don't have to look up before passing the ball. If he had been with a First Division club, there's no doubt that he would be a regular member of the England team by now. Chris Chilton is the best centre-forward in the country.

15

KEN WAGSTAFF

In February 1956 former England international Cliff Britton had insisted that he was finished with football forever after resigning as the manager of Everton. Britton, who had also managed Burnley, said: 'I am getting out of the game and going into the newspaper world. I have had some offers.' The following August he was back in football as Preston North End's manager and Hull City subsequently had to be very grateful for his change of heart. They put him in charge in July 1961, three months after his departure from Deepdale, and he built one of the most attractive footballing sides in the Tigers' history. In January 1963 City's chairman Harold Needler offered Britton a 10-year contract and gave the club £200,000 worth of shares in his Hoveringham Gravel business for team strengthening. Britton was patient and frugal until it became clear during the 1964–65 season that prolific marksman Chris Chilton needed some support. And he pepped up his attack by paying a club-record £40,000 to Mansfield Town for 21-year-old Ken Wagstaff, who had been the country's top goalscorer with 41 in all games during the 1962–63 season, in November 1964.

Britton had never paid more than £20,000 for a player, but his purchase of Wagstaff was the catalyst for putting his master plan in place. He had to move quickly because Brentford had already offered more than £30,000 for Wagstaff, who had started his career as a winger. But Britton knew what he was doing as he doubled his money on an outlay on a personal basis and Mansfield's manager Tommy Cummings said:

I am very sorry to lose Ken, but at least I know that he is joining someone who will look after him. Cliff Britton was my first boss in soccer when he signed me for Burnley and taught me a lot. I know he looks after players.

The fee beat the £22,500 that City had forked out to Stoke City for former England international defender Neil Franklin in February 1951 when Raich Carter had been in charge at Boothferry Park. But the deal did not only have a football link with Britton and Cummings, but also one with Carter and Wagstaff, who was born at Langwith, near Mansfield, in November 1942. The Mansfield Youth League had also nurtured the career of one of England's 1966 World Cup winners, Ray Wilson, and Wagstaff also started out with a local side—Woodland Imperial. But in May 1960 he got his big chance at Mansfield, who had appointed a new manager three months earlier—Carter.

Carter, Cummings' immediate predecessor, had succeeded long-throw expert Sammy Weaver, also an England international and an ex-Tiger, and later described Wagstaff as 'one of the finest centre-forwards I have ever seen and a player who is certain to play for England one day.' Wagstaff, who scored 93 times in 181 League games for the Stags, flourished as a productive goalscorer under Carter's tutelage and later paid due tribute to him:

> He was like a father to me and nursed me through my early games of football. That man really was a legend. Raich Carter was the real genius. He not only taught me how to play football, but also how to be a man. I never saw him play during his own illustrious career, but you could see his immense skill in his training sessions. I've spoken to a lot of older Hull City fans and they tell me that he was absolutely brilliant at Boothferry Park and I can believe them because Raich certainly knew the game inside out.

But Wagstaff's departure from Mansfield, where he had also been a teammate of David Coates, a regular in the Tigers' Third Division promotion side of 1958–59, caused an uproar. In fact, it prompted one angry letter to Cummings from an eight-year-old called Stephen Wright, who wrote: 'I go to see the Stags every week, but I am not going any more now that you have sold Waggy. I hoped we were going to win promotion to the Second Division, but we won't now.'

But he changed his mind about deserting the club when he was given a tour of the ground, met the remaining players and presented with an autographed photograph!

It did not take long, meanwhile, for Wagstaff to get into the goalscoring groove with the Tigers. He was ineligible to play straightaway because of the FA Cup rules, so he had to wait to make his debut in the League at home to Exeter City on November 21, 1964—three days before his 22nd birthday. But it was worth the short wait because it took him just 36 minutes to score for City—in a 3–1 win when Chris Chilton headed on a long kick by goalkeeper Maurice Swan. Ten minutes later Chilton himself made it 3–1—and a partnership bordering on goalscoring perfection was born. Ironically, though, there had been speculation that Wagstaff might have been signed to replace Chilton, who was immediately watched by Crystal Palace player-coach Ronnie Allen before they teamed up. Chilton, for his part, admitted that he had had no recollection of playing against Wagstaff when he was a Mansfield player, insisting: 'I couldn't remember that many players—just the centre-halves!' But he later confessed: 'Waggy was a great player—the nearest thing to Jimmy Greaves I've seen. I think you would have had the perfect footballer in every sense if you could have combined us both.'

Having scored on his City debut, Wagstaff found that he could not kick the habit because there were 14 goals in his first 11 League outings. He scored in his first six home League games for the club, including a hat-trick in a 4–0 Christmas home win over 10-man Port Vale, who had Albert Cheeseborough sent off after half an hour. It was City's last game of 1964 and Wagstaff made light of a tricky pitch: his first goal was a penalty, which he himself had won, but the second—in the 63rd minute—set him on the road to star status. It was written:

A spectacular goal by Ken Wagstaff brought the Boothferry Park crowd to their feet. He got the ball in the centre circle and went chasing down the middle like a jet-propelled engine. He was almost checked by one tackle, but burst through it by sheer force and then went through to the edge of the penalty area, where, as he was tackled for a second time, he cracked a great drive past Reg Davies. Wagstaff was laid out in the process, but the effect of having snow rubbed on the back of his neck by Chris Chilton and trainer Gus McLean's sponge soon brought him round!

He completed his hat-trick by heading home John McSeveney's 79th-minute centre as the Tigers gained momentum—a view that was intensified when Cliff Britton twice more splashed out more £40,000 fees on forwards Ian Butler and Ken Houghton from Rotherham United in the first fortnight of 1965. Ironically, Wagstaff himself had once had a spell as a junior at Rotherham . . .

In City's 26 League games starting with Wagstaff's debut, they lost only four and failed to score in only two. Wagstaff finished with 23 goals in 25 of them. But City were cruelly robbed of a promotion place after a disastrous Easter spell in which they took only one point out of a possible six. And in the way that football can often kick someone firmly in the teeth, the sequence included a 2–1 defeat on Wagstaff's return to Mansfield, who were also in the promotion race. In Wagstaff's FA Cup debut for the club earlier in the season Lincoln City's goalkeeper Malcolm White had defied him in particular with a lot of luck and most parts of his body and Mansfield's Colin Treharne adopted the same technique. Wagstaff did score at Field Mill with a comparatively-rare header from John McSeveney's corner after 65 minutes, but he admitted: 'I should have won it for us.' And in a tight finish to the Third Division season City were fourth, Mansfield also missed out in third place and Carlisle United and Bristol City went up instead.

The anti-climax was soon forgotten, though, because Wagstaff led the way as the Tigers went up in style as Third Division champions in 1965–66 and also reached the FA Cup quarter-finals. They scored 109 League goals with five forwards—Ray Henderson, Wagstaff, Chilton, Houghton and Butler—all getting into double figures. Although he managed only one more hat-trick—four in a 4–2 win at Brentford at Easter—Wagstaff led the way with 27 and added four more in Cup competitions, beating Bill Bradbury's post-war club record of 30 in a season in 1958–59. But Wagstaff did not set the club's post-war League record because Bradbury had got all of his 30 in the Third Division.

There were plenty of highlights and records that season and Wagstaff placed himself in the pantheon of the club's all-time heroes in a game which City did not even win. They were drawn at glamour boys Chelsea in the FA Cup quarter-finals after giantkilling episodes against Southampton and Nottingham Forest. City were not expected to win and their hopes were derided by Chelsea's manager Tommy

Docherty. In addition, the luck did not go City's way and they were 2–0 down with 10 minutes left. But then Wagstaff, whose career was often punctuated by a great sense of occasion, duly stepped up and scored twice to capture a 2–2 draw and it was written of his equaliser: 'Ken Wagstaff waltzed through a defence driven to tottering uncertainty and, as coolly as if he had just stepped out of a fridge, clipped home his second goal to earn a replay.' Wagstaff predicted a win in the replay at Boothferry Park on General Election day in March 1966 and the public believed him, but Chelsea won 3–1. At the same time, though, the comeback at Stamford Bridge had had all the hallmarks of Wagstaff's greatness as a marksman.

City never built on their 1966 promotion to continue their progress into the top flight, but they more than held their own in the Second Division because they were always capable of scoring goals. Wagstaff's tally of League goals in the following four seasons was a consistent 21, 17, 20 and 18 as he and Chris Chilton cemented their potent partnership, but he never had the chance to operate in the old First Division. And he said:

> It's no good being disappointed. Cliff Britton always said that he wouldn't sell Chris Chilton or me because our goals would keep him in a job for 10 years! And when Joe Harvey wanted to take us to Newcastle United, Harold Needler told him that he had a better chance of buying the town-hall clock. Chris was also a good player and we hit it off, both on the pitch and off it. We were different types on the pitch, but the friendship carried on off it. But all the players got on well in that promotion side and they were all good players.

And his mentor Raich Carter added: 'I felt it was a tragedy that Ken Wagstaff never played in the First Division. He was good enough to have been capped. He was good on the ground, he could make goals and he could score them.'

For his part, Chilton always acknowledged his partner's prowess:

> Ken was the best individual player in terms of scoring goals. There's got to be a charisma and an arrogance and a coolness about a goalscorer. He's got to be clinical, he's got to have the willpower to do it and he's got to be strong about it. And that's why those who can do it get all the accolades and the glory. If you put the assets of both of us in one package, you would have the nearest to the perfect footballer. His balance was better than mine. His ability was to keep

cool and he seemed to have that vision to think: 'If I strike now, it's going to be blocked.' So he would turn back, send the defender out of the way and then he would stick the ball in the net. Most of us would have hit it there and then because, once we'd got half a chance, we would tend to have wanted to strike at goal. Waggy was different.

The combination between me and Waggy became second-nature. I don't suppose you see that many who had the ability that we had of complementing each other. It didn't just come overnight—it probably took a year before it all started to knit into the right pattern. He was marvellous, but I just had to bring him to task once. He hadn't been at the club long. I received a ball in this particular game and Wag had finished up on the right-wing. As I chested it and turned, I looked and knocked the ball a few yards in front of him, knowing that the full-back had been sucked in. But Wag either wasn't ready for it or he didn't want to go for it, so it went out for a throw-in. He then turned to the crowd and gestured as if it weren't his fault, but it was mine. You don't do that, so I told him about it. I said: 'Don't ever do that to me!' But from that day on, that was it—we were buddies. It needed me just to let him know that I was as important as he was.

There were times when Wag went on strike while we'd been on the pitch. He wasn't averse to telling one or two of them what he wanted, which was fair enough. He'd won matches for them as much as anything, but we needed the service. I'd try to make the best of what service was coming, but there were occasions when Wag would say: 'If you can't play the ball in there where I want it, then I aren't running for it.' There were times when I would say to him: 'Wag, come on! Let's get on with it.' But he would say: 'No.' It was just one of his moods—he had those days. But it was just a phase because then he would get half a chance, he would turn somebody inside out, sit him on his backside and probably just stroke the ball into the back of the net. Then he would be back in business and happy with himself.

But I think that one of the reasons why Waggy and I really hit it off with each other was that we wouldn't try to score goals from stupid positions. If possible, we would try to play the other one in if he were in a better position. If I went in to the near post, then I knew very well that Waggy would be in that area somewhere behind me. I wouldn't try to head goals in at the near post or do something silly. I would let the ball hit me and just lift my chin. That's all there is to it. And Wag would do the same thing for me. Sometimes it wasn't just about the two of us scoring. It was about how much you could upset the opposition and drag people around. If Waggy and I were tightly marked by two central defenders, he might take one to one touchline, I would take the other one to the other and Houghy came through and rifled one in from 25 yards. It was still 'job done.'

People classed us as goalscorers, but we also had such an awareness of each other. We were quite conscious of the fact that I might have a half-chance, but might I have been able to set up Waggy, who would have a 100 per cent chance? Inevitably we would do that for each other. I didn't go along with that view that you had to be self-centred and mean. You've got to bring other people into the play. We did have an understanding.

Other teammates appreciated the wonder of Wagstaff. Andy Davidson, his 1965–66 title-winning captain, said:

Waggy could make the ball talk. Players tried to nail him, but he was too clever for them. I don't know why he didn't leave Hull City to go higher, but he was happy and he didn't want to. He was quick, but he didn't look it with his build. No-one could live with him over 10 to 15 yards. He would give defenders five yards and still get past them. Everything he did was natural.

Len Sharpe added: 'Waggy wouldn't have a shot for goal unless he felt he could score from where he was. He was also strong and hard to knock off the ball—just like Wayne Rooney.' Tom Wilson, who first played against Wagstaff for Millwall before joining City himself, said of him:

Waggy always said that he didn't like me to mark him because I would hold off before tackling him. He preferred defenders to be tight on his back so that he could turn them. At the same time Waggy was a difficult player to mark because he always had something up his sleeve.

And Ken Knighton observed: 'Waggy was such a clinical finisher—in fact, it was too easy for him—and he was good enough to have played for England.'

Davidson also eulogised about Wagstaff's ability to remain cool, calm and collected. Wagstaff himself believed that goalscorers were born rather than made although he paid tribute to Raich Carter for his influence at Mansfield and Cliff Britton for helping him to develop a positional sense:

It is a gift. When you're in the penalty area, you mustn't panic, but you should take your time. You must be good positionally and you don't need to belt the ball into the net when you can sidefoot it. I don't think that goalscoring can be taught because it's an instinct.'

Wagstaff, who reckoned that he first developed an appetite for goalscoring as a six-year-old, also relished the challenge of beating the best, including top England international goalkeepers of the day— Gordon Banks, Peter Bonetti and Peter Shilton. He recalled:

> I enjoyed scoring against top-drawer international goalkeepers such as Peter Bonetti at Chelsea and Gordon Banks against Stoke. I sat Gordon Banks down on his backside to score one in the FA Cup against Stoke City and put one to his other side when we met them again the following season. And it's nice to think that we put six past Peter Shilton in two matches against Leicester City in one season. We always said that we'd score against him if we shot low because we reckoned that he didn't get down too well. But I never feared any goalkeeper and you can't afford to do so. You miss some chances, but then you'll always score your fair share if you keep trying to take them. And that's why you must keep going when things aren't going well because you start scoring again if you do. At the same time I always thought that I could play a bit and I was always helping to make goals for others if I weren't scoring them.

The goals against Stoke in the FA Cup quarter-final in March 1971 again underlined his sense of occasion. Wagstaff scored after 14 and 33 minutes and was close to completing his hat-trick, but Stoke came back to win 3–2 after pulling back a goal just on halftime. Wagstaff's strike partner Chris Chilton gave an insight into his thinking that afternoon:

> He was really quiet in the dressing-room and I was a bit concerned that he was in one of his moods. We went across to the gym for the warm-up session, but he didn't want to do anything and he was having a little chunter to himself. As we came back round the end of the South Stand, he just stopped and said: 'I'll show that Banks.' That's all he said. Basically it was probably his way of psyching himself up. He just wanted to concentrate and he probably took it on as a personal challenge that he was going to show Gordon Banks what sort of a player Ken Wagstaff was. He had marvellous ability and there were only two or three players in the country then who could do that with that finesse and coolness. But that was his forte.

Wagstaff himself recalled:

> We thought we were on our way to the semi-finals of the FA Cup. There were more than 41,000 at Boothferry Park and they were going barmy as we led Stoke 2–0 just before halftime. They had Gordon Banks in goal and they were two of the sweetest moments in my life when I beat the great man in the first half.

And in February 1972 Wagstaff again showed his perceptive timing with the only goal of the game when City became FA Cup giantkillers in the fourth round at First Division Coventry City. Chilton was by then playing for Coventry, but, more appropriately, England's World Cup-winning manager Sir Alf Ramsey was watching. Wagstaff always remained loyal to the Tigers even though it was always accepted that he would also have been a force in the First Division, but he had been unsettled by the break-up of his partnership with Chilton in August 1971 and had asked player-manager Terry Neill to put his mind at rest. He said at the time:

> Terry said that he was not selling players, but now he's selling Chris. I could have understood it if it had been some other player for whom he had plenty of cover, but not Chris. Some time ago they could have sold me to Derby County, but they didn't and I want to know what the position is. There is no question of asking for a move even though I would like to play in the First Division, as everybody would. I would like to play in the First Division with City.

It was also just as well that Wagstaff and Chilton intuitively hit it off on the pitch because their preparation for away games apparently left something to be desired at times. Andy Davidson recalled:

> When we stayed in hotels on Friday nights for the long away trips, Cliff Britton always used to arrange for us to go to either the cinema or theatre locally. As soon as the lights went down, Chillo and Waggy would sneak out and find somewhere to have a drink while the film or play was on. And they always seemed to know when they were due to finish because they would creep back in just before the end so that they were never missed!

And even though Wagstaff and Chilton were good friends, there was also a fierce rivalry between the two at times. Chilton recalled:

> Waggy and I were playing golf at Springhead Park, we'd driven off at a par-five hole and I'd driven maybe 80 yards further than he had although he'd say it was only about five. It was his shot and I was waiting for him with some clubs in a bag on my shoulder. I was at a 45-degree angle from him and he'd got his back to me because he was left-handed. He whacked the ball with a wood and it came right off the heel of the club about only two feet off the floor and straight at me. Instinctively I turned away and lifted one leg, but it hit me

right in the calf muscle. It must have come at me about 150 miles an hour, so within 10 seconds my calf muscle had gone blue, pink, maroon and aubergine and it was as big as a rugby ball. I was in agony, but I limped on. But it was hopeless and I had to walk in. It was a day off, but I'd been in agony all night and the next morning I went in for treatment. I couldn't play on the Saturday, so Cliff Britton banned everybody from playing golf and I wasn't very popular. I got the blame because I was the one who missed the game. I could understand the manager saying that we weren't having it any more, but Cliff Britton was a marvellous golfer. They reckoned that he used to be able to play seven-handicap left-handed and six-handicap right-handed, so he loved his golf although he never played it while he was the manager.

In another instance at Springhead I drove through the green in one and my ball went into a hut, which was for people to shelter from heavy rain or whatever. Waggy, being the smart-arse he could be, said: 'You'll have to play out of there. It's the rules. You have to play out of the huts if you go in them.' So I went into the hut and worked out that I could get a punch at my ball if I hit it off the walls at certain angles and it was likely to shoot out of the door. It was bit like using the cushions on a snooker table. It went out and on to the green, but he was convinced that I'd picked it up and thrown it out. I said: 'That'll teach you.'

Throughout his career Wagstaff had few injuries, but in January 1975 he hurt his left knee in an FA Cup tie at Fulham and missed the rest of the season. He played in 10 League games in 1975–76 and also slotted in naturally in midfield in a Football League Cup tie against Sheffield United, but the end was near. The last of his 173 League goals for City came in a 3–2 win at Oxford United at the start of November 1975, but the following month his retirement was announced and he then joined the club's backroom staff. He had made 378 League appearances for the Tigers and remains seventh in their all-time list. Wagstaff, who is second in the club's all-time list of marksmen, then had a testimonial match in April 1976 when he scored in a 6–4 defeat against Billy Bremner's All-Stars in front of a 6,975 crowd and his mentor Raich Carter fittingly kicked it off, but the following month he left to coach George Cross in Australia.

In November 1976 he again trained with City—12 years to the week since he had first joined them—after his knee had shown a big improvement, but he was barred from making a League comeback because he had received disability insurance when he retired. Wagstaff went back to Australia, where he was eventually succeeded as manager of George Cross by his former City teammate Billy Wilkinson, before drifting into non-League football on his return to England. He played one game for Goole Town at Northwich Victoria during 1977–78, he turned out for local East Yorkshire sides Fenner's and Westfield Wanderers and he had a four-month spell as Bridlington Town's manager in the early part of the 1980–81 season. Wagstaff was also involved in a sports-shop venture before becoming a publican at the Plimsoll's Ship Inn and the Golden Ball in Hull. He then took over Marlborough Club in Hessle to the west of Hull, renaming it Waggy's, before having a brief spell at the Roos Arms in Roos to the east of the city.

Wagstaff had few setbacks during his long links with the Tigers. But in August 1970 he became the first City player to miss in a penalty shoot-out after they had drawn 1–1 with Manchester United after extra time at Boothferry Park in the Watney Cup. And in the 1990s he was temporarily banned by the club when he was elected as president of a pressure group called Tigers 2000, who were trying to oust the disastrous regime of the day.

But his value and popularity were always evident. A racehorse co-owned by Hull businessmen Cyril Wheeler and Wally Palmer, was named Waggy after him and became a regular winner at Redcar in 1968. And leading actor and long-standing City supporter Sir Tom Courtenay owned a Dalmatian dog called Wagstaff. He once brought it to Boothferry Park, where Wagstaff the dog was introduced to Wagstaff the player and goalkeeper Ian McKechnie apparently commented: 'The dog's better looking, but Ken's got more spots!' But Wagstaff, who was also a first-class rifle shot, will always be best remembered as a goalscorer supreme and it was once written of him: 'He could sniff a chance out of nothing—and take it.' As City's manager John Kaye observed when Wagstaff attempted his doomed comeback in 1976: 'There's nobody in the game to beat him when it comes to scoring goals.'

16

KEN HOUGHTON

There was a telling comment from seven-year-old Danny Williams when he travelled to Hull in January 1965. His father, Danny senior, was Rotherham United's manager and the youngster asked: 'Why do you bring them here in ones, dad? Why don't you bring a bus?' He was referring to the £40,000 departure of inside-forward Ken Houghton from Millmoor to join Hull City. He was the Tigers' second £40,000 capture from the Millers in successive weeks after left-winger Ian Butler's earlier arrival as manager Cliff Britton continued to spend the money at his disposal thanks to chairman Harold Needler's munificence.

Two months earlier Britton had broken the club's transfer record by spending £40,000 on forward Ken Wagstaff from Mansfield Town: now he equalled it twice more in rapid succession. The Tigers had tracked Houghton for two years and three months earlier they had had an £80,000 double deal for Houghton and Butler rejected. But they were promised first refusal. The impasse was broken when Butler asked for a move and then Rotherham, for whom he scored 56 times in 149 League games, decided that they also wanted to sell Houghton after 'reviewing their standing on the field and at the bank.' The two deals had at least ended one piece of long-standing speculation—that Britton was about to sign United's other inside-forward Albert Bennett, who eventually moved to Newcastle United.

Houghton reflected:

We were building a good side at Rotherham under Tom Johnston and Danny Williams and they must have seen something in me. Even though I once played at outside-right against Middlesbrough and never got a kick, I was told at one point that I had six games in which to prove myself, but I was hardly ever out of the side after that. We'd got a good forward-line together and they told us that nobody was going to leave. They even told us to move out of club houses and buy houses of our own, but in 12 months all five of us had gone. We used to have a pint in the Cross Keys in Rotherham every Tuesday night as a kind of bonding exercise and one week Ian Butler told us he thought he was going to Hull. Almost immediately Hull came in for me and Danny Williams said: 'You're not signing, but I'll come over with you anyway.' I didn't really know where Hull was and I was happy at Rotherham. I'd never dreamt of being transferred, but City manager Cliff Britton sold me the club so well that I couldn't wait to sign for them. It wasn't long before City went up and eventually Rotherham went down.

Houghton, whose parents Bill and Martha had seven children, was born in Rotherham in October 1939. He had four brothers and two sisters, he was the youngest of the seven and it meant that a down-to-earth outlook was soon instilled into him. And it was not long before he went below earth to earn a living. Houghton had initially played youth and reserve football as a centre-forward for Sheffield United alongside Jim Smith, later a much-travelled manager, but the management team of Joe Mercer and Dick Taylor left to go to Aston Villa. As a result, Houghton returned to Rotherham for a three-year stint as a miner at Silverwood Colliery in Thrybergh:

He recalled:

I had three brothers who went down the pit, as my dad did, but I don't remember him working much because he had tuberculosis. I played a bit for Silverwood as a centre-half, but then I had a trial at Rotherham and joined them straightaway as a centre-forward. I got £18 a week down the mines, but left to join Rotherham for £16 with £14 during the summer. But the family were pleased because I think that they probably had red-and-white eyes! Most of them came to watch me, but I used to get stick from them. We'd congregate at my mother's for Sunday tea, but the family gave me so much stick about my performances for a laugh. Even when I'd played well, they never mentioned it because it was all designed to keep my feet on the ground. I can remember scoring my first hat-trick for Rotherham against Bury and it never got a mention on the Sunday, but I have always remained level-headed that way because of it and I think it came from being in a mining fraternity.

Houghton was viewed as the last piece in Cliff Britton's promotion jigsaw when he left the Millers, for whom he had played at centre-forward in the two-legged first Football League Cup final against Aston Villa in 1960–61, and he said of his move at the time: 'It's a great set-up at Hull and the club obviously mean to go places. I think I shall be very happy and I shall certainly enjoy playing with Ian Butler again.' He played 10 games for City before he was on the losing side, he started to chip in with some goals and the promotion dream would have been achieved sooner than expected if it had not been for a disastrous Easter programme. Houghton reflected:

> Considering where we were when I joined the club, we did well even though we didn't get promotion in the end. But everybody was excited and the fact that we'd gone undefeated for a long time at one point lifted everybody up for the next season.

The 1965–66 season brought the Third Division title, a run to the FA Cup quarter-finals, a series of club records and 22 goals from midfield for Houghton in 45 League appearances. He also recorded five goals in cup competitions for an attractive, attacking side who failed to score in only three League games. And when wing-half Chris Simpkin missed his only game of the campaign as the Tigers became FA Cup giantkillers in February 1966 by beating Nottingham Forest 2–0 at home in the fourth round in front of 38,055 fans, Houghton coolly slotted into the defence and his performance was avidly acclaimed by his adoring public. Even Terry Heath, who was drafted into the forward-line at short notice and scored the two goals in fairy-tale style, admitted: 'Ken Houghton moved into a more defensive role and he had his best game of the season.' And respected sports writer Brian Taylor wrote:

> Houghton was here, there and everywhere, plugging defensive gaps, and he generally set City on the attack with sweeping, pinpoint passes whenever he got possession. It was one of the finest games he has played for the Tigers.

Only Houghton himself, it seemed, saw the tie, which ironically took place on the same day that former City hero Raich Carter was sacked as Middlesbrough's manager, in a different light because he insisted:

> It was one of the easiest games in which I ever played. I was only in the game every so often, so it was easy, but it annoyed me in a way because people kept mentioning it and yet Terry Heath had scored two goals. I played what was to become known as the sweeper's role and I was able to read the game. I was given plenty of room and I was allowed time to use the ball well, so I wouldn't say that it was my best game for the club because I had a lot of magic moments with City. I hardly made a mistake against Forest, but I always felt that I did well against First Division opposition. We did a great job tactically against Forest and that was because Cliff Britton's knowledge showed through. I admired Cliff so much as a manager, but I can remember that after that match he slated us and knocked me off my pedestal. I'd hit one bad pass during the game and Cliff brought me down to earth when we met to discuss it the following Tuesday because he kept harping on about it. I've never known such a perfectionist.

The FA Cup run ended with a 3–1 defeat to Chelsea after City had drawn 2–2 at Stamford Bridge against all the odds. One piece of adversity was the fact that future World Cup final referee Jack Taylor rejected a penalty appeal at a crucial stage when Houghton went near with a header during the first meeting. He ruefully reflected:

> Cliff Britton thought that we could beat them there because they didn't have the best home record, but they were murdering us and went 2–0 up. But we had a penalty denied when John Boyle handled a header of mine on the line. I don't think that the referee could believe that I'd headed it because it wasn't a strength of mine! But we hit back late on to draw 2–2 and probably only Waggy could have got those goals.

The inside-forward trio of Houghton, Wagstaff and local lad Chris Chilton could not stop scoring goals after promotion either as the fans were spoilt. Houghton was primarily there to help to create them, but he regularly chipped in, registering his first hat-trick for the club in September 1968 when City came from behind to win 3–2 at Millwall. He had some spells out with injury and his worth to the side was underlined in the same season. The Tigers topped the

Second Division table after a good start to 1968–69, but they fell away when Houghton started only six of the final 22 League games. He said:

> Waggy and Chillo always got the credit because they scored the goals and rightly so in that sense, but it was still a team game. In my last three years at Rotherham I played at centre-forward and inside-forward, but I fitted in at Hull in midfield because I could read the game and support the forwards. Cliff Britton was a great manager because he was very thorough. We played some great football, but a lot of it was planned. You'd practise moves under Cliff until you got them inch-perfect. We worked collectively for each other.

The contribution made by Houghton, who was once described by journalist Brian Taylor as 'the playmaker with the superbly-placed, superbly-weighted pass,' was always appreciated. Ex-Tiger Charlie Crickmore had left the club before Britton's spending spree, but he recalled:

> People talk about the arrival of Ken Wagstaff, but, for me, Ken Houghton was one of City's best signings because he could pass the ball well to both sides of the pitch and he was always involved in the game. When I faced City after I'd left, the managers would say that the most important thing for us to do was always to stop Houghton in midfield.

Teammate Chris Chilton added:

> Ken Houghton was the cultured passer of our side. He was a bit like Trevor Brooking in a sense. He would just let the ball do the work a lot of the time and he was a thinking player. He could hit passes from 10 yards to 60 yards accurately and he would score. When he arrived, the full team started to take a shape. Ian Butler gave me a supply which, as a striker, was brilliant because I'd got things coming in from wide positions. Then you had Houghy who would pick you out and slot balls up alongside you on the run. Then I had the added option of having another striker up alongside me with Wag and all his skill and strength. I'm sure it made me a better player and more confident. It looked easy for us to score goals. Ken Houghton and Ian Butler scored their fair share. All of a sudden you've got two average goalscorers with no disrespect to Ken and Ian, you've got a prolific goalscorer with Wag and then you've got a regular goalscorer with me. Things just developed from there.

Even though the quality of football was always exciting, City did not push on after promotion from the Third Division in 1966 and Houghton said: 'Cliff Britton thought that the team we had could have done the job of getting us into the First Division, so you have to respect him for being loyal.' But he was moved upstairs to a role as general manager in 1970 when Terry Neill was appointed as his successor as player-manager.

Houghton, meanwhile, had recorded his second hat-trick for City in a 4–2 win at Birmingham as he finished the 1969–70 season with nine goals from midfield in the final 10 League games. In all, he scored 16 goals in the League—only two less than strikers Chilton and Wagstaff. But the club needed new impetus and the Tigers were duly among the promotion contenders in Neill's first season before failing away at the death. Houghton said:

> We brought in Ken Knighton and Bill Baxter and it worked a treat for us on their debuts at Sheffield United. But after that we had nothing. It wasn't that they weren't good players, but we had done well before they came. Terry Neill was all right and wanted to get on with everybody.

Houghton, who became a close friend of Knighton and even scouted for him when he was Sunderland's manager, was the architect of another memorable piece of FA Cup giantkilling with City as the 1970s unravelled. In February 1973 he scored a 29th-minute winner when the Tigers beat West Ham United, who included Bobby Moore and Trevor Brooking, 1–0 at home in the fourth round. Houghton, who exacted some personal revenge because he had been injured in a Football League Cup tie at West Ham in 1970, recalled: 'I can't remember much about the goal except that Stuart Pearson and Phil Holme were involved and put West Ham under pressure. The ball ran free and all I had to do was to sidefoot it home.'

But the following summer Neill allowed Houghton to leave in a player-exchange deal with Scunthorpe United, for whom he was to score five goals in 33 League games, that brought their centre-half Steve Deere to Boothferry Park. The switch did not work out well because he said:

> It disappointed me when I left because I don't think that Scunthorpe wanted to sign Ken Houghton. Letting me go to them was only way in which their manager Ron Ashman would let Steve Deere go to Hull. But Ron Ashman immediately left to go to Grimsby and I was promised certain things at the Hull City end which weren't fulfilled, so I didn't enjoy my time at Scunthorpe at all. I had come from a very professional club at Hull, but, with due respect to Scunthorpe, they were like an amateur club at the time in comparison. They even did their match warm-ups in the clubhouse!

Houghton's contribution to one of the Tigers' most enthralling eras could never be underrated, though. He made 264 League appearances for them, leaving him 26th in the all-time list, and he scored 79 goals. That left him joined eighth with fellow sharpshooter Doug Clarke in the club's all-time list of marksmen: significantly, all those above them were arguably out-and-out strikers in today's parlance. The forward-line who subscribed so successfully to the club-record 102 League goals that earned City a title in 1965–66—Houghton, Wagstaff, Chilton, Ian Butler and Ray Henderson—scored a remarkable 565 for the club in total in the Third Division initially and then the Second Division. Furthermore, Houghton's goals were often spectacular because he was noted for his fierce shot and he recalled:

> My favourite goal for Hull was at Millwall when I volleyed one past Alex Stepney from a corner by Ian Butler. And I also enjoyed scoring with a similar volley at Aston Villa. The odd thing is that I scored both of them with my left foot, but I could hit them with both feet. It just came naturally from the time when I took penalties for Rotherham.

Houghton ran a newsagency in North Hull with prominent tennis umpire Alan Glaholm when he left League football and in the 1974–75 season he ventured into management for the first time—with non-League Scarborough. He recalled:

> I got to the FA Trophy final with Scarborough, but we'd played a lot of matches and lost 4–0 to Matlock Town. We were unbeaten in Northern Premier League tournaments and were playing Saturday and Tuesday nearly every week, but I enjoyed my time there. One of my proudest moments was when we beat Wimbledon 1–0 in the FA Trophy soon after they had beaten Burnley and then taken Leeds United to a replay in the FA Cup.

But in June 1975 Houghton contacted 'Boro's chairman Don Robinson to inform him of his resignation. Colin Appleton, later to have two spells as City's manager under Robinson's chairmanship, was returning to the club as general manager. Robinson had told Houghton by telegram, indicating that he wanted him to continue as a player only. Houghton said at the time: 'I did not think that it would be fair to Colin or myself to continue in such a position. I enjoyed my one year with Scarborough and thought we had done well to reach Wembley.'

But Scarborough was not to be Houghton's last resort in football. He indicated that he wanted to stay in the game and had a brief spell further down the east coast as Bridlington Town's player-coach, where he linked up with Ian Butler at a third club after York City had released him, before returning to Boothferry Park when City's manager, John Kaye, put him in charge of the club's youth development in May 1976. 'John rang me and I was chuffed to death because I never thought I'd come back to Hull City,' said Houghton.

City harshly sacked Kaye at the start of October 1977 and finally appointed Bobby Collins, the former Scottish international who had joined the coaching staff during the summer, as his successor as manager. Collins pondered the possibility of making Houghton his No. 2, but eventually plumped for Syd Owen, who had been one of his colleagues at Leeds United. But the management team did not last long and in February 1978 Houghton became City's caretaker manager with a brief to keep them in the Second Division. He failed and the Tigers were relegated in April 1978 after a 2–1 defeat at Orient. Houghton said at the time: 'It is hard to accept because I think that there is nothing worse in football than when you are down. You try to put on a brave face, but deep down it hurts.' But he was immediately rewarded with the manager's job on a long-term basis and it seemed that the fact that he had not sought an increase in salary had apparently impressed the board. Houghton observed: 'It is something I always wanted to do, but I wouldn't say that it was a pleasure at the moment.'

Houghton reinstalled the long-serving Andy Davidson as his assistant, having brought back another all-time hero, Chris Chilton, to look after the youngsters. And there was consolation in the fact that City's juniors, who had been coached by Houghton for most of the season, won the Northern Intermediate League title. Houghton also appointed former England international, Busby Babe and Manchester United manager Wilf McGuinness as first-team coach in the summer of 1978 and the Tigers, helped by 24 League goals from inspired £60,000 signing Keith Edwards, finished eighth in the Third Division in his first full season in charge. Houghton was given a further one-year contract as manager in early May 1979, but times were tough at the club. Three of the stars of 1966—Houghton, Davidson and Chilton—sought to regain the Second Division status that they had worked so hard to earn as players, but the 1979–80 season did not go well and money was scarce.

When City visited Brentford in December 1979, the party were put up at a London hotel that one of them described as 'a doss-house to save the club a few quid.' The Tigers lost 7–2 and soon afterwards Houghton, Davidson and McGuinness were fired. Houghton reflected:

> It was the worst day of my life when I got the sack as City manager. I don't regret taking over, but they were sacking managers right, left and centre, so I felt that I was being thrown in at the deep end a bit. I thought we were building a decent side, but the patience wasn't there. When we were told to sell our best players, I knew we were on to a loser.

Houghton then played locally for current Central Midlands League side Westella and Willerby and Hull Sunday League club St Peter's until he was 50: 'My last appearance was in a charity match at Bransholme when my old colleague Billy Wilkinson was back from Australia on a visit.' He also took a job as sales director with Davis Freight in Hull and then Immingham, but left a lasting legacy with his adopted club, Hull City. And it was not just as a player and in management because he was also the leader of the practical jokes that were part and parcel of the club's existence.

As a player, he would master manoeuvres of missing items from hotel rooms although he always insisted: 'I never touched any personal property.' On one occasion Houghton and 'the removal men' among his teammates offered an apprenticeship in their ways to young goalkeeper Peter Walters and he explained: 'We put him on look-out and, when he was looking the other way, we left his mattress up a nearby tree at Lilleshall!' And on the club's close-season tour of the West Indies in 1973 the players stayed in a hotel where they had small chalets for rooms. Revenge was sweet because Houghton apparently found a way into player-manager Terry Neill's chalet, took everything out and then put it back exactly as he had found it on the lawn outside. He mused: 'By that time I knew that I was leaving the club anyway!'

As a manager, he organised a party at his house in October 1979 and told City's commercial manager Arthur Anderson that it was a fancy-dress occasion. None of the other partygoers were told of such a prerequisite, but they were primed about what had been said to Anderson, who eventually knocked on the back door dressed in a red-and-black court jester's outfit replete with pointed feet and bells . . .

Houghton was also involved in an amusing escapade while working for Davis Freight in Immingham. He was walking round the docks one day when he was convinced that he saw his former City and Scarborough teammate Ray Pettit. Houghton kept calling to him, but Pettit walked on, kept his head down and repeatedly ignored him. It was only later that the Essex-based Pettit was able to explain to the rebuffed Houghton that he had been working for the investigations division of the Customs and Excise in London. The division specialised in inquiries into drugs, VAT evasion, fraud and smuggling and he had returned north on a top-secret, under-cover investigation when Houghton saw him!

Houghton, who was also ready to lead a sing-song whenever the opportunity arose and has continued to watch his adopted club regularly at the Kingston Communications Stadium, had been a cultured player in one of City's most exciting eras and later an underrated manager and coach. And his quiet, but steely determination and ready sense of humour mean that he was always one of the club's genuine nice guys.

17

GARRETH ROBERTS

Hull City's relegation from the old Second Division in 1978 proved to be a watershed in the club's affairs. The high hopes of the 1960s had evaporated, benefactor Harold Needler had died in 1975 and the club had lamentably lost their sense of direction and purpose. Furthermore, the situation would get much worse before it would get better, but at least a local hero was on the verge of emerging—midfield dynamo Garreth Roberts. City already had two of them in their ranks—loyal, long-serving stalwarts Malcolm Lord and Roger de Vries—but two more were in the pipeline. One was defender Peter Skipper, who would make his mark in two spells with the club after being signed from local football: Roberts, though, progressed through City's successful youth system, he would go on to captain them during two promotion seasons and he would move into second place behind Andy Davidson in the list of the club's all-time appearance-makers with 461 in the League.

Roberts, who was born in November 1960, was the product of City's junior team who had won the Northern Intermediate League title under two of the club's heroes of the 1960s—Ken Houghton and latterly Chris Chilton—in 1977–78 to offset the disappointment of the first team's relegation. The side also included Steve McClaren, who would go on to become England's manager, and Brian Marwood, who would make a cameo appearance as an England player. But while McClaren and Marwood would move away as players as they developed their lengthy and varied careers in football, Roberts stayed put. He was also the first of the three to be given his chance in League football as his career ran on parallel lines to that of Skipper for a while. Skipper made his League debut in a 5–3 defeat at Swansea in early March 1979: Roberts was on the substitutes' bench that night without coming on although manager Ken Houghton wrestled with his conscience afterwards as to whether he should have brought him on for Keith Edwards, who, oddly enough, became one of his best friends in football. Roberts said:

> Although I was glad to be part of it, we did take a bit of a pasting, so maybe it wouldn't have been a good time to go on. I had played mainly for the juniors at that point, so I was just starry-eyed and I didn't feel let down. Houghy was a great bloke who has stayed a friend. The main thing once you got your chance was that you kept the shirt and did yourself proud.

Hull-born Roberts did not have to wait long, though. He was omitted for the next game—at home to Brentford in midweek—but was then back on the substitutes' bench the following Saturday and this time his chance soon came. City beat Bury 4–1, Skipper scored his first League goal and Roberts made his bow after 33 minutes when striker Alan Warboys was stretchered off with damaged ankle ligaments. Warboys never played again for City, but in contrast it was the start of great things for Roberts who recalled:

> I came on for the old warhorse Alan Warboys and I was absolutely as nervous as hell even though there wasn't a big crowd, but it was still a dream come true because I was a local boy who had come through all the sessions under Fred Smith and Pete Sissons for youngsters on Tuesday and Thursday nights. I was also pleased that we won 4–1 and that I thought that I'd had a half-decent game.

Roberts immediately became a fixture because he started a League game for the first time against Colchester United three days later and he scored his first senior goal in a 2–2 draw at Carlisle during his fourth appearance:

> I hit a shot from the edge of the penalty box into the bottom corner, but the thing I remember most was that a few minutes earlier one of the

Carlisle players had gone over the top to me just below the knee and I could feel my fibula bend. It was the first time that it had happened to me and was one of the worst tackles ever on me.

Houghton added:

We immediately went into a successful run and Garreth never looked back, but he was one of those players I never had any fears about throwing into the side because I knew he would give everything and play the game the right way. You think that some players may have a chance of succeeding if they work at their games, but I had no doubt at all in my mind in Garreth's case. I doubt that there could ever be another Billy Bremner, but in those days Garreth looked as if he might be the next best thing.

Roberts further established himself with 44 League appearances during 1979–80, but Houghton was replaced as manager by Mike Smith and City only just staved off relegation to the Fourth Division for the first time. It was a temporary stay of execution because they finished bottom of the Third Division the following season and in early 1982 the club tumbled into receivership. Roberts mused: 'To have been at the club and not known just what was going on was very unsettling at the time.'

But his personal star was in the ascendancy because he recalled:

Mike Smith gave me the captaincy when I was in my early 20s and it was something of a poisoned chalice because there were a lot of senior players who made my life hell. There was some jealousy because they were fed up that they didn't get the job. It wasn't the best time in the club's history and there were cliques, but I was proud to be captain of my own local club and just kept at it. I was a captain who led by example rather than one who picked other people up. I got Billy Whitehurst to do that, I roomed with him for a few years and he turned out to be a good bodyguard on and off the pitch!

In the summer of 1982 extrovert Scarborough businessman Don Robinson took over as chairman, he appointed the experienced Colin Appleton as manager and the new regime brought instant promotion. Roberts again played in 44 of the 46 League games as the cobwebs were blown away and he said:

Don Robinson was great because he got people talking about the club and, when he first arrived, Colin Appleton was a good foil for him as manager. Don was the best chairman I worked under. He was great for the club at the time because he was just what was needed. I thought he was brilliant—a top man. Some of his quotes at the time about City being the first side to play on the moon were just plain daft. It was dead easy for people to take the mickey out of us after that, but it was Don's way of letting them know what a good team we were. He used to take us abroad for trips and up to Scarborough for a few days to keep us all together and he'd get us involved in all kinds of stunts. I can remember him getting me to feed some dolphins on one occasion. He told muggins to stand there with a fish in my teeth and this dolphin with its mouth wide open suddenly jumped up and took it!

In 1982–83 City went up from the Fourth Division as runners-up to Wimbledon and conceded just 34 goals. Third-placed Port Vale had the same defensive record—the joint best anywhere in the country that season. Appleton transformed the squad on a shoestring budget—in bleak comparison with his brief second spell in charge when Robinson reappointed him in 1989. And Roberts reflected:

> Colin was brilliant the first time because he set us on the right track, but it was very different the second time because there were a lot of players who would answer him back by then. He would organise a whole series of meetings and sometimes you'd wonder what points he was trying to make, but then about two days later you'd realise what he'd meant. He was a very deep thinker on the game and the answer was always there if you listened to everything he said. We kept virtually the same side for most of the season and it was also Colin's way of getting us all together. We went up with a 0–0 draw at Chester in a game which wasn't a classic, but there were plenty of highlights such as a 7–0 home win over Stockport County when I scored and Andy Flounders got a hat-trick. The way we were playing at the time typified the togetherness and camaraderie between all the lads.

The respect was mutual because Appleton said of Roberts' contribution to the successful campaign:

> Garreth was an integral and important part of our promotion year in 1983 as a busy midfield dynamo. That season Garreth, Steve McClaren and Billy Askew were superb in midfield. I knew that, if we were going to get some success in anything at the time, then part of it was

likely to be down to Garreth's consistent performances. He was always one of the names to go down on the teamsheet first.

Roberts played in 43 League games in 1982–83, but he was by now accustomed to life with the Tigers being something of a roller-coaster ride—even at the best of times. The 1983–84 season summed it up because it finished equally as dramatically as when City agonisingly missed out on promotion to the top flight at Oldham back in 1910.

City went into their last League game of the season at Burnley—which had been controversially postponed at the start of 1984 when the club's team coach failed to reach a playable Turf Moor in hazardous weather conditions—needing to win by three clear goals to pip Sheffield United for the third promotion place behind Oxford United and Wimbledon. But the Tigers, who had slipped slightly after remaining unbeaten in their opening 11 League games, managed to win only 2–0 and missed out by either a goal or a point. There was then added drama when Appleton resigned almost immediately afterwards to take over at Swansea.

Roberts recalled:

It was probably the most emotional game I ever played in because we needed to win by three clear goals to gain promotion. The build-up to it was intense because the situation gripped the whole city. The support we had at the game was unbelievable and to say that we were disappointed by the outcome was the biggest understatement imaginable. Brian Marwood gave us a good start with a goal from the edge of the box and then he and Steve McClaren began a move on the right. The ball came across and I struck what I thought was a certain goal, but a wandering Vince Overson knocked it over the bar with a flailing knee. That just about summed up our luck. Brian scored another great goal after halftime and there were still 25 minutes left, so we still had a chance, but it just wasn't to be. The feeling in the dressing-room after the match was awful. Everyone was so quiet and hardly anyone spoke for a long time. Some players just wandered off to find their own little space, collect their thoughts and try to put it all into perspective. It was so hard to believe that we'd lost our promotion chance by one goal after 46 games.

About 15 minutes after the game another bombshell hit us when Colin Appleton said he was resigning as manager. He said he had had enough and I think he would have resigned in any case—even if we'd gone up. There were repeated attempts by players to make him change his mind, but he was adamant about his decision. I think he was a big loss to the club because he had done such a good job in two seasons.

But there was some personal consolation for Roberts because it was his best season as a goalscorer from midfield with nine in the League. And in his eyes it included three of the best of the 47 that he was to score in his one-club career in League football.

The first two came within a fortnight of each other in mid-season in a 3–1 win at close rivals Bristol Rovers and a 1–0 home win over struggling Port Vale. Roberts said of the game at Rovers:

It was 1–1 when I scored two second-half goals to earn us the points and it was my second which stands out in the memory. There was a chase between their goalkeeper Phil Kite and Billy Whitehurst for a long through ball from Steve McClaren. Kite hacked it away and it came to me about 30 yards out, where I chipped it back over his head into the net. The linesman was flagging for offside, but the referee ruled that no -one was interfering with play, so the goal stood.

The winner against Vale came in different circumstances because he added:

We struggled to break them down, so there were only a little more than 15 minutes left when I finally scored. I picked up a clearance near the halfway line, went past two of their defenders, Colin Tartt and Geoff Hunter, and must have run about 40 yards with the ball before shooting from about 20 yards out. The ball flew into the top, right-hand corner of the net.

The third of Roberts' favourite goals that season came in a 4–1 win at eventual champions Wimbledon in April 1984 as City's promotion push maintained momentum and he recalled:

We had had a big build-up for the game because we'd stayed at Bishan Abbey from the middle of the week leading up to it. I was very pleased with my goal, which came just after halftime and made it 3–0 to us. I picked up a clearance about 20 yards out, let fly with my left foot of all things and the ball flew high into the net past Dave Beasant.

The amazing anti-climax of 1983–84 was replaced by joy the following season after Brian Horton had taken over as player-manager in succession to Appleton. This time City did finish third to go up into the Second Division behind champions Bradford City and Millwall and Roberts said:

> It was Brian Horton's first managerial job, but we first met him when he came out to Florida, where we'd gone at the end of the season. He took us for training and it was a great way for him to get to know the lads because we needed picking up after just missing out. Brian basically took up the slack and I think he knew we were still a good enough team to do well. He made a few changes here and there, but he made sure that we went out on the park feeling that nobody could beat us, especially at home. Everybody was working for each other and I think that Brian may compare that team favourably with any he managed.

Horton's arrival also provided Roberts with another bonus because he added:

> From a personal point of view, it helped that he was also a midfield player and he never surrendered to anyone—even in training sessions, which got a bit lively and tasty at times! At times Brian played with me in midfield, he could pass and tackle and he showed me how to play the position. He would tell me when to go and when to sit in and I gained a lot of experience from him. There were also times when he played me 'in the hole' because I think he saw something in the attacking side of my game.

For his part, Horton also recognised Roberts' effectiveness because he said:

> Garreth did very well in my first season in management when Hull won promotion. And while I know that I later took the captaincy away from him, I wish I hadn't done that because, looking back, it might have been a mistake on my part. Garreth twice helped his club to promotion as captain and proved himself to be a good player in the Fourth Division, the Third Division and the Second Division. And he might have played successfully in the First Division as well. I'm sure he had the ability, but players always need that little bit of luck.

In 1984–85 the Tigers comfortably made sure of promotion with three games remaining when they won 1–0 at Walsall at the end of their second run of five successive League wins since the start of March. Roberts recalled:

> Pete Skipper scored the all-important winner with a header from a corner at Walsall, but it was also a great result because they'd been on

the fringe of the promotion race themselves for most of the season. We could have had a far easier game in which we had to try to clinch promotion, but the fact that everyone worked hard to achieve victory made it all the more worthwhile. The second half was a continuous battle for us, but we were thoroughly competent and I shall always remember the celebrations on the pitch after we'd won.

I think it was about half-an-hour before we finally went back into the dressing-room, but the champagne still flowed a lot longer after that. There is no better feeling than clinching promotion at the end of the season, but this particular occasion was especially rewarding. It meant a lot because this win finally took us back into the Second Division only a year after we had missed out by just one goal in unfortunate circumstances. All the players and staff had shown a lot of character to bounce back immediately and do the job properly after such a big disappointment at the end of the previous season. It would have been a lot easier to have struggled in the middle of the table after the dramatic finish a year earlier, but the fact that we carried on and made sure the next season was very important and made up for the previous disappointment.

Roberts was never an ever-present for City in any season, but his record of League appearances was as consistent as ever in the Second Division—33 in 1985–86, 35 in 1986–87, 44 in 1987–88, 35 in 1988–89 and 36 in 1989–90. But his career was then to end with a relegation season. And it meant that it had just about come full circle, of course, because Roberts had initially made his mark as an apprentice when the first team went down in 1977–78.

The Tigers conceded lots of goals in the first half of 1990–91 when Stan Ternent was in charge, but Roberts was struggling with a knee injury. And it turned out that his last game for the club was the last one before Christmas 1990—a 2–1 defeat at Charlton. Early in 1991 Ternent was replaced as manager by Terry Dolan, who could not prevent relegation. City finished at the bottom of the Third Division, they were, in fact, embarking on the worst period in their history and Roberts, who had previously at least been granted a testimonial, was an absentee in the second half of the season.

The manner of Roberts' departure from League football, though, was shameful for such a loyal servant. He explained:

I knew my knee was bad because I'd been injured at Charlton. But the following month Terry Dolan became manager and he let me go even though he hadn't seen me play. I think it was all to do with finance. It wasn't the best way to go with the whole Terry Dolan thing. He offered me the youth coaching job one day and then changed his mind during the weekend. They didn't want me to play on, so it would have been a big step to retire at 31, but I would have enjoyed doing the job. I didn't think that I got what I deserved after 14 years because I left with a letter of one paragraph that just said: 'Thanks very much.' I thought it was a bit disrespectful, so I didn't finish in the right way.

The terse brevity of that last note was ominously similar to the official way in which Billy Bly, another long-serving City hero, was also told about his departure. And in Roberts' case he would have relished the chance to join the club's backroom staff because he said: 'I also felt very disappointed because I thought that I had a lot to offer on the coaching side.' There was some compensation, though, that much later he did return to help out with the coaching in the club's School of Excellence for a while.

The years did take their toll because Roberts, a keen tennis player who turned out at a good local level for Swanland, Cottingham and Beverley and East Riding—even after his football days were over— subsequently required operations for hip and knee replacements. And he has continued to retain his sporting links as an administrator with 15 years in sports development with local councils, a spell with the Services to Sport coaching agency and then as the coach development officer with the Humber Sports Partnership. And he admitted: 'I've been lucky because my work has always been to do with sport since I left football.'

But his playing days were often special as two former City players who were coaches at the club during the renaissance of the 1980s testified. Chris Chilton said:

Garreth was a super player. The years that he played in the game showed his tremendous qualities. Most small players have been wingers and you don't get many midfield players such as Garreth Roberts who go in and stick a boot through people, tackle and fight and can play.

And Dennis Booth added: 'Garreth always gave 100 per cent and never liked to be second-best in anything. He was a good servant to the club, he impressed me from the first occasion we met and he continued to do so.'

Roberts' height might usually have been given as just 5ft 5in, but he was a pocket battleship of a player with a huge heart that was always innate in his make-up. Former City coach Wilf McGuinness, a one-time Busby Babe who played and coached with both England and Manchester United, put it in perspective when he said:

> He will always be little Garreth because I'm only 5ft 6in myself, so there aren't all that many people I can say that to! Pound for pound Garreth was one of the best midfield players around. He was the type of player I always tried to be when I was a wing-half at Manchester United. There was no doubt that he was the kind of player that no team could do without.

18

TONY NORMAN

When former Wales manager Mike Smith took charge of Hull City at the start of 1980 in a blaze of publicity, he was handed loads of money to spend by the club's chairman Bob Chapman and personnel director Ian Blakey. It largely proved to be a disastrous decision because it ultimately led to the Tigers' financial ruin as they were relegated to the Fourth Division for the first time in 1981 and then went into receivership in February 1982. But one of the arrivals as part of Smith's spending spree was a bargain—goalkeeper Tony Norman.

Curiously, Norman had been a full-time professional at Burnley, who sold him to City for £30,000, but had not even had any experience of either first-team or reserve-team football. He recalled:

> I was at Burnley when Alan Stevenson and Gerry Peyton were the two main goalkeepers and Billy O'Rourke and I were in the youth team. I never played for the reserves, so it was completely different when I came to Hull to play for the first team. Mike Smith was the manager and knew me from Wales Under-21s and he just asked me if I'd come along because he said: 'I think you could do the job I want.' I wasn't overawed. It was a step up and time to move on. When I came to Hull, the football club were languishing and didn't seem to know which way to go. There was a lot going on with money, but I didn't take any notice. I got accepted and got on with the job. There were a lot of comings and goings and times changed because it started to become a

club where everybody would stick by everybody else. It wasn't Manchester United or Liverpool and the facilities weren't fantastic. I can remember that we would have to do runs under one of the stands, but Mike Smith and Cyril Lea just got with it.

Norman, a Welshman who was born in February 1958, was an integral part of the transformation that brought two promotions in three seasons, at one stage playing in a club-record 226 successive League games for the club. The sequence ran from August 1983 to September 1988 and left him in eighth place overall in City's all-time appearances list. Norman missed the last three games of the 1982–83 promotion season as his fellow Welshman John Davies deputised for him. But he then played in every League game for the next five seasons as well as the opening six Second Division matches in 1988–89. It was open to debate as to who had been the holder of the previous record because it was accepted in some quarters that forward David Mercer, whose son Tony became a featured singer in the *Black and White Minstrels' Show* on television, should be accredited with it. He played in 218 consecutive games, but it was not as black and white as it may have seemed, so to speak, because his run cut across the 1914–18 War when traditional League football was abandoned and replaced by regional competitions. It might have been argued, therefore, that the record broken by Norman had really belonged to the long-serving Andy Davidson, who played in 177 successive League games between 1962 and 1966.

Norman himself played down the significance of his record run in his usual modest manner because he said:

> I think it was all a bit daft on occasions because there was a spell when John Davies, our other goalkeeper, damaged his cruciate knee ligaments in a reserve game and was out for a long time. As a result, I was patched up to play when I got a knock because there wasn't an experienced alternative available. But it wasn't perfect and it became a case of just having to get on with it even when I picked up a few niggles.
>
> On one occasion I hurt my back in training and I'd have dropped out if there had been another readymade goalkeeper available, but I didn't. Yet I couldn't even bend down to tie up my boots—someone else had to do it for me! It was just a question of getting through the

game and hoping that everything didn't suddenly go pear-shaped, but it was absolutely crackers really. On another occasion I sprained my ankle in training on the Friday and they strapped me up to play the next day. The injury then eased, I played in the next few games as usual and then after about three weeks of it I was back to normal.

At the same time we were doing well. The spirit was so good then, we'd had a bit of success and I think my situation became part of our desire to keep things going. But I was never aware of any run of games. I'd just to go in and train and play and then train and play again. But whenever the unbroken run's been mentioned, I must admit that I have a secret pride in it and I reckon that it was worth being strapped up now and then.

There were occasions when Norman picked up knocks that forced him to leave the field. In March 1981 striker Craig Norrie had to take over in goal in a 0–0 draw at home to Chesterfield for the last 15 minutes when he was hurt. And during his long unbroken League run striker Andy Flounders went into goal for 13 minutes in a 2–2 draw at Millwall in December 1984 when Norman started to cough up blood after a clash with the burly John Fashanu.

He also had Cup absences while remaining an ever-present fixture in the League for so long. In May 1984 Paul Blackburn took over for an Associate Members' Cup quarter-final against Sheffield United and in bizarre circumstances in November 1986 Norman was ruled out of a Full Members' Cup tie at Southampton on the journey south when the coach jolted him. He explained:

We travelled down on the day of the match and on the coach we got changed from our tracksuits into our suits just before we stopped for something to eat. But all of a sudden the bus rolled on the motorway. That was all it was, but I was on one leg trying to put the other one into my trousers and my back clicked. From then it was dead simple: my back began to tighten up and soon became solid and we couldn't do anything to loosen it up.

And manager Brian Horton added:

We were pulling into a hotel at Luton to have lunch. The lads were in their tracksuits and I suggested that they changed to go inside. Tony was just changing his trousers when the coach lurched to one side and he felt his back go. We thought he'd be okay, but it was obvious he was still in pain when we got to Southampton.

City eventually lost 2–1 with defender Peter Skipper having to start the game in goal because there was no specialist substitute on the bench!

Norman's record League run ended at Oldham in his final season with City when he picked up an injury and Gavin Kelly replaced him in a 2–2 draw. Norman's sequence had previously been threatened before a game at Oldham, but he was passed fit in the end. At the same time he admitted that there were some venues that he hated:

> I never liked playing at Sheffield United, but I don't know why. I used to enjoy grounds where the fans were very close to you and for some reason it didn't seem that way at Bramall Lane. And artificial pitches were the worst invention ever. They had them at Oldham, Preston, QPR and Luton in those days and basically they put down a concrete base with a thin strip of carpet on top of it. I wasn't chuffed with any of the plastic pitches because it wasn't football. I wanted to play in the mud and not be in a situation in which another player had to put his finger on top of the ball when you kicked it because it wouldn't stay still. But that's what used to happen at Oldham in particular, where it could be very windy. The only person who benefited from the pitch at Oldham was Frankie Bunn after he had left Hull because he scored a record six goals against Scarborough in a Football League Cup tie on it for them!

And Norman knew all about football 'inventions' because he was also an innovator himself even though he was never entirely sure how he did it. But it happened in City's 1–0 home win over the old Wimbledon side in September 1983 when he decided to distribute the ball in a novel way by dropping it down just in front of him—sometimes either rolling it or tapping it outside the penalty box to gain further distance—and then kicking it off the ground as a calculated tactical measure. Wimbledon's manager Dave Bassett accordingly heeded the procedure and told his own goalkeeper, Dave Beasant, to make the most of it. The tactic then became part and parcel of the modern goalkeeper's armoury. But Norman admitted:

> I honestly don't know where I got the idea from. I don't know why I started to do it other than the fact that it was good for the way that we wanted to play at the time. We didn't have the biggest players upfront on some occasions, so I thought was easier to roll the ball out and then drill it. It meant that the kick looped in the air and the front

players could hold it up a bit better. And I found that it was more accurate. Dave Beasant has acknowledged that he started to do it at Wimbledon after he'd seen me do it and in the end everybody started doing it.

But there was always something completely different about Norman anyway. After all, he kicked the ball right-footed, but threw it out with his left arm. At cricket he is a right-handed batsman and a left-arm bowler. He plays golf right-handed, but writes left-handed . . .

If those were inconsistencies, then he provided consistency as a goalkeeper and one-time City hero Chris Chilton, who was on the coaching staff when Norman was signed, said:

> He was such a quiet, laid-back, unassuming lad. As an all-round goalkeeper, Tony was the best I played with or managed. He just had everything and was so dedicated. He was big, he was strong, he was good on crosses and he had quick feet and quick hands. He was a super goalkeeper and a nice bloke. He probably had everything except being 6ft 5in! He worked so hard at his game. He and John Davies were spot-on as professionals in the way they trained, the way they conducted themselves, the way they pushed themselves to the limit and the way they wanted to learn. We would put them through different things and they just thrived on it. And the fact that they were marvellous professionals rubbed off on others. It made a difference when the young guys who'd been on the fringe got into the side because they'd seen them training. They knew from them what they had to do to be first-teamers and they absorbed it. It was as if they'd been touched with a dye. They would then want to work hard and be solid professionals.

Norman's early days at Boothferry Park, though, were often difficult as he established himself in the side in succession to Eddie Blackburn. City's descent into receivership in early 1982 when Smith left meant that things got worse for him before they got better. But the club's revival was instilled by new chairman Don Robinson, who appointed Colin Appleton as manager.

Norman recalled:

> When you're in the bottom division and the receiver is called in, you can't get much lower. In fact, it was rock-bottom. It was just like falling to the bottom of the well and then slowly clambering up again. It was gradual, but at least it proved that there was bit of bounce left in

the club. I didn't know many chairmen at that stage, but Don Robinson brought in his own ideas. And in those days there was still room for a bit of romance in some departments of football, whereas it is just an out-and-out business today. Don had his own style, but he was an entrepreneur and a businessman who did things his own way and still gave the club a lift. His ways were fairly successful, he was approachable and at least he was in the right place then. And if we were beaten, then he'd feel it just much as the players and the supporters. On other occasions he might come into the players' lounge, put £20 behind the bar to buy the lads a drink and it was appreciated. He wasn't scared of going to the players and putting on a show. And at the end of nearly every season he would take us away on a tour. In fact, one November he just walked in after a game and said that in a couple of weeks or so we'd be going away to play a few games because we had a spare weekend. Then he explained that we were going to Bermuda for 10 days and leaving the Christmas shopping behind!

Don Robinson came up with all sorts of things, but he was a chairman who never interfered. Colin Appleton was quite forthright in telling you what was expected. I can remember that after our first defeat there was a bit of banter and a little smile and a laugh afterwards. The following week Colin reminded us that we had been beaten on the Saturday and told us to roll our sleeves up. He was his own man and was reclusive with the lads in terms of man management, but he was fantastic if you ever went to him with a problem. He made sure that he got the respect of the players and, even though he was never your best mate, he would still look after you. Colin had his own eccentricities, but he did the job his way and he was similar to Don in that respect. And, above all, he wanted to win things.

The outcome was promotion from the Fourth Division in Appleton's first season in charge when Norman made 36 League appearances and on only four occasions did he concede more than one goal in a game in them. The Tigers narrowly missed out on a second successive promotion in 1983–84, but they made up the following season, by which time Norman was well into his unbroken League sequence. It comprised five seasons without missing a League game, but promotion to the Second Division in 1984–85 was earned under a different regime after Brian Horton had succeeded Appleton. Norman said:

Brian had a different feel about him. He came out to Florida to meet us after we'd gone there for a trip at the end of the season and you couldn't work him out, but he had an intensity about him. He had his own way and his own standards. He was the only man I ever had a row with in a dressing-room and it happened twice. I was the quiet one, but I stood up for myself.

Once Norman had further underlined his consistency in the Second Division, international recognition ensued. The middle of three brothers, he was only just born in Wales at Mancot—four miles from the English border and six miles from Chester. But the call came in March 1986. He won five caps in all—making his debut as a substitute for Neville Southall against the Republic of Ireland in Dublin in a 1–0 win. The following month he kept a clean sheet in a goalless draw against Uruguay and then he was substituted in a 2–0 defeat against Canada. Norman was destined to be a long-term understudy to Southall, but he twice more played for Wales—during the summer of 1988 when he featured in wins in Malta and Italy. He reflected:

As at club level, my aim was to get into the team and stay there, but I went on more trips than I can remember without playing because of Neville Southall, who was usually the No. 1 choice. I was in the same squads as players such as Nev, Mark Hughes, Ian Rush and Gary Speed. They came from a different football world from me in some ways, but I was born in Wales and always wanted to be involved even if it meant driving for about eight hours to get to, say, Swansea to meet up.

When Norman's club-record League run ended early in the 1988–89 season, he was soon back in City's side after a one-game absence. He became a fixture again to clock up a total of 372 League appearances for the club, leaving him in eighth place in their all-time list, but it all came to a sudden end midway through that campaign. Norman's last game for the Tigers came on Boxing Day 1988 soon after chairman Don Robinson had organised his trip to Bermuda. Horton's successor as manager, Eddie Gray, stayed behind, one reason being to allow him to concentrate on prospective transfer business. It included selling Norman to Sunderland in a player-exchange deal.

He recalled:

I wasn't surprised because I knew that something was going on and everything had changed. Brian Horton would call me in and say they'd had a bid for me from such-and-such a club and that they'd been told that I wasn't for sale. And at least it was honest of him to put me in the picture. But Eddie Gray had told me that I could go if the club ever received the right kind of offer for me. What stunned me was how quickly it could happen when a bid did come in for me.

I didn't think a lot about the move at the time, but hindsight is the most marvellous tool in the world and it came as a surprise. I had been discussing another contract, but it never got signed. We'd had a break in Bermuda and played Bradford City on Boxing Day when one of the YTS lads came to tell me that Eddie wanted to see me. He said: 'We've accepted an offer for you and now it's down to you.' I said I'd go for talks, but then I had to ask him who the club was! I was told that Sunderland were involved and I went up to meet the manager Denis Smith, the chairman Bob Murray and the vice-chairman at the Tontine on the A19. Then I found that Iain Hesford and Billy Whitehurst were in the same hotel, discussing moves to Hull as part of the deal. I was gobsmacked and it hit home when I went up to Sunderland and the management team of Denis and Viv Busby said that there would be a Press conference to announce my signing. When I went into it, the room was full and TV stations were there, so I soon realised what it was like to become the club's record signing. It was different from what I'd been used to before. But I got to the FA Cup final and had a season in the top flight with Sunderland, so it was a good move for me.

The FA Cup final defeat in the 1992 final against Liverpool at Wembley provided Norman with one of the most remarkable incidents of his lengthy career because he said:

After the game I kept telling myself that I wasn't going to trip on the stairs coming down when we went for the presentations and then I looked at my medal. I realised that I'd got a winner's medal even though we'd lost 2–0, so I told the other lads to check their medals. We'd all got winners' medals, so I went over to Dean Saunders, who'd played for Liverpool and had been a teammate of mine with Wales, and told him to look at his medal. It was a runners-up medal, so it ended up with the two teams swapping our medals over!

Norman made 198 League appearances for Sunderland between the start of 1989 and the summer of 1995. He then had a spell at Huddersfield Town, where there was a reunion because Brian Horton had taken over as their manager, but he made just seven League appearances in two seasons, the last of his career being on New Year's Day, 1997. Norman had a brief time in non-League football at

Gateshead after he had returned to the North-East, where he became a police officer.

In August 2008 he returned to Sunderland as the goalkeeping coach in their Academy, where one of his successors was Alan Fettis, the former Northern Ireland international who had also been with the Tigers. The two goalkeepers had something else in common because they both scored for City as outfield players. Fettis actually scored in the League: Norman settled for the more modest atmosphere of an end-of-season friendly arranged by Don Robinson at Rudston and Kilham in May 1988. City had annually visited Kilham for social occasions in the early post-war years, but this time they played a game and won 10–0 before it was cut short because of bad light and again Skipper took over from him in goal.

Norman has latterly had his health problems, suffering from cardiomyopathy, which prompted him to do Alfred Wainwright's famed Coast-to-Coast Walk from St Bee's to Robin's Hood Bay in April 2005 to raise funds for the Children's Heart Foundation. He remarked: 'At one stage my back was the worst it had ever been when I was playing. Maybe the problem stemmed from bending down to pick the ball out of the net too often during my career!' His health condition has since improved, though, because he has been able to cut down on medication and embark on regular 10-mile bicycle rides before breakfast.

He has taken everything in his stride, though, continuing to prove that he is one of nature's good guys. The same could be said of his City teammate John Davies, who said: 'Tony Norman was a friend as well as my competitor for the goalkeeping jersey. But I thoroughly enjoyed my career at Boothferry Park and never regretted staying despite my few chances.' The trouble was that the sheer consistency of Davies's rival meant that he found himself in the same bracket as many of the forwards who tried to foil him—they failed to mount a Norman conquest . . .

19

BRIAN 'NOBBY' HORTON

Brian Horton made just 38 League appearances for Hull City, he was sent off in one of them and he did not score a goal for the club. But he has a special place in the Tigers' annals because he is the only person to help them to promotion as a manager, assistant manager and player. It all happened in two spells with the Tigers, both of which came about in intriguing circumstances. His first stint was as a player-manager, it nearly never happened and yet it brought instant success when it did. His second spell was as assistant manager and it brought even greater glory because it coincided with the Tigers reaching the top flight of English League football for the first time.

Horton, who was born in the West Midlands town of Hednesford in February 1949, had mapped out a playing career for himself as a midfield general, a leader and a winner when the first call came from City. It happened during the summer of 1984 when the club were looking for a new manager after Colin Appleton had resigned minutes after the Tigers had been pipped for a second successive promotion in the final game at Burnley.

Horton had had a spell at Walsall as a youngster in the mid-1960s without breaking into League football, so he then went back home into the non-League game with Hednesford Town, where he spent four years. He then made the most of his second chance in the League when Port Vale snapped him up and he initially became a first-team regular during the 1970–71 season. He made 236 League appearances for Vale, scoring 33 goals, but then switched Third Division clubs towards the end of the 1975–76 season by moving to Brighton and Hove Albion in a £30,000 deal. Horton skippered Brighton from the Third Division to the First Division, appearing in 218 League games for them and chipping in with another 33 goals. He then moved to Luton Town in a £100,000 deal in August 1981 and led them to the Second Division title, making 118 League appearances for them and contributing eight more goals.

Horton had always been in demand and someone who was well aware of his qualities was Appleton when he was in charge of the Tigers for the first time because he wanted to sign him as a player. But even though Appleton departed at the end of 1983–84, chairman Don Robinson knew all about Horton and plumped for him as City's new manager. Appleton admitted: 'It was all in the pipeline when I upped and went. I really rated him as a player.' It had been reported that Port Vale wanted Horton back as their player-coach, but Robinson stepped in first after consulting both Jack Charlton and Emlyn Hughes, later a City director. Hughes predicted that Horton would manage England and that was good enough for Robinson!

Even then things did not go entirely smoothly. Robinson briefly put Horton's appointment on hold after it had been leaked to the national Press. City were embarking on a close-season trip to America and Robinson insisted: 'We're going round Disneyworld, so we might bring back Mickey Mouse!' But once he had confirmation that Horton himself had not been responsible for the leak, Robinson went ahead with the appointment, eventually announcing it at a Press conference in Florida, to where Horton flew out. And Robinson said: 'He paid his own way over so that he could meet the lads. That just typifies the type of man Brian Horton is. He wants to be a winner.' And he was right.

City at once made up for their near miss by clinching their second promotion in three years thanks to Horton's magic touch, finishing third in the Third Division—seven points behind champions Bradford City and three points behind runners-up Millwall. More significantly, they were four points clear of Gillingham in fourth place. They won only two of their opening eight League games, but their challenge gradually gained impetus. They went 13 games without defeat and then twice won five matches in a row: and the last fixture of the second sequence brought promotion—three games from the end of the season.

It was especially fitting for Horton that the Tigers achieved their aim with a 1–0 victory at Walsall in May 1985. And he said:

> It was a bit special to achieve it at Walsall because all my family and friends were there. In fact, there were so many relatives that I couldn't get tickets for them all and they had to buy their own. It was tremendous to get promotion at Fellows Park because Walsall were my first club and they let me go on a free transfer, but there were no sour grapes. I left and my career took a turn for the better.

The all-important goal was scored after 19 minutes by defender Peter Skipper, who had been an ever-present in the three seasons since returning to his home-city club for a second spell. Further irony was eventually provided by the fact that Skipper himself later had a spell at Walsall and Horton observed: 'We scored a tremendous goal, which we had worked on in training. That deserved to win promotion.' Skipper responded: 'I have nothing but respect for what Brian Horton did.'

And two days later the Tigers entertained York City in a game watched by Appleton, who commented:

> Brian Horton has done tremendous work. You don't get the results if you don't make a majority of good decisions. Someone new taking over has still got to get the players going and the big thing was getting down to the task after the disappointment of just missing out, so this was all about motivation and getting on the right lines.

Horton maintained City's momentum in the Second Division as they finished sixth in the table in their first season in it. At the time it was their second-highest post-war finish. Don Robinson kept a tight rein on the purse-strings, but Horton developed a thriving youth policy and picked up a series of bargains, three of them—Garry Parker, Frankie Bunn and Ray Daniel—having been his teammates at Luton. City were less consistent in 1986–87—the first season of the play-offs—and were 14th, but they finished strongly and sent their Humber rivals Grimsby Town down.

It was also the season in which Horton's own playing career ended. The catalyst was his dismissal midway through the second half of a 5–1 defeat at Crystal Palace in December 1986. He was booked, then needed treatment after a clash of heads and was sent off for dissent before the restart. Horton, whose only previous dismissal had been at Grimsby 10 years earlier, needed stitches in his injury, but he said:

> I was disgusted with myself. I let myself and the team down. I get emotional during a game—I always have as a player—but I should have known better and will be fining myself. I got punched and reacted, which led to the first booking, but I asked for the sending-off. What could I say to the players after making the rules and then getting sent off? I left it to assistant manager Dennis Booth, who really blasted the players and said we were dreadful. Hopefully I won't have to play much longer.

The candid reaction was a measure of Horton the man, but, as he served his suspension, City found themselves on a run of eight League games without a win. In January 1987 it included a 4–0 defeat at Plymouth on Horton's return to the starting-line-up. He was booked after 30 minutes and brought on Andy Saville in his place 35 minutes later. City had conceded 17 goals in five games between Palace and Plymouth and soon afterwards Horton strengthened his squad by signing Charlie Palmer and Alex Dyer.

The Tigers' inconsistency continued in 1987–88. They were unbeaten in their opening 10 League games and were still well set at the end of 1987. But then they began 1988 with a 5–0 defeat at Aston Villa, they conceded 14 goals in their first four League games of the year and found themselves on a run of 13 Second Division games without a win. Horton brought back popular goalscorer Keith Edwards and snapped up another bargain with Wayne Jacobs from Sheffield Wednesday towards the end of the sequence, but Don Robinson panicked and sacked him.

It happened immediately after a 4–1 home defeat by Swindon Town in April 1988 when Horton deliberately fielded a youthful side with City's season petering out in a mid-table comfort zone. More ironic was the fact that the fixture had been rearranged after it had been postponed in late January. The question as to what might have happened if the game had gone ahead on the original date rather than nearly three months later was pertinent. Horton, who had had some flak from the fans since the home defeat by Sheffield United in late February, reflected:

> One or two players did very well for me, but one or two others didn't, yet in the end the public wanted me out. I wouldn't knock the chairman because he was very good to me when I first came to Hull in what was my first job as a manager, but I think that he felt that he had to do something because of the crowd. In hindsight I should never have sold Frankie Bunn, but he was given a hard time by the crowd and I did it to try to appease them.

Even then Robinson quickly tried to change his mind after realising that he might have reacted hastily. A delegation of senior players straightaway asked to see him when they heard about the sacking and tried to persuade him that he had made a mistake. Robinson then tried to reverse his decision, but Horton was adamant that he would never have the chance to fire him a second time. His judgment had to stand.

Those experienced players still respected his methods because goalkeeper Tony Norman said:

> Brian Horton was completely different from Colin Appleton and he was fairly young because he was a player-manager at the start. But he'd been there and done it as a player, so he had a bit of pedigree and you couldn't help but respect the fellow. He demanded effort, he'd built a solid foundation and we'd got something out of it simply because of his pure intensity.

And Garreth Roberts added: 'I once suggested to Brian Horton that maybe he was a bit too intense, so he grabbed hold of me and pinned me against a wall! But he was passionate and I don't mind people who are that way.'

The praise was justified because Horton was not out of the game for long and he was about to embark on a lengthy career in management with all its attendant ups and downs. He returned to football as assistant manager at Oxford United, where his former Brighton teammate Mark Lawrenson was in charge. But in October 1988 Lawrenson resigned after just eight months in the job because he had been kept in the dark about the transfer of Welsh international Dean Saunders to Derby County. The problem was that Oxford's eccentric chairman Robert Maxwell had sold Saunders to a club where his son Kevin was the chairman, so Horton soon found himself back in a managerial hot seat.

He stayed at Oxford until he was given the opportunity to manage in the top flight by Manchester City in August 1993. When he left Maine Road in May 1995, he remained in demand because two months later he took charge of Huddersfield Town, where he stayed until October 1997. Horton was soon back in management when he returned to face a tough task at his old club Brighton in February 1998, but he moved on again 11 months later. Another old club—Port Vale—came calling and he stayed at Vale Park for a further five years. When he moved on in February 2004, his exile from the game was again brief because he took on another challenge at Macclesfield Town two months later. Horton stayed until the start of October 2006, but he could hardly have been expected to predict his next move.

The Ex-Tigers' Association for former City players were planning a charity dinner dance at the club's Kingston Communications Stadium in February 2007 and they decided to invite Horton, whom they had always held in high regard, to be their guest of honour. A month before the function everything was confirmed in writing. A week before the function City's manager Phil Brown confirmed that he would take a table at it with his staff, including coach Steve Parkin. Brown, anxious to prove himself as a manager after being sacked by Derby in January 2006, and Parkin had a long conversation with Horton at the dinner dance as they socialised and fate dictated that one thing would lead to another.

Brown eventually offered Horton, who had twice gone back to his old clubs as a manager, the opportunity to return to City as his assistant. Horton did not have to think twice about accepting the role because he said: 'It was almost like unfinished business. I wanted to prove that Don Robinson made a mistake when he sacked me.'

The coincidence of the meeting at the dinner dance had sparked it all off and Horton added:

I didn't really know Phil as a friend, but I knew him a bit through football. He said that he wanted me to be the experienced one because that was what he'd lacked with him when he was at Derby. There was supposed to be a list of people for interview, but we met in Manchester, where we talked about football for about two hours and found that we agreed as to how it should be played. Phil always says

211

that the first time that he interviewed me was that night at the dinner in Hull, but I had no hesitation in accepting because the club had even more potential in the new stadium. I do like to prove people wrong and didn't forget it with regard to Don Robinson, but a long time had gone by and it had no bearing on everything when I went back to Hull as No. 2.

It was a change of role, though, for Horton after having been a manager five times since joining Lawrenson at Oxford as his assistant. But he was perfectly happy with it because he said:

I didn't sign a contract when I went to Oxford, but then Mark resigned over the Dean Saunders sale and I got the job. It was a totally different thing at Hull. I was going into what was more of a long-term situation with Phil as his No. 2. I'd had a good stint at being a manager, but Phil invited me to say what I felt and guide him and Steve Parkin. And it turned out that we became a tremendous team very quickly.

A further ironic touch was a report that chairman Adam Pearson had at one stage turned down the possibility of Horton returning to the Tigers' hot seat on an occasion when they were managerless. He had allegedly been concerned about the possible consequences of people returning to clubs after having left them. But both Pearson and Horton eventually did at Hull!

And Horton followed in a long line of distinguished ex-Tigers who had second spells at the club in a variety of major or minor roles on and off the pitch. The list includes David Menzies, Bert Mills, Cliff Woodhead, Ernie Bell, Raich Carter, Chris Chilton, Ken Houghton, Peter Skipper, Colin Appleton, Garreth Roberts, Keith Edwards, Billy Whitehurst, Steve Moran and Dean Windass twice.

City's new management team did not take long to be coherent because in 2007–08 they dramatically masterminded the achievement of the club's ultimate aim—the one that had deserted them so agonisingly back in 1910. But there was little indication at the start of the start of the season that it would end in glory. The Tigers won only three of their opening 11 League games, at one point dropping to 20th in the Championship table. But they slowly developed a habit of bouncing back immediately after a defeat and also gained momentum from the mid-season point onwards, at one stage losing only once in 12 League outings. City got up a head of steam at just the right time, winning their four games in March. And Horton explained: 'We had a break in Italy and everything gelled from there. There was a good thing going with the players and the staff and the fans got behind us. The system that we played worked and we got to Wembley through the play-offs.'

The Tigers finished third in the Championship behind champions West Bromwich Albion and Stoke City, overwhelmed Watford in the play-off semi-finals and then faced Bristol City in the final. It was the club's first visit to Wembley—old or new—and they duly won 1–0. And Horton had been full of confidence about the outcome because he recalled:

> I knew we would win it and I didn't think about losing the game. The ground seemed packed with our fans when we went out into the sunlight in the stadium and the winning goal by Dean Windass just capped it all off. I was choked when I walked into the stadium. I was trying to keep it low-key, but then I saw all our fans.

Horton and Windass might have been enrolled in City's hall of 'prodigal sons' and the parts that they played in finally erasing 98 years of hurt brought their personal wheels of fortune full circle with the club. After all, Windass had been freed by Horton at the end of his first, two-year spell at the club as an apprentice in the 1980s. But Windass still indicated his respect for Horton when he said:

> He's a very special man. I offered Brian the chance to have my man-of-the-match award at Wembley, but he wouldn't take it. He said that the winning goal was enough for him. We've got a fantastic relationship and he always said that I could go and prove him wrong. The low point of my career was getting released, but I needed that kick up the backside because I was a bit of a loose cannon when I was 18.

The Tigers then defied the awesome odds—and numerous gloomy predictions—by surviving in their first season in the Premiership. They included memorable wins at Arsenal and Tottenham Hotspur among their initial party pieces, enabling them to rise to third place in the table at one stage. They remained competitive for a while as the winning habit and elation of a promotion season held them in good stead, but reality set in and they won only one of their last 22 League games. City struggled for goals and eventually finished 17th—one point clear of Newcastle United in the first relegation place. It was still a difficult, daunting job done and Horton reflected:

> We said to ourselves: 'This is where the hard work starts now.' But Bob Shaw also played his part as chief scout with the players we brought in even though we knew that we might be gambling with only £1m. and £2m. players who might make mistakes. And, as it turned out, the first half of the first season in the Premiership was fantastic for everyone.

Not surprisingly, City found it equally as tough in their second season in the Premiership and this time they did not have the luxury of a strong start to maintain their buoyancy. The result was that in mid-March 2010 Adam Pearson, who had returned to the club the previous autumn, sacked Brown and Horton. He installed a new, short-term regime overseen by Iain Dowie as manager, but things did not improve because they won only one of their nine games in charge and City were relegated in 19th position. The management team, including Parkin, were on their way out, too.

Horton, in fact, reckoned that it might have been a different story if Brown's management team had remained intact because he said:

> I believe that we would have stayed up if we'd stayed there. There was none of the shouting for Phil to be out. The fans and the media hadn't turned against us. Normally you can read situations, but it totally shocked me. Phil, Steve and I said that we would want to work together again and in my case it would be a chance to prove Adam Pearson wrong.

And the opportunity duly arose midway through the 2010–11 season when Brown and Horton were reunited as a management team at Preston North End. Horton's approach, though, confirmed the impression that one of his major motivating forces for much of his football career has always been to fight back instinctively and make his point. He has always been driven, defiant, dogged and determined and it has ensured him a very special place in the Tigers' odyssey. And he, in turn, said of Hull: 'You form a bond with people. I like the people. I have had some incredible times at Hull City and the club will always be a big part of me.'

20

DEAN WINDASS

Hull City fans had long given up hope that the club would ever reach the top flight in League football because the catastrophe of the 3–0 defeat at Oldham in April 1910 had left its lasting legacy. There had been ups and downs accompanied by financial crises and the club had long been labelled as perennial under-achievers. They had twice tumbled into the fourth level of League football instead and they had even been threatened with dropping out of the League towards the end of the 20th century. The dream of competing as equals with the best clubs in the land had more often than not been a pipedream that was never destined to come true, but suddenly in May 2008 it finally did. On a sunlit afternoon at Wembley the Tigers reached what had become the Premiership by beating Bristol City 1–0 with a goal from an ageing local lad—Dean Windass.

The side who finally made it happen included two locals—Nicky Barmby, who had finally played for City after an illustrious top-flight career that included 23 appearances for England, and Windass. Both had scored in the Championship play-off semi-finals against Watford over two legs. But 39-year-old Windass was in his third spell with the Tigers, having being shown the door at 18 and then been sold to improve the ailing club's finances at 26. Consequently, the fact that he was to score the winner at Wembley meant that the Tigers' momentous achievement just could not have been scripted any better.

And if City had had to battle their way back from adversity as a club, then so had Windass, who was born in Hull in April 1969, as an individual. He had originally joined them as an apprentice, but he was not even a striker in those days. He was viewed as a central midfield player, but initially started out in City's junior side on the right-wing. He recalled: 'We had plenty of people who were quick such as Leigh Jenkinson, Neil Buckley and Mike Smith, but I wasn't very big, so I think they stuck me out there for my own protection.'

But the Tigers' youth policy under manager Brian Horton, which was administered by the club's former inside-forward Dave King in coaching terms, was then flourishing and there was plenty of competition among those who wanted to move up and make the grade as full-time professionals. This time Windass failed to make the cut and was told that he could go after two years with the club. He reflected:

> My ability was never in question. It was just my size. I was a bit of a late developer and they let me go. At that time Brian Horton didn't think I was strong enough. I can remember the meeting with him when he said: 'Sorry. We're not giving you a contract, but we do think you've got the ability.' He said that I was too small, I had to grow and mature and I would prove him wrong. You think your chance has gone, but I was working on a building site and I used to come home and go on a run every night to build myself up. What Brian Horton did for me was a big favour. It made me realise that you can achieve what you want if you put your mind to it.

And while there have been times when Windass has had a self-destruct streak—after all, he was amazingly sent off three times in one game while playing for Aberdeen—his heart has usually been in the right place and he is definitely a role model when it comes to battling back. Hundreds of youngsters are released by League clubs every summer: most of them feel sorry for themselves, they blame everyone and everything rather than themselves and they lack the Brian Horton hallmark of trying to bounce back and prove people wrong. But Windass took his lead from Horton, the manager who had released him, and slowly made his point.

After City had freed him, Windass even had a very brief spell in France with Montpellier, but it came to nothing. He then joined

Bridlington Town, but struggled to get into their first team at times. It was only when he joined Hull Sunday League side Northwood and then North Ferriby United that the fightback to prove himself gained momentum. One of Northwood's squad players to supply them with extra experience on special occasions, such as the national FA Sunday Cup, was ex-Tiger Geoff Barker, who was then North Ferriby's manager. He immediately recognised that Windass had talent and soon signed him.

Northwood's manager Peter Whinham, meanwhile, doubled up as Sunderland's chief scout and eventually took the revitalised Windass to Roker Park on trial when Denis Smith was in charge. That move finally alerted the Tigers, who had continued to ignore him, so they reacted quickly to spare themselves from embarrassment and duly invited him back. This time Windass was going to take his chance with both feet.

He had desire and, above all, he concentrated on his fitness. Windass put his new attitude into context:

> When I got my second chance, I knew that I never wanted to go back to a factory or a building site, so I tried to be a good trainer from 20 to 40 and would go out on runs on my days off. I know that I've been called a fat so-and-so, but I've never been overweight. I've never had pace, but it's just been my body shape. And even though I was one-paced, I was a strong runner when I got going and it was then a question of just using some football intelligence.

His father, John, reassured him because Windass added:

> My dad said: 'It's just one man's opinion.' At the time it was disappointing, but, looking back, I realise that I wasn't physically or mentally strong enough to play in Hull City's first team at 18. A manager has to make a thousand decisions. Sometimes they make a good one and sometimes they made a bad one, but they have to be made. You have to be mentally strong and in the end I fully understood why it had happened.

Windass started the 1991–92 season at North Ferriby and played in the first 10 games, but they were struggling to hang on to him. And after he had scored four goals in three games, another ex-Tiger Peter Daniel, who had taken over from Barker as North Ferriby's manager, knew that he could not stand in his way. City came calling, Windass wanted a second chance with them and he was immediately given his League debut. It came in a goalless draw at Swansea in October 1991 when he curiously wore the No. 2 shirt. This time he made the grade, his first goal came in his third outing—a 5–2 home win over Darlington—and he played in 32 League games in his first season.

Windass finished as the Tigers' top League marksman with seven goals in 1992–93, but the side were struggling to remain buoyant in what was by then the Second Division. They showed a marked improvement in 1993–94, though, and a lot of it was down to Windass, who dramatically established himself as a fans' favourite for the first time. He began the season with eight goals in five League games, including hat-tricks at Cambridge United and Bristol Rovers. Another mid-season hat-trick at home to Barnet followed and Windass again finished as City's leading League goalscorer, this time with a worthy 23.

He was again the Tigers' top League marksman with 17 in 1994–95, but the cash-strapped club were going nowhere. Consequently, the 1995–96 campaign was to be one of the worst in City's history as they were relegated to the fourth tier of the League for the second time, finishing bottom with only five wins in 46. Windass did not last the course because he had been attracting attention thanks to his goalscoring exploits and at the start of December 1995 he was sold to Aberdeen for a £700,000 fee.

Windass had made the grade, he would eventually end up playing in the Premiership and a League career that had once seemed so unlikely to happen at all became distinctly durable. He continued to raid the League goalscoring charts consistently with the exception of a spell in the top flight at Middlesbrough. But there were 21 in 73 games for Aberdeen, 15 in 33 games for Oxford United—where his former City colleague Malcolm Shotton was the manager—76 in 216 games in two spells at Bradford City, three in 37 games for Middlesbrough and six in 20 games for Sheffield United.

The Tigers' fortunes, meanwhile, had had been similar to those of Windass because they, too, had had to bounce back from adversity. In 1998–99 there were fears that they might even have been relegated from the League, but in 2002 they moved to a new ground, the Kingston Communications Stadium, and at once they made progress back up the Football League. But the eternal dream has still not been reached. But cometh the hour cometh the man . . .

By the end of the 2005–06 season Windass had played more games for Bradford than he had for anyone else, he had seemed to have become part of their football furniture and he had settled in the West Riding. But then he returned to the Tigers—initially on loan— and almost unwittingly the seeds had been sown for them to achieve their ultimate goal together.

The loan deal was sealed in mid-January 2007 and the circumstances were decidedly strange. Windass, after all, exchanged one relegation battle for another. As it was, Bradford went down from League 1 after winning just two of their final 19 games. Significantly, they had been in mid-table when Windass signed off with both of their goals in a 2–2 draw at home to Swansea City. But the Tigers were 19th in the Championship when Windass began his third spell with them. As it was, they finished two places lower, but one spot above the relegation zone. And in the end survival was comfortable, especially because Windass had shown his sense of occasion with a hat-trick against fellow strugglers Southend United. What added to the intrigue was that Windass finished as the leading League goalscorer with two clubs, both of whom had been relegation contenders, that season—11 for Bradford, who failed to avoid the drop, and eight for the Tigers, who did.

The outcome was that on mid-summer's day in 2007 City's manager Phil Brown turned the loan deal into a long-term one. Windass was 39, he cost the Tigers £150,000 and he had effectively moved back up two divisions. But City's showing in the first half of the 2007–08 season was modest and Windass missed the second half of it when the side suddenly gained momentum at just the right time. It meant that the Tigers' leading League goalscorer for the second successive season was a loan signing—Yorkshireman Fraizer Campbell from Manchester United. City finished third and found themselves in the play-offs, in which they beat Watford by a 6–1 aggregate at the semi-final stage. It then meant that the Tigers were going to Wembley for their first time in their history. And cometh the man, cometh the goalscorer . . .

On May 24, 2008, the ghost of 98 years earlier when John 'Jackie'

Smith and his teammates missed out on the top flight at the last hurdle was finally exorcised when the Tigers beat Bristol City 1–0 in front of a crowd of 86,703, the biggest ever to watch them. Windass, described by one publication at the time as a 'one-time frozen-pea packer,' kept his cool to volley home the winner from Campbell's cross and teammate Nicky Barmby summed it up succinctly: 'It was great technique to hit a ball that way and it looked as if the script had been written for him.'

And time has certainly not dimmed the memories of the magic moment for Windass himself because he still says:

> I had a sense of something special because we'd been playing well since Christmastime and had done well against Watford in the play-off semi-finals. And I felt that, if someone was going to score a winner at Wembley, it was either going to be me or Nicky Barmby with the Hull-born connection. Every youngster wants to play at Wembley and I thought I'd missed my chance when Neil Warnock left me out of the side for the play-off final when I was at Sheffield United. So it meant that I was quite blessed to score the winner there at 39 years old. And it really was Roy of the Rovers stuff, considering the status of the game. Phil Brown had told me after the semi-finals that I would be starting the game, but I'd been carrying a calf injury, so he warned me to be careful in training and that he might play me for only about 70 minutes. But the goal came in the 39th minute, so maybe it was meant to be written about for years.
>
> For a few moments it's almost something that you don't think you've done. But then you look back at it and see the goal on video, so you realise that it's true after all. Nicky Barmby was at the back of the penalty box and the Bristol defenders were dropping back, so I thought that, if I'd stayed out of it, then I'd got a chance of a shot on goal. Fraizer Campbell then gave me an inch-perfect pass and I knew straightaway that it was inviting me to volley it. And then I knew it was a goal as soon as it left my right foot. It was just like a golf drive when you know exactly where the ball's going because you feel that you've hit it straight down the middle.

Windass was replaced by fellow striker Caleb Folan 19 minutes from the end and Barmby and Campbell were also substituted. And Windass admitted: 'I couldn't watch the game in the last 10 minutes.' And Brown added: 'It was nice for me to look up at the big screen late in the game to see Dean Windass with his arm around Nicky Barmby like long-lost friends. It was a fitting scene to see the two Hull lads and it was also very fitting that Dean got the winning goal.'

Windass's winner also paved the way for skipper Ian Ashbee to become the first player to appear for the Tigers in all four divisions of the Football League. But in some quarters the occasion actually became excessively exaggerated as there was even talk of naming a road in Hull in honour of Windass, who kept his celebrity status well in its context himself, though, because he said: 'I don't like it when it's just about me. People talk about me being a legend, but that's daft. Legends are people who fight in wars. I only play football and score goals.'

And John Windass discovered shortly before his death in 2011 that his son's Wembley fame did not quite encompass everything. John was well-known as a singer on the clubland circuit in the Hull area under the stage name of John Daniels and on one occasion he watched the television in a club after setting everything up for the evening's entertainment. Dean suddenly appeared on screen in his role as a football pundit and John proudly told the club's staff: 'That's my lad.' But the insistent reply came back: 'No, it's not. That's Dean Windass. He can't be your lad because you're John Daniels!'

But things could have not got better for City and Windass on that warm Wembley afternoon. In one sense, though, they could get worse for Windass because he was itching to play regularly in the Premiership again. But Brown had to weigh up sentiment against reality. As a result, having got the Tigers to their promised land, Windass had few chances to milk it even though he still firmly believed in himself. In 2008–09 he made four appearances as a substitute and then just one in the starting line-up in the club's first top-flight season. He was accredited with a scrambled goal at Portsmouth in one of the substitute appearances and his start came in a 5–1 defeat at Manchester City when Brown controversially delivered his team talk on the pitch when they were 4–0 down by halftime.

It was the last of Windass's 236 League games for the Tigers and he had scored 77 goals in them, leaving him joint 10th with Arthur Temple in the club's all-time list. And Windass could not quite match the record of another City forward who was also born on April 1—Eddie Burbanks. He became the club's oldest League player when he played his last League game for the club just a few days after his 40th birthday towards the end of the 1952–53 season.

Windass reflected on the beginning of the end of his own lengthy League career:

> I was getting on towards 40 by this time and tried to make sure that I went back for pre-season training fitter than anyone else. A lot of people said that they were surprised that Phil Brown didn't start me in Hull's first game in the Premiership at home to Fulham, but he never played me regularly and dangled me on a string a bit. I was disappointed about the way it turned out, but I respect the decision that had to be made.

In the second half of the season Windass was loaned to Oldham Athletic, with whom he went into goal and kept a clean sheet at Leicester after Greg Fleming had been dismissed. He had also adopted the role in an emergency during a game for Bradford at Southend in 2005. Windass also scored his last League goal for Oldham—against Northampton Town, whose coach Ian Sampson had been a teammate at Bridlington and Northwood, and it left him tantalisingly on 199 in his time in League football in England and Scotland. It was an excellent return for someone who had been supposed to make goals rather than score them at the outset of his career.

But Windass had a natural flair for goalscoring because he said: 'When I played upfront, I believed that I'd score goals because I knew when to get into the penalty box and what positions to take up. It was instinctive.' As City's supporters knew only too well, it was matched only by his strong sense of occasion.

In 2009–10 Windass, having left the Tigers for a third time, played six more League games for Darlington, where he had a short spell as player-coach, assisting former England international Colin Todd, who had been one of his managers at Bradford. Windass had by then amassed a total of 634 League appearances, the last of them being as a substitute against Bournemouth in September 2009.

And even though he became involved in media work, Windass still could not give up playing. He could not resist the temptation to return to the Northern Counties East League when he made his debut for Barton Town Old Boys, whose manager David Anderson was a teammate of his when they were juniors with City in the 1980s and later at Northwood, on August Bank Holiday Monday in 2010. He promptly scored a hat-trick against Yorkshire Amateur and insisted: 'It may be just a bit of fun for me, but I know it's a serious game for Barton.' Later in the season Windass, whose son Josh has been involved in Huddersfield Town's youth set-up, also signed for Scarborough Athletic, who had been managed by his father-in-law Brian France. In fact, he married into something of a footballing dynasty because the family links have included his former City teammates Mike Smith and Darren France and one-time Port Vale manager Lee Sinnott, whose son Jordan has also been in Huddersfield's Academy ranks.

And Windass's unbridled enthusiasm made sure that he would also volunteer to play regularly in charity games for the Ex-Tigers' Association as soon as he realised that his League days were finally over, proving to be a big draw as he returned to the playing-fields of the East Riding. His longevity had been exemplary, but nothing will diminish the magic memory of the Wembley wizardry from Windass, which was even recorded for posterity by Hull singer—songwriter Geoff Lawes, who was at the game, with his song 'Hull City Heroes', which also refers to Barmby and Campbell, who were involved in the build-up to the historic goal.

Its words are:

It's of three local heroes, this story I shall tell,
One of them was born in 'Ull and another one was as well,
The third was not so lucky, but we love him just the same,
And all three lads are a joy to watch when they play the beautiful game.

CHORUS:
'Deano, Deano!' was the Tiger nation's roar,
The day we went to Wembley and watched Dean Windass score,
Nick Barmby raced for 30 yards with the ball in his control,
He passed to Campbell, who crossed to Dean, who hammered it in Bristol's goal.

Dean Windass comes from Gypsyville, just close to Boothferry Park,
He was raised in the shadow of the stadium where City used to lark,
They say, if you cut Deano, his blood flows amber and black,
But I wouldn't try that if I were you 'cause Deano always gets you back.

Now what about Nick Barmby? Well, his school was Kelvin Hall,
He's a giant of English football, all of 5 feet 7 tall,
He's often played for England and his caps are such a crop,
When he gives up larking football, he can open a milliner's shop.

And finally Fraizer Campbell, whose cross helped Deano score,
His football skills are unsurpassed, but his geography is poor,
How else could a lad from Huddersfield let himself be quite so blighted,
As to sign for a team from Lancashire like Manchester United?

It's of three local heroes, my story you've heard tell,
One of them was born in 'Ull and another one was as well,
The third was not so lucky, but we love him just the same,
And all three lads are a joy to watch when they play the beautiful game.

And Lawes' tribute has started to find a place in folklore itself because he said:

I have sung the song at clubs in the local area and at folk festivals in the North of England. It always goes down well and there have been occasions when the fans of Deano's other clubs such as Aberdeen and Bradford City have been present and have joined in the chorus with enthusiasm, later reminiscing about what a great character he was when he played for them.

As with some of the Tigers' other legends, Windass himself had to fight against adversity to establish himself as a hero. But maybe no-one has done it in such dramatic fashion. Dean Windass finally exorcised the ghost that had haunted the majority of Hull City players. Windass made sure in his 39th year in the 39th minute of the club's first appearance at Wembley that the elusive dream finally came true and 98 years of disappointment and anti-climax were finally erased from a collective memory. It was the stuff of which legends are made.